ACCOUNTING BASICS
for Community Financial Institutions
SECOND EDITION

PAUL J. SANCHEZ, CPA

Accounting Basics for Community Financial Institutions
Copyright © 2004, 2009 by Financial Managers Society, Inc.

All rights reserved. No part of this publication may be reproduced or transmitted in any form or by any means, electronic or mechanical, including photocopy, recording or any information storage or retrieval system, without the written permission of the publisher.
The technical information and opinions presented herein do not necessarily reflect the viewpoint of the Financial Managers Society, Inc., or its individual members, and the Society, its editors and staff assume no responsibility for such expressions of opinion or statements. The Financial Managers Society, Inc., assumes no liability for inadvertent errors or omissions in this publication.

Financial Managers Society, Inc.
100 West Monroe
Suite 810
Chicago, IL 60603
1-800-ASK-4FMS (275-4367)
www.fmsinc.org

Printed in the United States of America

CONTENTS

About FMS ix
About the Author xi
About This Book xiii
Acknowledgments xv

PART 1 ACCOUNTING BASICS

Chapter 1—Basic Accounting 3
What Is Accounting? 3
Accounting System Concepts 4
    Types of Accounts 4
    The Fundamental Accounting Equation 6
    Double-Entry Bookkeeping 6
Accounting Cycle Activities 8
    Recording Transactions in a Journal 9
    Posting from the Journal to the Ledger Accounts 10
    Preparing a Trial Balance 10
    Preparing End-of-Period Adjustments 12
    Preparing the Balance Sheet 13
    Preparing the Income Statement 17
    Preparing and Posting Correcting Entries 21
    Closing the Books 21
    Preparing a Post-Closing Trial Balance 26
Appendix A—Single-Step Income Statement 27
Appendix B—Multiple-Step Income Statement 28
Appendix C—Condensed Income Statement 29
Appendix D—Summary of Accounting Cycle Activities 30

Chapter 2—The GAAP Self-Regulatory Framework 31
Generally Accepted Accounting Principles 32
Revenue Recognition 32
    Realized/Realizable Revenue 32
    Earned Revenue 33
Expense Recognition 33
Accruals and Deferrals 34
    Accruals 34
    Deferrals 34
Conceptual Framework 35
    Entity Concept 35
    Going Concern Concept 35

Stable Monetary Unit 36
Fair Value 36
Consistency/Comparability 36
Revenue Realization/Recognition 37
Securities 38
Doctrine of Conservatism 38
Matching/Materiality 38
Asset Valuation 39
Fair Value Assets 39
Fair Presentation/Full Disclosure 39
The Rule Makers 40
Securities and Exchange Commission 40
American Institute of Certified Public Accountants 41
Committee on Accounting Procedure 41
Accounting Principles Board 41
Financial Accounting Standards Board 42
GAAP Hierarchy 43
FASB Codification 44
Scope of New Codification 44
Cross-Reference Report 45
Issuance of New Standards 45
Verification Period 45
SOX and PCAOB 46
What Went Wrong? 46
Independence 46
Public Company Accounting Oversight Board 47
Appendix A—Issuance of an FASB Statement on Financial Accounting Standards 49
Appendix B—International Financial Reporting Standards 50

PART 2 COMMUNITY FINANCIAL INSTITUTION ACCOUNTING

Chapter 3—Accounting Uniqueness in Community Financial Institutions ... 57
Unique Characteristics of Community Financial Institution Accounting 58
Daily Balancing and Posting to Trial Balance 58
Recording Deposits 58
Recording Withdrawals 61
Balancing Accounts 61
Single-Entry Tickets 61
Continuous Departmental Accountability 63
Drafts 63
Checks 63

  Certified Checks 64
  Cashier's Checks 65
  Cash Items.. 66
  Clearing and Exchange Items 66
  Due from Correspondents 68
  Interest Bearing Deposits... 68
Proof Function 69
Separate Ledger and Memo Accounts 69
Paper versus Electronic Documents 70

Chapter 4—Basic Business Functions and Risks of Community Financial Institutions 71

Business Functions of Community Financial Institutions 71
  Funding..71
  Lending..76
  Investing 78
  Fee-Based Services 83
  Support Activities... 84
  Internal Accounting, Reporting and Compliance Activities.......................85
Business Risks Faced by Community Financial Institutions 85
Appendix—FHLB Borrowings 90

Chapter 5—Internal Controls in Community Financial Institutions....... 93

Recent Internal Control Initiatives 93
The COSO Report..94
  Internal Control Definition...95
  Internal Control Objectives.. 96
  Internal Control Components 96
  Relationships between Objectives and Components 96
  Effectiveness...97
  Adequacy... 98
  Documentation 99
Comparison of FDICIA and SOX.. 100
Sarbanes-Oxley Provisions...101
  Prohibited Services Used by Community Financial Institutions 101
  Audit Committee Responsibilities 102
  Management Internal Control Responsibilities 102
  Auditor Internal Control Responsibilities......................................105
PCAOB Actions and Criticisms 106
  Excessive Costs Related to Internal Control Work............................107
  Litigation 108

Chapter 6—Typical Financial Statements of a Community Financial Institution 109
GAAP Financial Statements 109
Balance Sheet 110
Income Statement. 110
Statement of Cash Flows 110
Statement of Changes in Stockholders' Equity 111
Notes to the Financial Statements 111
Additional Annual Report Information 111
Auditor's Report 111
Supplemental Data 111
Management's Discussion and Analysis 112
Financial Statement Examples. 112

Chapter 7—Left-Hand Side of the Balance Sheet 121
Cash and Cash Equivalents 122
Balance Sheet Presentation 123
Right of Setoff. 123
Footnote Disclosure 124
Money Market Investments 125
Securities Available-for-Sale 125
Securities Portfolio. 125
Footnote Disclosure 126
Loans 130
Types of Loans 130
Loan Payment and Amortization 133
Footnote Disclosure 134
Unearned Interest. 135
Reserve for Loan Losses 140
Net Realizable Value 140
Activity in the Reserve Account 140
Approach to Determining the Allowance 142
Loan Classifications 144
Controversy 148
Footnote Disclosure 148
Premises and Equipment 150
All Costs Included 150
Depreciation 150
Footnote Disclosure 150
Accrued Interest Receivable. 151

Other Assets 152
    Customer Acceptance Liability 152
    Investments Accounted for under the Equity Method of Accounting 152
    Nonmarketable Securities 153
    Other Real Estate Owned 153
    Accounts Receivable 153
    Prepaid Items 154
Appendix A—Determining the Allowance Account 155
Appendix B—Subprime and Negative Amortizing Loans 157

Chapter 8—Right-Hand Side of the Balance Sheet, Income Statement and Statement of Cash Flows ... 161
Right-Hand Side of the Balance Sheet 161
    Liabilities 162
    Shareholders' Equity 166
The Income Statement 167
    Interest Income 167
    Interest Expense 167
    Net Interest Income 167
    Other Income 168
    Other Expenses 168
    Provision for Income Taxes 168
    Current Income Statement Deficiencies—No Segment Information 172
Statement of Cash Flows 173

Chapter 9—Ratio Analysis ... 175
Ratio Analysis for Financial Institutions 175
    Profitability Ratios 176
    Capital Ratios 177
    Asset Quality Ratios 178
    Liquidity Ratios 178
    Productivity Ratios 179
Limitations of Ratio Analysis 180
Peer Group Analysis 180
Fictitious Depository Corporation Ratios 181
    Profitability Ratios 181
    Capital Ratios 185
    Asset Quality Ratios 185
    Liquidity Ratios 186
    Productivity Ratios 186

Chapter 10—Unique Accounting Issues for Community Financial Institutions 187
Accounting for Nonrefundable Fees 187
Accounting for Investments 190
    Recording Marketable Securities Transactions 191
    Accounting for Premiums and Discounts on HTM Securities 197
Accounting for Loan Impairments 198
Accounting for Derivatives 203
    Types of Derivatives 203
    Use of Derivatives to Manage Interest Rate Risk 206
Accounting for Transfers of Financial Assets 212
Securitizations 213
Accounting for Other Real Estate Owned and Its Sale 213
    Booking OREO 213
    Methods of Sale of OREO 215
    Accounting for the Sale of OREO 218

Chapter 11—Current Trends 223
Related Party Disclosures 223
Future Expectations 227
    Future Auditing Expectations 227
    Future Consulting Expectations 227
    Future Accounting Expectations 228
Recent Trends 228
    Fair Value Trend 228
    Risk Disclosure Trend 229
    Balance Sheet Emphasis Trend 229
Appendix—Fair Value Information 231

PART 3 FINANCIAL STATEMENTS
Balance Sheet (Figures 6.2 and 6.3) 238
Income Statement (Figure 6.4) 240
Statement of Cash Flows (Figure 6.5) 242
Selected Supplemental Data (Figure 9.1) 244
Financial Ratios (Figure 9.2) 245

GLOSSARY 247

INDEX 275

About Financial Managers Society, Inc.

The Financial Managers Society, Inc., (FMS) is the only individual membership society exclusively devoted to serving the needs of finance and accounting professionals from financial institutions. Our more than 1,500 members are CFOs, controllers, CEOs, COOs, treasurers, investment officers and internal auditors from banks, thrifts and credit unions.

FMS offers career-enhancing education, targeted news and research, national leadership opportunities, a voice in shaping regulations and accounting principles and connections with other industry professionals.

The mission of the Financial Managers Society is to enhance the professional development of financial personnel within financial institutions.

The Society accomplishes this mission in the following ways:

- Offering premier education and information to members and others within the financial services industry regarding accounting, financial management, regulatory, operational, auditing and other industry issues
- Providing forums for the exchange of information and practical applications
- Articulating industry and member concerns to regulatory and accounting policy-setting bodies
- Providing members with opportunities for technical, personal and leadership growth and development

Learn more about FMS at www.fmsinc.org.

About the Author

Paul J. Sanchez, CPA, CBA, CFSA, is the president and owner of Professional Services Associates (www.sanchez-psa.com), a consulting, professional training and development business that services corporate clients (auditors, controllers, etc.), CPA firms and others.

He was an assistant professor at Long Island University—C.W. Post Campus as well as an adjunct lecturer at City University of New York. Paul was Vice President—Professional Development for the Audit Division of a regional bank and Director of Professional Practices and Vice President of a money-center bank where he directed professional practice development and training for internal auditors. He was on the technical staff of the Auditing Standards and Examinations Division of the American Institute of Certified Public Accountants (AICPA). He practiced public accounting in the New York office of Deloitte where he was involved as a firm recruiter and an in-house professional development instructor. Prior to its merger with a national CPA review company, he was an owner and instructor for auditing and financial accounting seminars for Person/Wolinsky CPA Review Courses, a company that prepared candidates to pass the Uniform CPA Examination.

Paul is a frequent lecturer and instructor for accounting, auditing, banking and other public and in-house seminars, workshops and other presentations. He is the author and publisher of "The Ideas and Analysis Letter: The Sanchez Take," a monthly business editorial opinion letter. (Go to www.sanchez-psa.com for information.)

He wrote the first edition of *Accounting Basics for Community Financial Institutions* (Financial Managers Society, 2004).

About This Book

This second edition of *Accounting Basics for Community Financial Institutions* provides an easy-to-absorb overview of what is often considered a confusing topic. It gives newcomers to the financial services environment a concise, straight-forward introduction to community financial institution accounting. For more experienced personnel, it's a welcome refresher.

To facilitate its use by readers of all levels, the book is divided into three parts: (1) Accounting Basics; (2) Community Financial Institution Accounting; (3) Financial Statements.

Readers who have little or no background or experience in accounting are urged to read the entire book—particularly Part 1, which deals with general accounting and the accounting framework.

Those with basic accounting experience but with little or no exposure to financial institution accounting might prefer to begin with Part 2.

Part 3 is a perforated section that contains copies of the sample financial statements that are introduced throughout the book. The perforated statements can be removed for easy reference while you read the chapters that explain them.

The extensive glossary and index help readers locate the meanings of abbreviations, acronyms, concepts and words quickly, easily and efficiently.

The book has been updated to reflect the significant changes in the accounting profession since the first edition. Changes include developments in the area of codifying the Financial Accounting Standards Board (FASB) authoritative accounting pronouncements and the gradual movement toward international financial reporting standards (IFRS). Additional information has been provided about the Sarbanes-Oxley Act (SOX), the Public Company Accounting Oversight Board (PCAOB) and responsibilities relating to effective internal controls.

This edition details the approach to determining the proper allowance for loan losses—especially in light of the apparent blatant disregard for credit risk that characterized subprime and negative amortizing loans. Other significant changes focus on accounting for other real estate owned (OREO), fair value accounting, accounting for securitization, Federal Home Loan Banks (FHLB) borrowings and Income Statement display deficiencies.

Overall, this second edition of *Accounting Basics for Community Financial Institutions* provides current thinking about accounting matters. It gives community financial institution personnel the basic information they need to successfully understand financial services accounting.

Acknowledgments

Some say "the second time around is easier." That might be true of some aspects of life, but I'm not sure it applies to the revision of a book. Writing an accounting text is no small task—even the second time around. After the many favorable comments I received about the first edition, I was challenged to keep the book alive and current.

The successful completion of any book is the result of the patient efforts and hard work of many people. I especially thank the wonderful folks at FMS for again giving me the opportunity to put many accounting ideas and concepts into a form that will continue to benefit individuals at community financial institutions. I thank Dick Yingst, President and CEO of FMS, for taking another chance with the publication of this second edition. I appreciate his continued concern with satisfying the accounting needs of FMS member organizations. Many thanks to Diane Walter who, before her retirement from FMS, saw the need for an updated text. Her initial prodding and her belief in the need for an update inspired me to take on the project and to persevere throughout the process. I also thank Jennifer Vimarco who took over as Director of Professional Development after Diane's retirement and kept the project on target and moving along smoothly toward completion.

My thanks and appreciation go to the FMS Council members who took valuable time out of their schedules to read, edit, comment, criticize and praise: Dustin A. Cuttriss, CPA, Manager of BKD, LLP, in Fort Wayne, IN; Sydney K. Garmong, Executive of Crowe Horwath, LLP, in Washington, DC; John Klimowich, SVP/Controller of Columbia Bank in Fair Lawn, NJ.

I'm especially grateful for the patient, professional design expertise of Linda Gipson of Gipson Design Studio. I also thank my editor, Sherry L. Powley of Powley Editorial Consulting. Her ability to translate and edit my sometimes boring accounting words into easy-to-read presentations still amazes me.

Finally, I sincerely thank the many students of accounting who have attended accounting classes I've conducted over the years. Those students always managed to teach the teacher. Their questions and intellectual probing of issues make accounting an exciting, never-ending challenge for me. I thank all my students and attendees at my training sessions for their questions, opinions and enthusiasm. They are the ones who make it all worthwhile for this old accounting teacher. Their thirst for accounting knowledge and my attempts to quench that thirst are reflected throughout this text. I thank them all.

Paul J. Sanchez, CPA
Professional Service Associates
www.sanchez-psa.com

PART ONE

ACCOUNTING BASICS

CHAPTER 1

Basic Accounting

This chapter is a basic accounting primer for those who have little or no accounting experience, and it provides a good review for those who want to sharpen their accounting knowledge. The chapter presents the building blocks needed to understand basic accounting and explains the nuts and bolts of accounting—the debits and credits.

After studying this chapter you should be able to
- define *accounting*
- state the fundamental accounting equation
- differentiate among types of accounts: assets, liabilities, owner's equity, revenue and expense
- explain the double-entry bookkeeping system
- distinguish between the balance sheet and the income statement
- summarize the accounting cycle activities

What Is Accounting?

Accounting is a field of business that records, classifies and interprets the economic transactions of a business enterprise. Many persons are involved with accounting—from the preparation of basic household accounts to the preparation of corporate financial statements in accordance with *generally accepted accounting principles (GAAP)*. GAAP is a technical accounting term that encompasses the rules and procedures necessary to define acceptable accounting practice at a particular time to ensure that financial statements are properly presented. GAAP is explained in Chapter 2.

Every business must strive to be *profitable* and stay *solvent*. Accounting provides information about how well the business is attaining those goals.

Individuals use the recording, classification and interpretation of economic transactions for various reasons.

1. **INTERNAL USERS**—This category includes all levels of management personnel within a business who are responsible for the planning and control of operations. Accounting gives these users information that helps them see whether the business is meeting goals and where problems exist.

2. **EXTERNAL USERS**—This category includes all individuals who are not directly concerned with day-to-day operations but who are indirectly related to the business (for example, lenders, investors, regulators, the public). Accounting gives these users information that helps them determine whether the business is operating in a safe and sound way and helps them decide whether to invest in (or lend to) the business.

Accounting System Concepts

Accounting uses a method of capturing transaction data that is referred to as the *accounting system*. The accounting system is a record-keeping method that encompasses the entire process of recording, classifying, reporting and interpreting transaction data.

The accounting system involves three major steps.
- The system manually or electronically records the dollar amounts of completed transactions, such as the sale of a product or purchase of office supplies.
- It then classifies those transactions into logical categories called *accounts*.
- The accounting system finally summarizes the logically classified transactions into reports called financial statements.

The *financial statements* (principally the balance sheet and income statement) are the synthesis of massive amounts of data representing financial transactions. Financial statements are usually the final product of accounting. (The balance sheet and income statement are discussed later in this chapter.) Decision makers interpret the financial statements and use the information from them to plan and control operations and to make business decisions.

This book focuses on the accounting system's creation of financial statements. The accounting system provides other reports (for managerial review, tax compliance, governmental review, etc.) that are not the focus of this book.

However, before we can discuss how the accounting system actually operates, you need to understand the following concepts:
- Types of accounts
- The fundamental accounting equation
- Double-entry bookkeeping

TYPES OF ACCOUNTS

An *account* is a device for grouping additions and subtractions that apply to items included in the financial statements. Accounts keep track of what the business owns, owes, spends, receives, incurs or earns. Accounts are maintained for items such as office equipment purchased, utility bills paid, payroll expenses, postage costs and taxes paid or incurred. The accounting system classifies the transactions of the business to accounts.

Individual accounts are grouped into the following types:
- Assets
- Liabilities
- Equity
- Revenue
- Expense

Asset Accounts

Asset accounts accumulate balances for the items the business *owns*. These include cash, inventory, receivables (unpaid bills or other money not yet received for goods or services sold) and fixed assets, such as buildings or computer equipment.

Liability Accounts

Liability accounts accumulate the balances the company *owes*. These include accounts payable (a current business expense that will be paid for at a later time), short-term debt and long-term debt.

Equity Accounts

Equity accounts represent the value of the initial infusion of cash into the business plus the profits or minus the losses of the business.

How equity is determined is partly affected by the type of business ownership. Many financial institutions are *corporations*, which means their ownership is divided into transferable shares of capital stock. Organizers incorporate in a state. The corporate entity becomes a legal "person" in the state. Investors infuse cash (equity) into the business by purchasing shares of capital stock and thereby becoming *stockholders*. Stockholders can sell all or part of their shares at any time. The bank often pays a return to the stockholders in the form of cash *dividends*.

Equity of a bank corporation includes the amounts received by the business for the sale of the capital stock plus profits (or losses) after payment of cash dividends.

Revenue Accounts

Revenue accounts accumulate the values of the goods or services the business sells. Revenue accounts are considered temporary (usually one year) accounts. At the end of the accounting period (the one year), the corporation transfers revenue account balances to the equity account called "income summary."

Expense Accounts

Expense accounts accumulate the amounts the organization spends, or incurs, to run the business (cost of goods sold, salaries, heat, power). They are also temporary (usually one year) accounts. At the end of the period (the one year), the business transfers expense account balances to the equity account called "income summary."

The balance in the income summary account is transferred to the equity account called "retained earnings."

Note: If the revenue account balances are greater than the expense account balances, the business has *net income*.

$$\text{REVENUE} - \text{EXPENSE} = \text{NET INCOME}$$

The net income (revenue less expense) increases the business's equity.

THE FUNDAMENTAL ACCOUNTING EQUATION

Another important accounting concept is the fundamental accounting equation:

$$\text{ASSETS} = \text{LIABILITIES} + \text{EQUITY}$$

When the financial statements are created, assets must equal the total of liabilities plus equity. As discussed above, revenue and expense accounts are closed out at the end of the accounting year and the balances are transferred to equity.

The fundamental accounting equation always remains balanced. This concept is more fully explained later in this chapter.

DOUBLE-ENTRY BOOKKEEPING

A time-honored system used in accounting is *double-entry bookkeeping*. In its simplest form it can be viewed as a method for recording transactions by tracking where cash comes from and where it goes. The method is called double-entry bookkeeping because every transaction affects at least two accounts. Here's how this works.

First, assume we are using a manual accounting system. Although computers do much of the tedious work of accounting, it is easier to understand what the computer is doing if you think through the process as if it were performed on paper. Then, you will be able to understand how the computer system performs a number of these steps for you.

Debits, Credits and T Accounts

To understand double-entry bookkeeping, think of each account as a large letter T, as shown in Figure 1.1.

FIGURE 1.1 "T" ACCOUNT FORMAT FOR DOUBLE-ENTRY BOOKKEEPING

Name of Account	Account Number
Debit Side ("To")	Credit Side ("From")

For the simplest double-entry cash transaction, the business records an amount of money being transferred between two accounts.

- When funds are transferred *to* an account, the system uses the term *debit* and records the amount on the left side of the T account.
- When funds are transferred *from* an account, the system uses the term *credit* and records the amount on the right side of the T account.

When you are trying to decide whether to record an amount as a debit or credit, always ask yourself, "Is the cash going *to* (debit) the account or *from* (credit) the account?"

For example, assume Sam is buying office supplies with $100 cash. If Sam recorded this transaction in a personal accounting system, he would list a $100 credit to the right side of the cash account because the funds are coming *from* this account. Then, he would list a $100 debit to the left side of the office supplies expense account because the funds are going *to* purchase office supplies.

See Figure 1.2 to see how this transaction would be entered into the T accounts. Businesses group transactions into accounts that cover a category such as office supplies rather than have separate accounts for each type of office supply. You will learn more about this classification system later in this chapter.

FIGURE 1.2 ENTERING A TRANSACTION AS A DEBIT AND A CREDIT

Cash	
Debit Side ("To")	Credit Side ("From")
	$100

Home Furnishings Expense	
Debit Side ("To")	Credit Side ("From")
$100	

At times, certain transactions may affect more than two accounts. However, we should note two critical aspects of double-entry bookkeeping at this point.

Every transaction has at least one debit and one credit. And, for every transaction, the total debits (left-side amounts) equal the total credits (right-side amounts).

The balance between all accounts is the essence of double-entry bookkeeping.

Credits and Debits by Type of Account

Now, let's look at how transactions are entered as debits and credits in the different types of accounts.

Initially the corporation sets up each account as one of the following types: (1) asset, (2) liability, (3) equity, (4) revenue, (5) expense. Account types do not appear in the formal accounting records. The bookkeeper, accountant, etc., must know the different types and how they are affected by various transactions.

- Asset accounts have debit (or positive) balances. A new asset is a debit to the account because it increases what the business *owns*.
- Liability accounts have credit (or negative) balances. A new liability is a credit to the account because it increases what the business *owes*.

- Equity accounts should have credit balances because assets generally exceed liabilities. Thus, the debit balance asset accounts minus the credit balance liability accounts would need a credit balance equity to retain the notion that debits equal credits.
- Revenue accounts have credit balances. A cash sale gets cash for the business. Therefore, the business debits cash and credits sales (the revenue account).
- Expense accounts have debit balances. Cash paid for heat, power, salaries, etc., requires a credit to cash and a debit to an expense account.

Figure 1.3 shows a chart to help you remember how to enter transactions in the different types of accounts.

FIGURE 1.3 HOW DEBITS AND CREDITS AFFECT DIFFERENT TYPES OF ACCOUNTS

Type of Account	Debit (To account)	Credit (From account)
Asset	Increase	Decrease
Liability	Decrease	Increase
Equity	Decrease	Increase
Revenue	Decrease	Increase
Expense	Increase	Decrease

Accounting Cycle Activities

The accounting system is a cycle that usually involves the following activities:

1. Recording transactions in a *journal*
2. Posting transactions from the journal to *ledger accounts*
3. Preparing a preliminary *trial balance* to ascertain whether the debits equal the credits
4. Preparing end-of-period adjustments to record transactions needed but not yet journalized
5. Preparing the financial statements (income statement and balance sheet)
6. Preparing and posting correcting entries
7. Closing the books
8. Preparing a post–closing trial balance

Each procedure is detailed in the remainder of the chapter.

The corporation records its transactions into a journal (and later into separate ledger accounts) as debits and credits. The total of the debit balance accounts must equal the total of the credit balance accounts.

RECORDING TRANSACTIONS IN A JOURNAL

A *journal* is the original, chronological record of all transactions that occurred. The journal shows all the information about all transactions in one place and provides an explanation for each transaction. It is the chronological history of all the events in the life of the business.

As an example, assume the following. J. Jones creates the J. Jones Company, Inc., a business that plans to sell financial consultation services to the public. Mr. Jones acquires all of the 1,000 shares of capital stock of the corporation and transfers $360,000 to the business. The business then makes transactions that affect its balance sheet. Figure 1.4 shows the journal entries for the corporation's transactions. (The type of account for each entry is given in parentheses after the entry.)

FIGURE 1.4 GENERAL JOURNAL ENTRIES

	General Journal			Page 1
Date	Account Titles and Explanation	L/P*	Debit	Credit
20XX Jan 3	Cash (assets) Common Stock (equity) Issued 1000 shares of no par common stock for $360,000 to J. Jones	01 40	360,000	360,000
4	Land (asset) Cash (asset) Bought land for cash	20 01	282,000	282,000

5	Building (asset)
	   Cash (asset)
	   Due to XYZ Co. (liability)—Accounts Payable
	Acquired building; Paid part cash; balance payable
	   within 90 days to XYZ Company.
		21
		01
		30
			72,000	30,000
				42,000

10	Due from ABC Corp. (asset)—Accounts Receivable
	   Land (asset)
	Sold the unused part of the land at cost to ABC Corp.
	   Due within three months
		03
		20
			22,000	22,000

15	Office Equipment (asset) Due to Smith Co. (liability) Purchased office equipment on credit from Smith Co.	22 30	10,800	10,800
21	Cash (asset) Due from ABC Corp. (asset)—Accounts Receivable Collected part of receivable from ABC Corp.	01 03	3,000	3,000
29	Due to Smith Co. (liability)—Accounts Payable Cash (asset) Made partial payment of the liability to Smith Co.	30 01	6,000	6,000

*L/P = *ledger page*

Note that asset accounts, such as cash, land, building, due from ABC Corp., are increased with debits and are decreased with credits. Liability accounts, such as due to XYZ, Co. and due to Smith Co., are increased with credits and decreased with debits.

Also note that all the debits equal all the credits.

POSTING FROM THE JOURNAL TO THE LEDGER ACCOUNTS

Next, all transactions are taken from the journal and put into ledger accounts. A *ledger account* is a separate T account that is an asset, liability, equity, revenue or expense account. Each ledger account is numbered; the number identifies the account. After a journal transaction is posted to a ledger account, the number of that account is entered in the L/P (ledger page) column of the journal (see Figure 1.4).

After the accountant posts the entries from the journal to the ledgers, the accounts in the ledgers appear as in Figure 1.5. The posting of the transaction entries from the journal to the ledger accounts leads to the establishment of the account balances. After the postings are made and the determination of ledger account balances is complete, a trial balance is created.

PREPARING A TRIAL BALANCE

The *trial balance* is a listing of all account balances. As previously noted, total debit balance accounts must equal total credit balance accounts. This balance between accounts is essential. Figure 1.6 shows a trial balance for the transactions discussed above.

FIGURE 1.6 TRIAL BALANCE

J. Jones Company, Inc.
Trial Balance
January 31, 20XX

Cash	$ 45,000	
Accounts receivable	19,000	
Land	260,000	
Building	72,000	
Office equipment	10,800	
Accounts payable		$ 46,800
Common stock		360,000
	$ 406,800	$ 406,800

FIGURE 1.5 JOURNAL ENTRIES POSTED TO LEDGER ACCOUNTS

Cash					Account 01
Date	Explanation	Ref	Debit	Credit	Balance
20XX					
Jan 3		1	360,000		360,000
4		1		282,000	78,000
5		1		30,000	48,000
21		1	3,000		51,000
29		1		6,000	45,000

Accounts Receivable					Account 03
Date	Explanation	Ref	Debit	Credit	Balance
20XX					
Jan 10		1	22,000		22,000
21		1		3,000	19,000

Land					Account 20
Date	Explanation	Ref	Debit	Credit	Balance
20XX					
Jan 4		1	282,000		282,000
10		1		22,000	260,000

Building					Account 21
Date	Explanation	Ref	Debit	Credit	Balance
20XX					
Jan 5		1	72,000		72,000

Office Equipment					Account 22
Date	Explanation	Ref	Debit	Credit	Balance
20XX					
Jan 15		1	10,800		10,800

Accounts Payable					Account 30
Date	Explanation	Ref	Debit	Credit	Balance
20XX					
Jan 5		1		42,000	42,000
15		1		10,800	52,800
29		1	6,000		46,800

Common Stock, No Par					Account 40
Date	Explanation	Ref	Debit	Credit	Balance
20XX					
Jan 3		1		360,000	360,000

Note: The "Ref" (reference) column gives the journal page number on which the entry originally appears.

Trial Balance Assurances

The trial balance provides "proof" that the total debit balances agree with the total credit balances. This provides the following assurances.
1. Debit and credit amounts for all transactions are equal.
2. The debit or credit balance of each account has been correctly computed.
3. The balances in the accounts are mathematically accurate.

Trial Balance Errors

If the debit and credit totals of the trial balance are not in agreement, one or more of the following typical errors may have occurred.
1. A debit balance was listed in the credit column of the trial balance, or vice versa.
2. Arithmetic mistakes were made in balancing accounts.
3. Clerical errors were made in copying account balances into the trial balance.

The trial balance does not prove that transactions have been correctly recorded. If, for example, a payment of cash were erroneously recorded by crediting the land account instead of the cash account, the trial balance would still balance. The trial balance simply proves the debits and credits are equal.

The trial balance not only provides assurance that the ledger is in balance but it also serves as a device for the preparation of financial statements. For example, the trial balance can very easily be used to "draw" the formal balance sheet that appears in Figure 1.7.

PREPARING END-OF-PERIOD ADJUSTMENTS

After creating the trial balance and correcting errors found, the next step is preparing adjustments. These adjustments record transactions that do not appear in the journal but are needed to accurately reflect assets, liabilities, income and expenses for the period covered by the statements. Adjusting entries can be classified as follows.

1. **COSTS THAT MUST BE ALLOCATED TO MORE THAN ONE PERIOD**—An example is a building cost debited to an asset account. The cost is then debited to an expense account (depreciation expense) over the estimated useful life of the building.
2. **REVENUE COLLECTED IN ADVANCE**—An example is a service company receiving fees from clients in advance of providing the service. When the fees are received, the cash account is debited and a liability account (deferred fees) is credited. Each accounting period requires an adjustment in which deferred fees is debited and fee income (a revenue account) is credited.

3. **UNRECORDED EXPENSES**—An example is wages incurred but not yet paid. An adjusting entry is needed to debit salary expense and to credit wages payable.
4. **UNRECORDED REVENUE**—An example is a service company that may have provided service but hasn't yet collected the cash or billed the client for the service. An adjustment is needed to debit a receivable account and to credit fees earned (a revenue account).

To keep the J. Jones Company example simple, no adjusting entries are noted because the recorded transactions are handled on a *cash basis*. This is a method of accounting that credits income when cash is received and debits expenses when cash is disbursed.

This book does not focus on the various adjustments that fall into the four categories above. The reader should know that there is a part of the accounting process that requires adjustments for the four categories.

The adjustments are needed to take the accounts from a cash basis and put them on an *accrual basis*, which is required by GAAP. The accrual basis of accounting means that the company recognizes income or expense independent of when the cash is actually received or disbursed. It credits revenues in the accounting period in which they are earned and charges or debits expenses in the accounting period in which they are incurred. That is, the company recognizes income when it sells (or delivers) goods or when services are performed, separately from when the cash is actually received. For example, a furniture company would recognize income for selling a chair on the date it delivers the chair and sends out the invoice to the customer. The customer may pay for the chair several weeks later.

The company recognizes expenses in the period when the related income is recognized—independent of the date when cash is paid out. For example, the furniture company recognizes the expense of delivering the chair in the accounting period in which the company bills for the chair, even if the company pays the delivery company in the next accounting period.

PREPARING THE BALANCE SHEET

The *balance sheet* is the culmination of the accounting cycle activity. It displays the fundamental accounting equation (Assets = Liabilities + Stockholders' Equity) *as of* a single point in time (the period end date). The balance sheet is sometimes referred to as the *statement of financial position*. Among other things, the balance sheet is useful for

1. determining the liquidity of the business
2. assessing the business's financial flexibility
3. providing information about returns on investments
4. evaluating the financial structure of the business
5. reviewing the financial health of the business in accordance with GAAP

The very simple trial balance in Figure 1.6 was used to create the not-as-simple balance sheet in Figure 1.7.

FIGURE 1.7 BALANCE SHEET

J. Jones Company, Inc.
Balance Sheet
As of 1/31/XX

Assets		Liabilities & Owner's Equity	
CURRENT ASSETS		**CURRENT LIABILITIES**	
Cash	$ 45,000	Accounts Payable	$ 46,800
Accounts Receivable	19,000		
Total current assets	64,000		
NONCURRENT ASSETS		**EQUITY**	
Land	$ 260,000		
Building	72,000	Common Stock	
Office Equipment	10,800	(1,000 shares authorized,	
Total noncurrent assets	$ 342,800	issued and outstanding)	360,000
		Total liabilities &	
Total assets	$ 406,800	owner's equity	$ 406,800

As in this example, balance sheets often classify assets and liabilities as current or noncurrent. The J. Jones Company, Inc., has only a few current assets and only one current liability. It has no noncurrent liabilities. These and other terms used on the balance sheet are discussed below.

Current Assets

Current assets are items the business owns that it can reasonably expect to convert into cash, sell or consume within one year (or within the operating cycle, if it is longer). Specific current assets include cash and cash equivalents, short-term investments, receivables, inventories and prepaid expenses.

- **CASH**—This includes cash on hand (coins, currency, undeposited checks, money orders and drafts) and deposits in banks. Cash that is restricted in use or cash restricted for a noncurrent use would *not* be included in current assets.
- **CASH EQUIVALENTS**—These include short-term, highly liquid investments that are readily convertible to known amounts of cash and are so near their maturity dates that they present insignificant risk to changes in value because of changes in interest rates. Generally, only investments with original maturities of three months or less when the investment is made are considered cash equivalents. Examples include Treasury bills, commercial paper, money market funds, etc.
- **SHORT-TERM INVESTMENTS**—These assets include all readily marketable securities.
- **RECEIVABLES**—These include accounts receivable, notes receivable, receivables from affiliates, receivables from officers and employees, etc. Generally, the accounts receivable account is used for trade activity. For example, for J. Jones Company, Inc., accounts receivable would be used for the receivable created when it sells its consulting services.
- **INVENTORIES**—These assets include goods on hand that are held for sale. The basis of evaluation and the methods of pricing must be disclosed.
- **PREPAID EXPENSES**—These expenses include assets created by the prepayment of cash or the incurrence of a liability. They expire and become expenses with the passage of time, usage or events (for example, prepaid rent and prepaid insurance).

Noncurrent Assets

Noncurrent assets are items the business owns that it cannot reasonably expect to convert into cash, sell or consume within one year (or within the operating cycle). They generally include long-term investments; property, plant and equipment; and intangible assets.

- **LONG-TERM INVESTMENTS**—These assets consist of investments in debt and equity securities intended to be held to maturity, tangible assets, investments held in sinking funds, pension funds, amounts held for plant expansion, cash surrender values of life insurance policies, etc.
- **PROPERTY, PLANT AND EQUIPMENT**—These include machinery, equipment, buildings, vehicles, furniture, fixtures, natural resources, land, etc.
- **INTANGIBLE ASSETS**—These are trademarks, patents, copyrights, organizational costs, etc.

Other Assets

Other assets are accounts that do not fit into the current or noncurrent categories. Examples include long-term prepaid expenses, deferred taxes, noncurrent receivables, restricted cash, etc.

Current Liabilities

Current liabilities are amounts the business owes that it expects to liquidate using current assets or the creation of other current liabilities. They generally include

1. obligations arising from the acquisition of goods and services entering the operating cycle
2. collections of money in advance for the future delivery of goods or performance of services
3. other obligations maturing within the current year to be met through the use of current assets

Current assets minus current liabilities equal *net working capital (NWC)*. NWC represents the margin of safety available to meet the financial demands of the operating cycle. During each operating cycle, current assets are converted to cash. Much of the cash is used to pay the current liabilities and to replenish inventories. The balance is extra liquid resources available to do other things beyond what is required to "operate" the business on a short-term basis (for example, buying or creating inventories using vendor debt, selling inventories on credit, collecting receivables from customers).

The extra resources can be used for nonoperating items such as

- buying more fixed assets
- paying down long-term debt
- paying dividends to owners

NWC is the measure of the extra resources generated beyond what is needed to run the business.

Noncurrent Liabilities

Noncurrent liabilities are amounts the business owes that it does not expect to liquidate using current assets or the creation of other current liabilities. They generally include the following.

1. **OBLIGATIONS ARISING THROUGH THE ACQUISITION OF ASSETS**—For example, the business acquires a building to conduct its operations. The business takes a mortgage to finance the building acquisition. The mortgage payable is a long-term (noncurrent) liability.
2. **OBLIGATIONS ARISING OUT OF THE NORMAL COURSE OF OPERATIONS**—For example, the business defers the payment of some compensation costs for its key employees until future years. The portion of the compensation that is payable immediately is wages payable—a current liability. The deferred portion is deferred compensation payable—a noncurrent liability.

3. **CONTINGENT LIABILITIES INVOLVING UNCERTAINTY AS TO POSSIBLE LOSSES**—For example, the business could be sued for negligence, patent infringement or a host of other claims. The business, if found guilty of the charge, would have to make payments. The possibility of making payments is a contingent liability. When it becomes probable that the business will have to pay, and when the amount to be paid is reasonably estimable, the contingent liability becomes a real liability and is recorded. Some part of the liability may be noncurrent.
4. **NONCURRENT CAPITAL LEASE OBLIGATIONS**—For example, certain leases for accounting purposes are treated as "capital leases." These leases are recorded as installment purchases. A noncurrent asset is debited (usually it is coded "asset under capital lease") and a noncurrent liability is credited (usually it is called "liability under capital lease").

Other Liabilities

Other liabilities include accounts that do not fit into the current or noncurrent categories. They include deferred credits, deferred income taxes payable, etc.

Equity

The *equity* is the amount of net assets (Assets – Liabilities = Equity) of the business.

Shareholders' equity arises from investments by owners. In the balance sheet of J. Jones Company, Inc., the initial investment in 1,000 shares for $360,000 is shown in the equity section. Generally, equity is increased by *additional* owners' investments or *net income* and is reduced by distributions to the owners or *net losses*. If additional shares were sold for cash or other assets, the equity would increase. The sale of common stock is credited to an equity account called "common stock."

As the business earns revenues and incurs expenses, the difference is added to or deducted from equity in an account called "income summary." If revenue exceeds expenses, the income summary account is increased. If expense exceeds revenue, the income summary account is decreased. The balance in the income summary account is transferred to the retained earnings equity account. (See Closing Entries for Revenue Accounts below for details about closing revenue and expense accounts and transferring their balances to the income summary account.)

Equity is reduced when cash leaves the business in the form of a cash dividend to the owner(s). The *dividend* is a distribution of accumulated earnings. Since the business credits the retained earnings equity account when it has earnings, it debits that account when it distributes such accumulated earnings. For J. Jones Company, Inc., there was no cash dividend.

PREPARING THE INCOME STATEMENT

The *income statement* (also known as the *statement of income or statement of earnings*) measures performance for a given period. It is used to determine profitability. It is also used to determine value and creditworthiness.

The income statement can be presented in three formats: (1) single-step format, (2) multiple-step format or (3) condensed format.

- The *single-step income statement* displays two groups—revenue and expenses. Expenses are deducted from revenues to arrive at net income or loss, except for income tax expense, which is reported separately as the last item on the income statement. See Appendix A at the end of this chapter for an example.
- The *multiple-step income statement* displays more information. It separates operating transactions from nonoperating transactions and matches costs and expenses with related revenues for functions such as cost of sales, selling, etc. See Appendix B at the end of this chapter for an example.
- A *condensed income statement* displays revenue less total expense by group (for example, selling, administrative). The details for the groups are shown in supplementary schedules or notes. See Appendix C at the end of this chapter for an example.

When revenue and expenses are included in a cycle, the business must produce an income statement *before* creating the balance sheet.

Note that in our example so far, the J. Jones Company's accounting cycle for January 20XX did not include any revenue or expense items. Now let's add revenue and expenses to our J. Jones example so that we can revise the balance sheet and prepare an income statement.

Assume the following additional transactions for the J. Jones Company, Inc., during January 20XX. On January 15 the business received cash of $5,000 for providing financial consultation services to a client. On January 30 it paid $600 for utility service (telephone, power, etc.) and $2,000 for office workers. These revenue and expense transactions are entered in the journal and posted to the ledger accounts. Figure 1.8 shows the journal entries.

FIGURE 1.8 REVENUE AND EXPENSE JOURNAL ENTRIES

General Journal				Page 2
Date	Account Titles and Explanation	LP	Debit	Credit
20XX				
Jan 15	Cash	01	5,000	
	Revenues – Fees	50		5,000
	Sold consulting services			
30	Salaries Expense	60	2,000	
	Utilities Expense	61	600	
	Cash	01		2,600
	Paid salaries and utilities from January 20XX			

The additional entries are posted to the ledger accounts. Figure 1.9 shows the cash, revenues-fees, salaries expense and utilities expense account entries.

FIGURE 1.9 REVENUE AND EXPENSE LEDGER ENTRIES

Cash					Account 01
Date	Explanation	Ref	Debit	Credit	Balance
20XX					
Jan 3		1	360,000		360,000
4		1		282,000	78,000
5		1		30,000	48,000
21		1	3,000		51,000
29		1		6,000	45,000
15		2	5,000		50,000
30		2		2,600	47,400
18		2			

Revenues-Fees	Account 50				
Date	Explanation	Ref	Debit	Credit	Balance
20XX					
Jan 15		2		5,000	5,000

Salaries Expense	Account 60				
Date	Explanation	Ref	Debit	Credit	Balance
20XX					
Jan 30		2	2,000		2,000

Utilities Expense	Account 61				
Date	Explanation	Ref	Debit	Credit	Balance
20XX					
Jan 30		2	600		600

Figure 1.10 shows the revised trial balance after the addition of the revenue and expense transactions.

FIGURE 1.10 REVISED TRIAL BALANCE

J. Jones Company, Inc.
Trial Balances
January 31, 20XX

Cash	$ 47,400	
Accounts Receivable	19,000	
Land	260,000	
Building	72,000	
Office Equipment	10,800	
Accounts Payable		$ 46,800
Common Stock		360,000
Revenues-Fees		5,000
Salaries Expense	2,000	
Utilities Expense	600	
	$ 411,800	$ 411,800

The revenue and expense transactions require an income statement. Figure 1.11 is an income statement that displays the transactions of January 20XX.

FIGURE 1.11 INCOME STATEMENT

J. Jones Company, Inc.
Income Statement
For the month ended 1/31/XX

REVENUES

Fees		$ 5,000
EXPENSES		
Salaries Expense	$ 2,000	
Utilities Expense	600	
Total expenses		2,600
Net income		$ 2,400

Note that the income statement displays revenue minus expense to arrive at net income. The net income increases the equity of the business. Note how that is reflected in the balance sheet in Figure 1.12, which has been revised to incorporate the revenue and expense transactions.

FIGURE 1.12 REVISED BALANCE SHEET

J. Jones Company, Inc.
Balance Sheet
As of 1/31/XX

Assets			Liabilities & Owners Equity	
CURRENT ASSETS			**CURRENT LIABILITIES**	
Cash	$	47,400	Accounts Payable	$ 46,800
Accounts Receivable		19,000		
Total current assets		66,400		
NONCURRENT ASSETS			**EQUITY**	
Land	$	260,000		
Building		72,000	Common Stock, No Par	
Office Equipment		10,800	(100,000 shares authorized,	
Total noncurrent assets	$	342,800	issued and outstanding)	360,000
			Net income for 1/XX	2,400
			Total equity	$ 362,400
			Total liabilities &	
Total assets	$	409,200	owners equity	$ 409,200

The equity section clearly reflects the change in equity that results from the net income. Both financial statements—the balance sheet and the income statement—are needed to present the impact of the transactions in their entirety.

This was a very simple presentation. Nevertheless, the concepts are the same for a large or a very small business. The types of journals and ledger accounts change from business to business based on the specific circumstances. The basic accounting cycle (journalizing, posting, obtaining account balances and trial balance creation), however, does not change.

PREPARING AND POSTING CORRECTING ENTRIES

At this point in the cycle, the books and records reflect GAAP. However, mistakes, such as unintentional mathematical errors, improper postings or misapplications of GAAP, may still exist. Internal auditors or others often detect these errors before the books are closed. The organization must make correcting entries to remove the errors in order to prepare proper financial statements.

CLOSING THE BOOKS

The financial statements are easier to understand when we recognize how the income statement and balance sheet are related. The balance sheet shows the amount of owner's equity as of the balance sheet date. The income statement explains the change in owner's equity resulting from the profitable (we hope) operations of the business. The income statement therefore provides the link between the prior and current balance sheets.

The balance sheet accounts are "real" accounts; the account balances carry forward from the last day of the old year to the first day of the new year.

The income statement accounts are "temporary" accounts. At the end of each year they are reset to a zero balance. How is this done? By using *closing entries*.

The balances in all the income statement accounts are transferred to a fictitious account called *income summary*. Each revenue and expense account is "zeroed out," and each balance is transferred to the income summary account. The closing entries will put all the revenue balances (credits) into the income summary account as a credit and all the expense balances (debits) into the income summary account as a debit. If revenues are greater than expenses, the income summary will have a credit balance (profit). If expenses exceed revenues, the income summary account will have a debit balance (loss).

Closing Entries for Revenue Accounts

Revenue accounts have credit balances. Closing a revenue account, therefore, means transferring its credit balance to the income summary account. This transfer is accomplished by a journal entry debiting the revenue account in an amount equal to its credit balance, with an offsetting credit to the income summary account. The only revenue account of J. Jones Company, Inc., was revenues-fees, which has a credit balance of $5,000 at January 31. Figure 1.13 shows the journal entry to close that revenue account. Figure 1.14 shows the revenues-fees ledger account and the transfer of its $5,000 credit balance to the income summary account.

FIGURE 1.13 JOURNAL CLOSING ENTRY FOR REVENUE ACCOUNT

General Journal				Page 3	
Date	Account Titles and Explanation		LP	Debit	Credit
20XX					
Jan 31	Revenues-Fees		50	5,000	
	Income Summary		99		5,000
	To close the Revenues-Fees account				

FIGURE 1.14 LEDGER CLOSING ENTRY AND TRANSFER TO INCOME SUMMARY

Revenues-Fees				Account 50	
Date	Explanation	Ref	Debit	Credit	Balance
20XX					
Jan 15		2		5,000	5,000
31	To close Revenues-Fees account	3	5,000		-0-

Income Summary				Account 99	
Date	Explanation	Ref	Debit	Credit	Balance
20XX					
Jan 31	To close Revenues-Fees account	3		5,000	5,000

Closing Entries for Expense Accounts

Expense accounts have debit balances. Closing an expense account means transferring its debit balance to the income summary account. The journal entry to close an expense account, therefore, consists of a credit to the expense account in an amount equal to its debit balance, with an offsetting debit to the income summary account.

The J. Jones Company ledger has two expense accounts. One compound journal entry is made to close both accounts. (A *compound journal entry* is one that includes debits to more than one account and/or credits to more than one account.) Figure 1.15 demonstrates the compound journal entry for J. Jones Company, Inc.

After this closing journal entry is posted, the two expense accounts have zero balances and the income summary account has a credit balance of $2,400, as seen in Figure 1.16.

FIGURE 1.15 COMPOUND JOURNAL CLOSING ENTRY FOR EXPENSE ACCOUNTS

General Journal				Page 3
Date	Account Titles and Explanation	LP	Debit	Credit
20XX				
Jan 31	Income Summary	99	2,600	
	Salaries Expense	60		2,000
	Utilities Expense	61		600
	To close the Expense accounts			

FIGURE 1.16 INCOME SUMMARY ACCOUNT BEFORE TRANSFER TO RETAINED EARNINGS ACCOUNT

Salaries Expense					Account 60
Date	Explanation	Ref	Debit	Credit	Balance
20XX					
Jan 30		2	2,000		2,000
31	To close the Expense accounts	3		2,000	-0-

Utilities Expenses					Account 61
Date	Explanation	Ref	Debit	Credit	Balance
20XX					
Jan 30		2	600		600
31	To close the Expense accounts	3		600	-0-

Income Summary					Account 99
Date	Explanation	Ref	Debit	Credit	Balance
20XX					
Jan 31	To close Revenue-Fees account	3		5,000	5,000
31	To close the Expense accounts	3	2,600		2,400

Closing the Income Summary Account

As shown in Figure 1.16, the two expense accounts have now been closed, and the total $2,600 formerly contained in those accounts appears in the debit column of the income summary account. The revenues-fees account balance of $5,000 earned during January appears in the credit column of the income summary account. Since the credit entry of $5,000 representing revenue is larger than the debit of $2,600 representing expenses, the account has a credit balance of $2,400—the net income.

The net income of $2,400 earned during January causes the owner's equity to increase. The credit balance of the income summary account is, therefore, transferred to the retained earnings account by the journal entry shown in Figure 1.17.

FIGURE 1.17 JOURNAL ENTRY TO TRANSFER INCOME SUMMARY ACCOUNT BALANCE TO RETAINED EARNINGS ACCOUNT

	General Journal			Page 3
Date	Account Titles and Explanation	LP	Debit	Credit
20XX				
Jan 31	Income Summary	99	2,400	
	Retained Earnings	41		2,400
	To close the Income Summary account for January by transferring the net income to the Retained Earnings account.			

After this closing entry is posted, the income summary account has a zero balance, and the net income earned during January appears in the retained earnings account as shown in Figure 1.18.

The income summary account is a balance sheet account that appears in the owner's equity section of the balance sheet. It has a credit balance and presents the accumulated earnings available for dividends.

FIGURE 1.18 INCOME SUMMARY ACCOUNT BALANCE AFTER TRANSFER TO RETAINED EARNINGS ACCOUNT

	Income Summary				Account 99
Date	Explanation	Ref	Debit	Credit	Balance
20XX					
Jan 31	To close Revenues-Fees account	3		5,000	5,000
31	To close the Expense accounts	3	2,600		2,400
31	To close Income Summary account	3	2,400		-0-

	Retained Earnings				Account 41
Date	Explanation	Ref	Debit	Credit	Balance
20XX					
Jan 31	To close Income Summary account	3		2,400	2,400

PREPARING A POST–CLOSING TRIAL BALANCE

After the income statement accounts are closed, the corporation can prepare a post–closing trial balance such as the one in Figure 1.19.

FIGURE 1.19 POST–CLOSING TRIAL BALANCE

J. Jones Company, Inc.
Trial Balance (Post Closing)
January 31, 20XX

Cash	$ 47,400	
Accounts Receivable	19,000	
Land	260,000	
Building	72,000	
Office Equipment	10,800	
Accounts Payable		$ 46,800
Common Stock		360,000
Retained Earnings		2,400
	$ 409,200	$ 409,200

The income statement accounts are closed. The balance sheet accounts are ready to be carried forward. The books are closed.

APPENDIX A

XYZ Company, Inc.
Example of Single–Step Income Statement
For the Year Ending 12/31/XX
(amounts in thousands)

REVENUES

Net sales	$	5,000
Dividend revenue		400
Rental revenue		600
Total revenues		6,000

EXPENSES

Cost of goods sold		2,000
Selling expenses		500
Administrative expenses		300
Interest expense		100
Income tax expense		1,250
Total expenses		4,150
Net income	$	1,850

APPENDIX B

XYZ Company, Inc.
Example of Multiple-Step Income Statement
For the Year Ending 12/31/XX
(amounts in thousands)

Sales revenue			
Sales		5,100	
Less: Sales discounts	$ 40		
Sales returns and allowances	60	100	
Net sales revenue		5,000	
COST OF GOODS SOLD			
Merchandise inventory, Jan. 1, 20XX		500	
Purchases	2,000		
Less purchase discounts	50		
Net purchases	1,950		
Freight and transportation—in	50	2,000	
Total merchandise available for sale		2,500	
Less merchandise inventory, Dec. 31, 20XX		500	
Cost of goods sold			2,000
Gross profit on sales			3,000
Selling expenses			
Sales salaries and commissions	210		
Sales office salaries	70		
Travel and entertainment	60		
Advertising expense	50		
Freight and transportation—out	40		
Shipping supplies and expense	30		
Postage and stationery	20		
Depreciation of sales equipment	15		
Telephone and telegraph	5	500	
Administrative expenses	150		
Officers' salaries	50		
Legal and professional services	30		
Utilities expense	20		
Insurance expense	20		
Depreciation of building	10		
Depreciation of office equipment	10		
Stationery, supplies and postage	5		
Miscellaneous office expenses	5	300	800
Income from operations			2,200
OTHER REVENUES AND GAINS			
Dividend revenue		400	
Rental revenue		600	1,000
			3,200
OTHER EXPENSES AND LOSSES			
Interest on bonds and notes			100
Income before income tax			3,100
Income tax			1,250
Net income for the year			$ 1,850

APPENDIX C

XYZ Company, Inc.
Example of Condensed Income Statement
For the Year Ending 12/31/XX
(amounts in thousands)

Net sales		$ 5,000
Cost of goods sold		2,000
Gross profit		3,000
Selling costs (see Note 10)	$ 500	
Administrative costs	300	800
Income from operations		2,200
Other revenues and gains		1,000
		3,200
Other costs and losses		100
Income before income tax		3,100
Income tax		1,250
Net income for the year		$ 1,850

NOTE 10—SUPPLEMENTARY SCHEDULE OF SELLING COSTS

Sales salaries and commissions	$ 210
Sales office salaries	70
Travel and entertainment	60
Advertising expense	50
Freight and transportation—out	40
Shipping supplies and expense	30
Postage and stationery	20
Depreciation of sales equipment	15
Telephone and telegraph	5
Total selling expenses	$ 500

APPENDIX D

Summary of Accounting Cycle Activities

1. **JOURNALIZE TRANSACTIONS**—Enter all transactions in the general journal, creating a chronological record of all events of the business.
2. **POST TO LEDGER ACCOUNTS**—Post debits and credits from the general journal to the proper ledger accounts. This creates a record classified by accounts.
3. **PREPARE A PRELIMINARY TRIAL BALANCE**—Prove the debits and credits equal in the ledger.
4. **PREPARE END-OF-PERIOD ADJUSTMENTS**—Make adjustments such as depreciation, amortization, accruals and deferrals at this point. The adjustments, unless they are corrections of errors, are noncash entries that must be made to generate GAAP financial statements.
5. **PREPARE FINANCIAL STATEMENTS**—An income statement is needed to show the results of operations for the period. A balance sheet is needed to show the financial position of the business at the end of the period.
6. **PREPARE AND POST CORRECTING ENTRIES (IF ANY)**—Journalize and post all correcting entries that might be the result of mathematical errors, conceptual errors in applying GAAP, etc.
7. **PREPARE AN ADJUSTED TRIAL BALANCE**—Prove the debits and credits equal in the ledger again.
8. **JOURNALIZE AND POST THE CLOSING ENTRIES**—The closing entries zero the revenue and expense accounts and transfer net income or net loss to income summary. The income summary balance is then transferred to the retained earnings account. The closing entries also prepare the balance sheet accounts for recording the transactions of the next period.
9. **PREPARE AN AFTER-CLOSING TRIAL BALANCE**—Prove that the ledger remains in balance after posting of the closing entries.
10. **PREPARE FINANCIAL STATEMENTS**—Same as step 5 above with any corrections.

CHAPTER 2

The GAAP Self-Regulatory Framework

This chapter provides an overview of generally accepted accounting principles (GAAP) and the self-regulatory mechanism that promulgates GAAP in the United States. It distinguishes between cash basis and accrual basis accounting, explains accounting terminology and presents important concepts. The chapter discusses the key accounting governmental agency—the Securities and Exchange Commission (SEC)—and the key private-sector professional associations. It also presents several important banking-related pronouncements of the Financial Accounting Standards Board (FASB).

After studying this chapter you should be able to
- distinguish between *cash basis* and *GAAP* financial statements
- define *generally accepted accounting principles (GAAP)*
- explain the revenue recognition principle
- describe the expense recognition principle
- explain the following terminology:
  – realized and realizable
  – earned
  – incurred
  – cause-and-effect relationship
  – immediate recognition
  – systematic and rational allocation
- distinguish between accrual and deferral
- explain the following basic GAAP concepts:
  – entity concept
  – going concern concept
  – stable monetary unit concept (historical cost)
  – consistency/comparability
  – revenue realization/recognition
  – doctrine of conservatism
  – matching/materiality
  – asset valuation
  – fair presentation/full disclosure
- identify the organizations involved in GAAP

- summarize the activities of the following groups:
  - Securities and Exchange Commission (SEC)
  - American Institute of Certified Public Accountants (AICPA)
  - Financial Accounting Standards Board (FASB)
- list the major types of FASB pronouncements
- classify the various account pronouncements into the five tiers in the GAAP hierarchy

We saw in Chapter 1 that cash drives the transactions through the accounting cycle. We also learned that cash basis financial statements were not acceptable according to generally accepted accounting principles (GAAP). An organization should present its financial statements in accordance with GAAP. What exactly does that mean? This chapter defines GAAP and explores the principles and concepts that make up GAAP's conceptual framework.

Generally Accepted Accounting Principles

GAAP is a technical term that encompasses the conventions, rules and procedures needed to define acceptable accounting practice at a particular time. Principles such as those detailed in this chapter have evolved over years, and most preparers and auditors of financial statements recognize them.

The principles of revenue recognition, expense recognition, accruals and deferrals are cornerstones on which the conceptual framework of GAAP is built. GAAP's conceptual framework includes nine central concepts: (1) entity; (2) going concern; (3) stable monetary unit (historical cost); (4) consistency/comparability; (5) revenue realization/recognition; (6) doctrine of conservatism; (7) matching/materiality; (8) asset valuation; (9) fair presentation/full disclosure. This chapter details those principles and concepts.

GAAP also involves governmental regulators and their pronouncements. Over the years, the federal government has designated several organizations as GAAP rule makers. This chapter introduces the regulators as well as their roles, activities and pronouncements. Since various regulators issue pronouncements, an organization may have difficulty determining which pronouncement to use at a particular time. The conclusion of the chapter details the CPA profession's hierarchy for the application of GAAP pronouncements.

Revenue Recognition

The *revenue recognition principle* is a cornerstone of GAAP. It requires that revenues and gains be recognized (recorded; booked; incorporated into the financial records as assets, liabilities, equity, revenue or expense) when measurable and when realized or realizable or earned.

REALIZED/REALIZABLE REVENUE

Revenues are *realized* or *realizable* when goods or services or other assets are exchanged for cash or claims to cash. When goods are sold to a customer who can and will pay for them later, the selling entity should recognize revenue when the title to the goods is transferred to the buyer.

For example, when a retailer sells shirts to a customer, the customer takes the shirts and agrees to pay within a certain time frame or on account. The buyer owns the shirts at the time of sale, and the sale is recorded in the retailer's journal as follows:

Debit:	Accounts Receivable	$XXX
Credit:	Sales Revenue	$XXX

EARNED REVENUE

Revenues are *earned* when the entity has substantially completed all the requirements needed to obtain the benefits. If the sale requires the seller's future performance, the revenue is not recognized until substantially all of the required performance is completed.

For example, if the entity sells energy (gas, oil, etc.) for future delivery and payment is not due until delivery is made, no entry is recorded. The future commitment, however, creates a possible liability (a contingency) that requires disclosure in the footnotes to the financial statements.

Even if the selling company receives cash at the time of the agreement for the promise to make delivery in the future, no revenue is recognized. The entity has not substantially completed its part of the agreement.

The journal entry to record the cash follows:

Debit:	Cash	$XXX
Credit:	Liability	$XXX

No revenue is recognized. The requirement to record revenue only when it is realized or earned—the revenue recognition principle—is a central principle of GAAP.

Expense Recognition

Another cornerstone of GAAP is the *expense recognition principle*, which requires that expenses be recorded when incurred. Generally, expense recognition is based on the following concepts.

- **CAUSE-AND-EFFECT RELATIONSHIP**—Expenses and costs related to a period are matched against revenue in the period of sale (for example, the cost of goods sold and sales commissions).
- **IMMEDIATE RECOGNITION**—Expenses are recognized in a period when no future benefit exists, or when no clearly evident relationship with revenue exists (for example, advertising or research and development costs).
- **SYSTEMATIC AND RATIONAL ALLOCATION**—Expenses are charged against future revenues and/or future periods (for example, depreciation, amortization).

Accruals and Deferrals

GAAP transaction recognition uses the accrual and deferral basis of accounting for revenue and expense recognition.

Accruals and deferrals, like the revenue and expense recognition principles, are cornerstones of GAAP.

ACCRUALS

Accruals are recorded transactions that affect the income statement but have no effect on cash flows.

For example, as of December 31, 20X0, an entity may have "earned" interest on a note receivable although interest will not be paid until February of 20X1. At year-end 20X0, an entry would be made as follows:

Debit:	Accrued Interest Receivable	$XXX
Credit:	Interest Revenue	$XXX

The same is true for a note payable. If the entity incurred interest costs but the interest is not payable until the following accounting period, an entry such as the following is needed for GAAP purposes:

Debit:	Interest Expense	$XXX
Credit:	Accrued Interest Payable	$XXX

In both cases the income statement is affected (recorded revenue or recorded expense), although no cash has changed hands. The revenue or expense is accrued.

DEFERRALS

Deferrals are the opposite case. Cash is received or paid, but the cash transaction has no impact on the income statement.

For example, assume a landlord receives one year's rent in advance. When the cash is received, the entry is as follows:

Debit:	Cash	$XXX
Credit:	Deferred Rental Income	$XXX

The deferred rental income account is a liability account. It is reduced when the rent is actually earned. For each month during the year, the landlord records 1/12 of the deferred amount as revenue as follows:

Debit:	Deferred Rental Income	(1/12 of $XXX)
Credit:	Revenue	(1/12 of $XXX)

On the other hand the lessee (renter) would make the following journal entries to record the payment of rent in advance:

| Debit: | Prepaid Rent Expense | $XXX |
| Credit: | Cash | $XXX |

Each month, the renter would record one month's actual rent expense incurred:

| Debit: | Rent Expense | (1/12 of $XXX) |
| Credit: | Prepaid Rent Expense | (1/12 of $XXX) |

Accruals and deferrals attempt to properly match costs with related revenues.

Conceptual Framework

As previously mentioned, nine basic concepts (the conceptual framework) underlie GAAP: (1) entity; (2) going concern; (3) stable monetary unit (historical case); (4) consistency/comparability; (5) revenue realization/recognition; (6) doctrine of conservatism; (7) matching/materiality; (8) asset valuation; (9) fair presentation/full disclosure. Each is presented below.

ENTITY CONCEPT

The *entity concept* is the most basic concept in accounting. The transactions of each entity are accounted for separately. This allows for proper measurement of the operating performance and the financial position of each entity independent of all other entities. The entity concept applies equally to all types and sizes of organizations.

The entity concept requires that the financial statements of each entity include all departments, divisions, branches, subsidiaries, etc. Financial statements can be displayed for each entity in a group, including the parent entity, or for the consolidated entity. In the latter case, all significant intercompany transactions and balances must be eliminated.

GOING CONCERN CONCEPT

Under the *going concern* (or *continuity*) *concept*, in the absence of contrary evidence, accountants assume the entity will continue operating for the foreseeable future (at least one year subsequent to the balance sheet date). The alternative to a going concern is an entity that is "going out of business."

If there are no substantial doubts about the continued existence of the entity, the financial statements should be prepared and displayed in accordance with GAAP.

If a going concern problem exists, the financial statements should reflect liquidation accounting. *Liquidation accounting* shows all assets on the balance sheet at values that the business expects to realize when the assets are sold; it shows liabilities on the balance sheet at the values it expects to pay for the liabilities. These amounts would be substantially different from GAAP amounts.

STABLE MONETARY UNIT

Accounting information is expressed primarily in monetary terms. The monetary unit is the prime means of measuring assets. This measure is not surprising given that money is the common denominator in business transactions. In the United States, the monetary unit is the dollar.

The *stable monetary unit (historical cost) concept* ignores the effect of inflation. It says, "A dollar is a dollar, regardless of time." A year 2010 dollar is equal to a year 1910 dollar for accounting purposes. (This certainly is not the case for economic purposes.)

The business records and maintains all assets and liabilities at historical cost. Each asset and each liability on the balance sheet is the sum of all the individual dollar amounts added over time.

FAIR VALUE

In recent years accounting rule makers have moved toward fair value accounting. This has been a gradual, steady movement not without vocal, serious critics who do not believe the stable monetary unit concept should be abandoned.

For more about recent fair value accounting requirements, see the Appendix to Chapter 11.

CONSISTENCY/COMPARABILITY

Consistency and comparability are closely related concepts that are essential components of the GAAP conceptual framework.

Consistency

The *consistency concept* deals with the period-to-period application of the same accounting principles ("last in first out" inventory method versus "first in first out" inventory method; accelerated versus straight-line depreciation, etc.). Alternative GAAPs exist in a number of cases—most notably how inventories enter and leave the business and how rapidly fixed assets are "used up."

Comparability

The *comparability concept* deals with the period-to-period display of accounting information (financial statements) in the same manner. The Financial Accounting Standards Board encourages comparability in order to make useful analysis possible from business to business and from period to period.

The comparability principle directs each entity to produce accounting information that is comparable over time. To achieve consistency, entities must follow the same accounting practices from period to period. Otherwise, a financial statement user cannot tell whether changes in income and asset values result from operations or from the accounting practices used.

GAAP allows an entity to make changes in its accounting methods, but the entity must disclose the accounting change, the reasons for the accounting change and the effect of the accounting change on net income. This disclosure is made in a footnote to the financial statements.

REVENUE REALIZATION/RECOGNITION

Simply put, the *revenue realization/recognition concept* states that revenues should not be recognized (recorded, "booked") until they are realized. Revenue should be recorded in the period earned.

Some revenues, such as interest and rent, accrue with the passage of time. The accountant records the amount of such revenue earned over each period. Other revenues are earned by selling goods or rendering services. Identifying when these revenues are earned depends on more factors than the passage of time.

Under the revenue realization/recognition concept, three conditions must be met before revenue is recorded: (1) the seller has done everything necessary to expect to collect from the buyer; (2) the amount of revenue can be objectively measured; (3) collectibility is reasonably assured. In most cases, these conditions are met at the point of sale or when services are performed. The amount of revenue to record is the value of the assets received—usually cash or a receivable.

However, situations may arise in which the amount of revenue or the timing of recording the revenue is not easily determinable. Depending upon the circumstances, accountants commonly choose among three revenue recognition methods: (1) collection; (2) installment; (3) percentage-of-completion.

Collection Method

The *collection method* is used only if the receipt of cash is uncertain. Under this method, the seller waits to record the sale until cash is received. When financial institutions sell Other Real Estate Owned (OREO), they often use this revenue recognition method.

Installment Method

The *installment method* is a collection method used for installment sales. In a typical installment sale, the buyer makes a down payment when the contract is signed and pays the remainder in installments. The gross profit percentage on the installment sale is calculated. That percentage is applied against cash collections to arrive at the amount of revenue to recognize when cash is collected.

Percentage-of-Completion Method

Construction projects often extend over several years. The accounting issue for the construction company is when to record the revenue. The most conservative approach is to record all revenue earned when the construction project is completed. This is the *completed-contract method.*

The preferred method of revenue recognition in such circumstances is the *percentage-of-completion method.* Revenues are recognized as the work is performed. Each year the company estimates the percentage of project completion. One way to make this estimate is to compare the cost incurred for the year with the total estimated project cost. This percentage is then multiplied by the total project revenue to compute the construction revenue for the year. Construction income for the year is revenue minus cost.

SECURITIES

Some pronouncements provide differing methods of accounting for similar assets. For example, SFAS 115 sets forth the accounting for investments, and the accounting method depends on the type and management's intent.

Under SFAS 115 debt and equity securities must be put into one of the following three categories when they are acquired:
- Held-to-maturity
- Trading
- Available-for-sale

At each balance sheet date the appropriateness of the classification must be carefully reassessed.

Held-to-Maturity Securities

This category includes securities that the company has positive *intent* and *ability* to hold until they mature. These should be measured at amortized cost.

Trading Securities

This category includes securities that the company plans to sell in the near term. These should be measured at fair value in the balance sheet with corresponding unrealized gains and losses recognized in the income statement.

Available-for-Sale Securities

This category includes securities that cannot be classified as "held-to-maturity" or "trading." These should be measured at fair value in the balance sheet with corresponding unrealized gains and losses recognized in other comprehensive income in the stockholders' equity section.

In these cases the unrealized gains or losses are recognized—either in the income statement (for trading securities) or in the balance sheet stockholders' equity section (for available-for-sale securities).

DOCTRINE OF CONSERVATISM

The *doctrine of conservatism* concept states that accounting should never anticipate gains or profits but should always book (recognize) losses when they are probable. This means certain *loss contingencies* (probable losses for which amounts are reasonably estimable) should be recognized. On the other hand, accounting should not recognize *gain contingencies* (probable gains) until they are realized.

MATCHING/MATERIALITY

Like consistency and comparability, matching and materiality are closely related components of the GAAP conceptual framework.

Matching

The *matching principle* governs the recording and reporting of expenses. It requires that expenses related to revenue be recorded in the same period as the revenues. Income is revenue minus expense. The company first measures its revenues, then identifies and measures all the expenses it incurred during the period to earn the revenues. To *match the expenses against the revenue* means to subtract the expenses from the revenues.

Some expenses are easy to match against particular revenues. For example, cost of goods sold relates directly to sales revenue; commissions and fees paid for selling the goods, delivery expense, sales supplies expense, etc., relate to sales revenue.

Other expenses (depreciation, salaries, etc.) are not so easily linked to particular sales because they occur whether any revenues arise or not. Accountants usually match these expenses against revenue on a time basis. For example, straight-line depreciation of a 20-year building assigns one-twentieth of the building's cost to expense each year.

Materiality

The *materiality concept* requires that the financial statements not include a dollar misstatement or omission that would adversely influence the financial statement reader. Financial statements, indeed, include errors and omissions. These errors or omissions, however, should not be so significant that reliance upon the financial statements leads to bad decisions by investors, creditors or regulators.

ASSET VALUATION

The *asset valuation concept* requires that assets initially be recorded at cost and then be adjusted to reflect proper accounting values.

Receivables should be valued at *net realizable value* (the amount that is expected to be collected). That is why financial institutions need a loan loss reserve account.

Inventories should be valued at the lower of cost or market (LOCOM).

FAIR VALUE ASSETS

Once again, if certain assets have been selected to be displayed at fair values, the cost, net realizable value and LOCOM concepts are superseded by the fair value "rules."

Note that held-to-maturity securities are at cost while trading and available-for-sale securities are at fair value. Although different bases are used, both honor the asset valuation concept.

FAIR PRESENTATION/FULL DISCLOSURE

Fair presentation and full disclosure are another pair of related components that make up the GAAP conceptual framework.

Fair Presentation

Fair presentation requires that a full set of GAAP financial statements with all appropriate disclosures be presented by the organization to the regulators and the public.

Full Disclosure

The *disclosure principle* holds that a company's financial statements should report enough information for readers to make knowledgeable decisions about the company. The company should report relevant, reliable and comparable information about its economic affairs.

Disclosures should include information about
- significant accounting principles
- probable losses
- accounting changes
- subsequent events
- business segments

Disclosures are made on the face of the financial statements (parenthetically) or in footnotes to the financial statements. The footnotes are an integral part of the financial statements.

In summary, GAAP represents the conventions, rules and procedures that define acceptable accounting practice at a particular time. Many principles (like those discussed above) have evolved over the years and are recognized by most preparers, readers and auditors of financial statements.

The Rule Makers

The Securities and Exchange Commission (SEC), the American Institute of Certified Public Accountants (AICPA) and the Financial Accounting Standards Board (FASB) are responsible for formally or informally developing GAAP.

SECURITIES AND EXCHANGE COMMISSION

In 1929 the public saw the stock market crash, the financial institutions fail and the economy collapse. The public looked to the government to fix the problem. Because of the failure of the system that was in place at the time, the government introduced many reforms. The creation of the Securities and Exchange Commission was among those reforms.

Prior to 1929, no organization issued accounting standards. The federal government established the *Securities and Exchange Commission (SEC)* to help develop and standardize financial information presented to stockholders—among other duties. The SEC is a federal agency that administers the Securities Exchange Act of 1934 and several other acts.

Most companies that issue securities to the public or are listed on a stock exchange are required to file annual, audited financial statements with the SEC. The SEC also prescribes the accounting practices and standards that publicly owned companies must follow, and it exercises oversight over all corporations listed on the major stock exchanges.

Since its inception, the SEC has relegated its accounting practices responsibilities to the private sector. The SEC encouraged the creation of a private-sector standard-setting body. The SEC believes the private sector has the resources and talent to develop appropriate accounting standards and can probably do so in an efficient and effective fashion. Accounting standards have generally developed in the private sector (through AICPA and FASB pronouncements). This is likely to continue in the foreseeable future.

The SEC's partnership with the private sector continues today. The SEC has acted with restraint and has relied on the AICPA and FASB to regulate the accounting profession and to develop and enforce accounting standards.

The SEC's involvement in the development of accounting standards has varied over the years. In some cases the private sector attempted to establish a standard, but the SEC refused to accept it. In other cases the SEC prodded the private sector into taking quicker action on certain reporting problems (for example, accounting for investments in debt and equity securities). The SEC responds to FASB exposure drafts and provides the FASB with advice.

The SEC has the authority to establish accounting principles but has relegated its duty to the private sector. The private sector seeks and values the views of the SEC. The private sector formulates and implements the standards based on all informed input.

Publicly owned companies are required to submit their financial statements to the SEC. If the SEC believes that an accounting or disclosure irregularity exists in the financial statements, it sends a deficiency letter to the company. Deficiency letters are usually resolved immediately. If the company disagrees with the letter, the SEC has the power to issue a *stop order* that prevents the company from issuing securities or trading securities on the exchanges. Criminal charges may also be brought by the Department of Justice for violations of certain laws.

The SEC, in effect, is the watchdog over the integrity of financial reporting for publicly traded companies.

AMERICAN INSTITUTE OF CERTIFIED PUBLIC ACCOUNTANTS

The *American Institute of Certified Public Accountants (AICPA)* is the national professional organization of Certified Public Accountants (CPAs). The AICPA has been a significant player over the years in the development of GAAP.

COMMITTEE ON ACCOUNTING PROCEDURE

At the urging of the SEC, the AICPA appointed the *Committee on Accounting Procedure (CAP)* in 1939. CAP was composed of practicing CPAs. It issued 51 Accounting Research Bulletins from 1939 to 1959. This case-by-case approach failed to provide the structured body of accounting principles that was both needed and desired. In response to the need for a more conceptual approach, the AICPA created the Accounting Principles Board.

ACCOUNTING PRINCIPLES BOARD

The *Accounting Principles Board (APB)* was formed in 1959. Its major purposes were to
1. advance the written expression of accounting principles
2. determine appropriate accounting practices
3. narrow the areas of difference and inconsistency in practice

To achieve these objectives, the APB's mission was to develop an overall conceptual framework to assist in the resolution of problems and to perform appropriate research on issues before finalizing pronouncements.

Unfortunately, the APB came under fire. It was charged with lack of productivity and failing to act promptly to correct alleged accounting abuses. It was replaced by the FASB.

FINANCIAL ACCOUNTING STANDARDS BOARD

The accounting profession created the *Financial Accounting Standards Board (FASB)* in 1973 to replace the Accounting Principles Board as the accounting rule-making body in the private sector. The FASB was formed so the accounting profession could avoid governmental rule making.

The FASB's purpose is to establish and improve standards of financial accounting and reporting. The developed standards are designed to guide and educate issuers, auditors and users of financial statements.

The FASB relies on the input and expertise of a variety of groups formed for various projects. It also relies on the *Financial Accounting Standards Advisory Council (FASAC)*, which is responsible for consulting with the FASB on major policy and technical issues and for helping select task force members. The FASB also has its own staff of professionals to help with research.

To establish financial accounting standards, the FASB believes it should be
1. responsive to the needs and viewpoints of the entire economic community, not just the public accounting profession
2. in full view of the public, operating through a "due process" system that allows all interested persons the opportunity to express their views

The FASB issues five major types of pronouncements: (1) Standards; (2) Interpretations; (3) Financial Accounting Concepts; (4) Technical Bulletins; (5) Emerging Issues Task Force Statements. They are discussed below.

Standards

The FASB issues financial accounting standards that are considered generally accepted accounting principles. Those standards are called *Statements of Financial Accounting Standards (SFASs)*.

See Appendix A to this chapter for the steps the FASB takes in the evolution of a typical FASB Statement of Financial Accounting Standards.

Interpretations

Interpretations represent modifications or extensions of existing standards. The interpretations have the same authority as standards. Interpretations, however, do not require the FASB to operate in full view of the public through the due process system that is required for FASB Standards.

Financial Accounting Concepts

In November 1978, the FASB issued the first in a series of *Statements of Financial Accounting Concepts* as part of its conceptual framework project. This is part of the effort to move away from the problem-by-problem or "knee-jerk" approach to standard setting.

Concepts set forth fundamental objectives that the Board will use in developing standards of financial accounting and reporting. They are intended to form a conceptual framework that will consistently serve as a tool for solving existing and emerging problems. *A Statement of Financial Accounting Concepts does not establish GAAP.* Concepts statements, however, pass through the same due process system as do standards statements.

FASB Technical Bulletins

The FASB is frequently asked to provide guidance on implementing or applying FASB Standards or Interpretations, APB Opinions and Accounting Research Bulletins. Timely guidance on financial accounting and reporting problems is needed in the rule-making arena. Technical bulletins are issued in the following situations.

1. The Technical Bulletin is not expected to cause a major change in accounting practice for a number of enterprises.
2. Cost of implementation is low.
3. Guidance provided by the Bulletin does not conflict with broad fundamental accounting principles.

Emerging Issues Task Force Statements

In 1984 the FASB formed the *Emerging Issues Task Force (EITF)*. The EITF is composed of 13 members who represent CPA firms and preparers of financial statements. Observers from the SEC and AICPA also attend EITF meetings. The EITF's goal is to reach a consensus on how to account for new and unusual transactions that may create inconsistent financial reporting practices.

The SEC regards EITF statements as preferred accounting and requires persuasive justification for departure from them.

GAAP Hierarchy

Over the years many pronouncements have been issued to identify GAAP. The CPA profession has developed a GAAP hierarchy for those pronouncements. The hierarchy has five tiers or levels. The pronouncements in Tier 1 constitute the highest level of GAAP authority. Tier 2 is next and so on.

Some pronouncements are contradictory. When contradictory pronouncements or inconsistencies are present, preparers of financial statements must select the accounting approach in the highest level of authority. Figure 2.1 shows the GAAP hierarchy for for-profit entities.

FIGURE 2.1 GAAP HIERARCHY

Tier One
- FASB Statements
- FASB Interpretations
- APB Opinions
- AICPA Accounting Research Bulletins

Tier Two
- FASB Technical Bulletins
- AICPA Industry Audit and Accounting Guides
- AICPA Statements of Position

Tier Three
- Consensus Positions of the FASB Emerging Issues Task Force
- AICPA Practice Bulletins

Tier Four
- AICPA accounting interpretations
- "Qs and As" published by the FASB staff
- Industry practices widely recognized and prevalent

Tier Five ("Other Accounting Literature")
- Other sources of information, including FASB Concepts Statements, textbooks, professional journal articles, etc.

FASB Codification

On January 15, 2008, the Financial Accounting Standards Board (FASB) released the FASB Accounting Standards Codification (the codification) for an extended verification period.

The codification disassembled and reassembled thousands of accounting pronouncements (including those of the FASB, EITF and AICPA) to organize them under approximately 90 topics.

The codification is not intended to change U.S. GAAP. It is part of the FASB's efforts to reduce the complexity of accounting standards and to facilitate international convergence.

After completing the verification period, the FASB is expected to formally approve the codification as the single source of authoritative U.S. accounting and reporting standards, other than guidance issued by the Securities and Exchange Commission (SEC).

SCOPE OF NEW CODIFICATION
- The codification includes literature issued by a standard-setter within all four levels in the GAAP hierarchy.

- The codification provides GAAP guidance only. It does not include guidance for non-GAAP matters such as Other Comprehensive Basis of Accounting (OCBOA), cash basis, income tax basis or regulatory accounting principles.
- The codification includes relevant authoritative content issued by the Securities and Exchange Commission (SEC) and select SEC staff interpretation and administrative guidance. An "S" precedes the SEC section codes.
- The codification does not include standards for state and local governments.

CROSS-REFERENCE REPORT

The codification includes a cross-reference report that allows users to identify where current standards reside in the codification or the source material that populates a specific location.

However, certain standards that served to amend other literature may no longer appear in the codification by the standard number. For example, SFAS 151, *Inventory Costs*, was an amendment of Accounting Research Bulletin (ARB) 43, chapter 4. In the cross-reference report, users will no longer see SFAS 151; rather the amended material is reflected in ARB 43.

Users should be aware of this when reviewing the codification, as some standards may appear to be "missing," but are in fact incorporated into the standard(s) that they revised or updated.

ISSUANCE OF NEW STANDARDS

Once the codification becomes authoritative, the FASB will no longer consider new standards authoritative in their own right. Instead, new standards will serve only to update the codification and provide the historical basis for conclusions of a new standard.

New standards will include the standard and an appendix of codification update instructions. This combination will be codification update YY-XX where YY is the last two digits of the year and XX is the sequential number for each update. For example, 09-01, 09-02 and so on.

VERIFICATION PERIOD

The codification is available for comment during the "verification" period. During that period, FASB has noted that the intent of the verification is not to debate the underlying requirements of GAAP, but to verify that the codification appropriately captures them.

After completing the verification period, FASB is expected to formally approve the codification as the single source of non-SEC authoritative accounting and reporting standards, and it will supersede all then-existing non-SEC accounting and reporting standards.

The FASB currently expects to approve and make the codification authoritative as of July 1, 2009.

SOX and PCAOB

In 2002, the rules changed as the result of many financial irregularities that occurred at publicly owned companies. The business community and the general public were shocked by the number and magnitude of widely publicized accounting irregularities and the length of time over which they took place. The implications of the Enron scandal and other fraudulent financial reporting cases were far-reaching and will affect accounting for a long time.

WHAT WENT WRONG?

The fraudulent financial reporting fiasco that occurred in the early 2000s cannot be associated with one single event or issue. Aside from the fraud perpetrated by management, questions were raised on what appeared to be a long-growing coziness between outside auditors and their clients.

Some CPA firms had shifted their focus from auditing to consulting. The lucrative consulting business was too much of a temptation for CPA firms. Some CPA firms even did audits at reduced prices in order to tap into the consulting services.

Many asked, "How could the CPA perform an *independent* audit if so much revenue from consulting fees was at risk?" As a result, Congress passed the Sarbanes-Oxley Act of 2002 (SOX) in order to improve accountability by management, strengthen independence rules and enhance disclosure. The SEC also issued numerous rules to implement the provisions of SOX.

In addition to providing new rules for auditors, SOX put in place many provisions—including monetary penalties—impacting management.

INDEPENDENCE

A cornerstone for the CPA external auditor is independence. In all matters relating to the audit, the auditor must have independence in mental attitude.

SOX—the response to the many serious accounting irregularity cases—addressed auditor independence very harshly.

A summary of the four SOX auditor independence sections follows.

1. **PROHIBITED SERVICES**—The act prohibits an issuer's registered public accounting firm from performing certain specified categories of services for that issuer under any circumstances (whether or not preapproved by the audit committee) "contemporaneously" with any audit. These services include: (i) bookkeeping; (ii) financial information systems design and implementation; (iii) appraisal or valuation services; (iv) fairness opinions, or contribution-in-kind reports; (v) actuarial services; (vi) internal audit outsourcing services; (vii) management or human resources services; (viii) broker or dealer, investment adviser or investment banking services; and (ix) legal services and expert services unrelated to the audit. The Board is authorized

to exempt issuers or firms from the prohibitions on a case-by-case basis—an authority that might be exercised, for example, in cases where the discontinuation of an auditor's provision of a nonaudit service to a client would result in extreme hardship to the company.

The act contemplates that an issuer's auditor (for example, a registered public accounting firm) may continue to perform any other nonaudit services (including "tax services," which could encompass a broad range of services) for the issuer, but only if approved in advance by the issuer's audit committee. The act provides that all auditing and nonauditing services provided to an issuer by its auditor must be preapproved by the issuer's audit committee and that such approval must be disclosed in the issuer's periodic reports.

2. **AUDIT PARTNER ROTATION**—A registered public accounting firm may not perform audit services for an issuer if either (1) the lead (or coordinating audit) partner who has primary responsibility for the audit or (2) the audit partner who reviews the audit has performed audit services for such issuer for five consecutive fiscal years.

3. **AUDITORS MUST REPORT DIRECTLY TO AUDIT COMMITTEES**—Each registered public accounting firm that performs an audit for any issuer must timely report to the audit committee:
   - All critical accounting policies and practices used
   - All "alternative treatments" of financial information within GAAP that have been discussed with management officials of the issuer, ramifications of the use of such alternatives and the treatment preferred by the accounting firm
   - Other material written communications between the accounting firm and the issuer's management, such as any management letter or schedule of unadjusted differences

4. **COOLING-OFF PERIOD**—A registered accounting firm may not perform for an issuer any audit service if the CEO, controller, CFO, CAO or any person serving in an equivalent position for the issuer was employed by that auditor and participated in any capacity in the audit of that issuer during the one-year cooling-off period preceding the date of the initiation of the audit. This provision only applies to individuals at the accounting firm who actually worked on the issuer's audit and would not extend to individuals at the accounting firm who did not work on the issuer's audit.

PUBLIC COMPANY ACCOUNTING OVERSIGHT BOARD

The Public Company Accounting Oversight Board (PCAOB) was created by SOX. The PCAOB is a private-sector, nonprofit corporation that oversees the audit of public companies. Its goal is to protect the interests of investors and further the public interest in the preparation of independent audit reports.

Duties of this independent PCAOB include, among other things, the following:

1. Register public accounting firms that prepare audit reports for issuers
2. Establish or adopt, or both, auditing, quality control, ethics, independence and other standards relating to the preparation of audit reports for issuers
3. Conduct inspections of registered public accounting firms
4. Conduct investigations and disciplinary proceedings concerning, and impose appropriate sanctions where justified upon, registered public accounting firms and associated persons of such firms

Although SOX put the auditing rule-making mechanism into the government sector, it left the accounting rule-making mechanism in the private sector (FASB).

Public accounting firms that perform audits of public companies must register with the PCAOB. The PCAOB has established audit standards that deal with issues such as the following:

- Audit work paper retention
- Required concurrent or second partner reviews of audit reports
- Description of the scope of internal control testing in an auditor's report and the findings from such testing
- Evaluation by the CPA of client internal controls in place
- Monitoring quality control standards of registered CPAs

The Board inspects the registered public accounting firms to assess compliance with rules and procedures. Inspections are performed annually for CPA firms with more than 100 public company clients and every three years for those with 100 or less.

The SEC has oversight and enforcement authorities over the PCAOB.

APPENDIX A

Issuance of an FASB Statement on Financial Accounting Standards

A new FASB Statement requires the support of five of the seven Board members. FASB Statements are considered GAAP, and they must be followed. All Accounting Research Bulletins and Accounting Principles Board Opinions that were in effect when the Financial Accounting Standards Board came into existence continue to be effective until amended or superseded by FASB pronouncements.

To avoid misconceptions of the term "principles," the FASB uses the term "financial accounting standards" in its pronouncements.

The due process system of developing new FASB Standards is very important. The steps the Board uses when developing and issuing standards follow:

1. A topic is identified and placed on the Board's agenda.
2. A task force of experts is formed to define problems, issues and alternatives related to the topic.
3. FASB technical staff conducts research and analysis.
4. A *Discussion Memorandum (DM)* is drafted and released to the public.
5. A public hearing is held (usually 60 days after release of the DM).
6. The Board reviews and evaluates the input received from the public.
7. The Board deliberates on the issues and issues an *Exposure Draft (ED)*.
8. After at least a 30-day exposure period, the Board evaluates all responses to the ED.
9. A committee studies the ED in relation to the public responses, reevaluates its position and revises the ED, if necessary.
10. The full Board gives the revised draft final consideration and votes on issuance of a Statement.

APPENDIX B

International Financial Reporting Standards
IFRS

Accounting rule makers have always attempted to develop one set of accounting standards that can be used on a global basis.

International standards, known as IFRS, have been issued by the International Accounting Standards Board (IASB), an independent accounting body based in London.

PRINCIPLES-BASED STANDARDS

IFRS are "principles-based" standards, unlike GAAP, which are "rules based."

IFRS establish broad rules and dictate specific treatments. IFRS consist of the following:
- International Financial Reporting Standards (IFRS)—Standards issued after 2001
- International Accounting Standards (IAS)—Standards issued before 2001
- Interpretations originated from the International Financial Reporting Interpretations Committee (IFRIC)—Issued after 2001
- Interpretations of the Standing Interpretations Committee (SIC)—Issued before 2001

FRAMEWORK

The IFRS framework states that the objective of financial statements is to provide information about the financial position, performance and changes in the financial position of an entity that is useful to a wide range of users in making economic decisions.

SOME BASIC IFRS AND GAAP SIMILARITIES

1. The underlying assumptions are the same.
   - **ACCRUAL BASIS**—The effect of transactions and other events are recognized when they occur, not as cash is received or paid.
   - **GOING CONCERN**—The financial statements are prepared based on the presumption that an entity will continue in operation for the foreseeable future.
2. The qualitative characteristics of financial statements are
   - understandability
   - relevance
   - reliability
   - comparability

3. The statement of financial position (balance sheet) comprises:
   - **ASSETS**—Resources controlled by the entity as a result of past events and from which future economic benefits are expected to flow to the entity.
   - **LIABILITIES**—A present obligation of the entity arising from past events, the settlement of which is expected to result in an outflow from the entity of resources embodying economic benefits.
   - **EQUITY**—The residual interest in the assets of the entity after deducting all its liabilities.
4. The statement of comprehensive income (income statement) comprises:
   - **INCOME**—Increases in economic benefits during the accounting period in the form of inflows or enhancements of assets or reductions in liabilities.
   - **EXPENSES**—Decreases in economic benefits.
5. An item is recognized in financial statements when the following are true:
   - It is probable that a future economic benefit will flow to or from an entity and
   - When the item has a cost or value that can be measured with reliability.

SOME BASIC IFRS AND GAAP DIFFERENCES

1. Property, plant and equipment (PPE) are measured initially at cost.

   Cost can include borrowing costs directly attributable to the acquisition, construction or production if the entity adopts such a policy consistently.

   PPE may be revalued to fair value if the entire class of assets to which it belongs is so treated (for example, the revaluation of all office equipment). Surpluses on revaluation are recognized directly on equity, not in the income statement. Deficits on revaluation are recognized as expenses in the income statement.

   The cost or valuation of an asset is depreciated over its estimated useful life down to the recoverable amount.

   Depreciation is recognized as an expense in the income statement unless it is included in the carrying amount of another asset.

   Depreciation of PPE used for development activities may be included in the cost of a recognized intangible asset.

   The depreciation method and recoverable amount are reviewed at least annually. In most cases the method is "straight line," with the same depreciation charge from the date when an asset is brought into use until it is expected to be sold or when further economic benefits cease to be obtained.

Other patterns of depreciation such as "reducing balance" are used if assets are used proportionately more in some periods than others.

2. Inventory is stated at the lower of cost and net realizable value, which is similar in principle to lower of cost or market (LOCOM) in GAAP.

   Cost comprises all costs of purchase, costs of conversion and other costs incurred in bringing items to their present location and condition.

   Where individual items are not identifiable, the "first in first out" (FIFO) method is used, such that cost represents the most recent items acquired. "Last in first out" (LIFO) is not acceptable.

   Net realizable value is the estimated selling price less the costs to complete and costs to sell.

3. Receivables and payables are recorded initially at fair value.

   Subsequent measurement is stated at amortized cost.

   In most cases, trade receivables and trade payables can be stated at the amount expected to be received or paid. It is necessary to discount a receivable or payable that has a substantial credit period.

   If a receivable has been impaired, its carrying amount is written down to its recoverable amount—the higher of value in use or its fair value less costs to sell.

   Value in use is the present value of cash flows expected to be derived from the receivable.

4. Borrowings are stated at amortized cost using the *effective interest rate method*. This requires that the costs of arranging the borrowing are deducted from the principal value of the debt and are amortized over the period of the debt.

5. Provisions (for example, uncertainties) are liabilities of uncertain timing or amount.

   Provisions are recognized when an entity has, at the balance sheet date, a present obligation as a result of a past event, when it is probable that there will be an outflow of resources (for example a future cash payment) and when a reliable estimate can be made of the obligation.

   Restructuring provisions are recognized when an entity has a detailed plan for the restructuring and has raised an expectation among those affected that it will carry out the restructuring.

6. Revenue is measured at the fair value of consideration received or receivable.

Revenue for the sale of goods cannot be recognized until the entity has transferred to the buyer the significant risks and rewards of ownership of the goods.

Revenue for rendering of services is accounted for to the extent that the stage of completion of the transaction can be measured reliably.

7. Employee costs are recognized when an employee has rendered service during an accounting period.

   This requires accruals for short-term compensated absences such as vacation (holiday) pay.

   Profit sharing and bonus plans require accrual when an entity has an obligation to make such payments at the reporting date.

8. Income taxes payable for current and prior periods are recognized as liabilities to the extent they are unpaid at the balance sheet date.

   Deferred tax liabilities are recognized as taxable temporary differences at the balance sheet date, which will result in tax payable in future periods.

   Deferred tax assets are recognized for deductible temporary differences at the balance sheet date if it is probable that there will be future taxable profits against which they can be offset.

   There are exceptions to the recognition of deferred taxes in relation to the following:

   a. Goodwill (for deferred tax liabilities)
   b. Initial recognition of assets and liabilities in some cases
   c. Investments and interests in subsidiaries, branches, jointly controlled entities and associates, provided certain criteria are met

9. IFRS cash flow statements show movements in cash and cash equivalents.

   This includes cash on hand and demand deposits, short-term liquid investments readily convertible to cash and overdrawn bank balances that readily fluctuate from positive to negative.

   IFRS cashflow statements do not show movements in borrowings or net debt.

   Cash flow statements may be presented using either a direct method, in which major classes of cash receipts and cash payments are disclosed, or using the indirect method, whereby the profit or loss is adjusted for the effect of noncash adjustments.

   Items on the cash flow statement are classified as operating activities, investing activities and financial utilities.

CONVERGENCE OF GAAP AND IFRS

The FASB and the IASB have done quite a bit to converge the content of IFRS and GAAP.

The goal is that by the time the SEC allows or mandates the use of IFRS for U.S. publicly traded companies, most or all of the key differences will have been resolved.

The specific differences between IFRS and U.S. GAAP are disappearing. Significant differences such as the following still remain:

- IFRS do not permit last in first out (LIFO) as an inventory costing method.
- IFRS use a single-step method for impairment write-downs rather than the two-step method used in GAAP, making write-downs more likely.
- IFRS have a different probability threshold and measurement objective for contingencies.
- IFRS do not permit "curing" debt covenant violations after year-end.
- IFRS guidance regarding revenue recognition is less extensive than GAAP and contains relatively little industry-specific instruction.

The greatest difference between IFRS and GAAP is that IFRS provide much less overall detail.

FUTURE OF IFRS IN THE UNITED STATES

In August 2008, the SEC unanimously approved a roadmap that might require use of IFRS as follows:

Large Companies by the year	2014
Midsize Corporations by the year	2015
Small Businesses by the year	2016

This follows the February 2007 SEC movement to allow foreign entities to submit their financial statements using IFRS rather than U.S. GAAP.

The SEC proposal that IFRS reporting begin with 2014 filings is consistent with a 2008 AICPA survey showing that a majority of AICPA members polled believed it would take three to five years to prepare for IFRS.

PART TWO

COMMUNITY FINANCIAL INSTITUTION ACCOUNTING

CHAPTER 3

Accounting Uniqueness in Community Financial Institutions

This chapter examines certain unique banking matters and accounting characteristics of particular importance to community financial institutions. It shows how accounting for financial institutions differs from accounting for industrial companies.

After studying this chapter you should be able to

- describe the unique characteristics of banking and financial institution accounting
- explain the need for daily balancing and posting to the trial balance
- identify the entries for customer deposits and withdrawals
- distinguish between general ledger accounts and subsidiary ledger accounts
- identify the internal control that reconciles the deposit liability account of the general ledger with the individual deposit liability accounts of the subsidiary ledger
- explain the single-entry ticket approach in financial institution accounting
- explain continuous departmental accountability in the financial institution
- define *drafts* and *checks* and distinguish between them
- summarize the differences between certified checks and cashier's (official) checks
- list the journal entries associated with a certified check
- explain, compare and contrast the significance of the following items:
  – cash items
  – clearing and exchanges
  – due from correspondent
  – interest bearing deposits
- summarize the entries required when a check is dishonored (an NSF check)
- list the steps the Proof Department takes to prove deposits and collect cash for financial institution customers' check deposits
- distinguish between *due from* and *due to* accounts and the related accounting
- list the Proof Department's daily activities
- explain ledger and memo accounts

Unique Characteristics of Community Financial Institution Accounting

Depository institutions have unique characteristics that differ in many respects from those of the typical industrial company—wholesaler, retailer, manufacturer.

One obviously unique feature is that depository institutions have no inventory. A financial institution does not sell merchandise. It has no goods for sale. This eliminates many accounting problems associated with inventory, such as finished goods, work-in-process, pricing, lower of cost or market valuations, LIFO (last in first out) and layers.

Depository institutions are in the unique service business of handling *other people's money (OPM)*. The depository institution receives OPM, usually in the form of deposits from one group (depositors), and recycles the OPM to another group (borrowers). (Chapter 4 addresses financial institution activities other than deposit taking and lending.)

The deposit/loan, receipt/payment services create unique accounting practices for the depository institution. Unique characteristics of financial institution accounting include (1) daily balancing and posting to trial balance; (2) single-entry tickets; (3) continuous departmental accountability; (4) proof functions; (5) separate ledger and memo accounts. This chapter discusses each practice.

Daily Balancing and Posting to Trial Balance

Depository institutions must know exactly what their customers' deposit and loan balances are on a daily basis, so daily posting of transactions and the production of a daily trial balance and balance sheet are required. The accounting cycle (from initial recording of journal entries to trial balance) described in Chapter 1 usually occurs monthly for the typical industrial company; it occurs daily for the depository institution.

The customer's (depositor's) right—and need—to know exactly how much he or she has on deposit drives the daily cycle. A financial institution cannot tell a customer who makes a balance inquiry to "come back at the end of the month when the books are closed." Thus, daily balancing is necessary. The next sections demonstrate sample entries for recording deposits and withdrawals and present the essential internal control that ensures that all accounts balance.

RECORDING DEPOSITS

The *deposit account* is a liability account; it is the *due to customer* account. Its credit balance represents the customer's funds currently held by the depository institution. Following are the basic, redundant journal entries the depository institution uses to record deposits:

Debit:	Cash	$XXX	
Credit:		Deposits	$XXX

The financial institution usually has a general ledger deposit account for each type of deposit, such as savings and demand deposit. The financial institution also establishes a *subsidiary ledger* for each customer. A subsidiary ledger is a group of accounts with individual balances that in total equal the balance in a general ledger account.

For example, when deposits are made, the above entry is made in the journal and posted to the general ledger liability account for deposits. At the same time, the individual customer deposit accounts in the subsidiary ledger are credited. For example, assume a total deposit of $5,500 for all customer accounts consisted of the following deposits:

Customer	A	$	1,000
Customer	B		2,000
Customer	C		1,100
Customer	D		900
Customer	E		500
Total		$	5,500

The following sections show the entries the financial institution must make to record the deposit in the general journal, the general ledger and the subsidiary ledgers.

General Journal Entry

The general journal entry for the $5,500 deposit would be as follows:

Debit:	Cash	$5,500	
Credit:		Deposits	$5,500

General Ledger Entry

Figure 3.1 shows the general ledger for the deposit account after the $5,500 recording.

FIGURE 3.1 GENERAL LEDGER ENTRY

Deposits (General Ledger A/C)

	Balance	$100,000
	Deposit	5,500
		$105,500

Subsidiary Ledger Entries

Assume the total on deposit for all customers was $100,000 prior to the $5,500 deposit, and the subsidiary ledger had the following balances in the customers' accounts.

Customer	A	$ 40,000
Customer	B	30,000
Customer	C	15,000
Customer	D	10,000
Customer	E	5,000
Total		$100,000

Figure 3.2 shows the subsidiary customer ledger accounts after the appropriate portion of the $5,500 deposit is posted to each customer's account.

FIGURE 3.2 SUBSIDIARY LEDGER ENTRIES

Customer A	
Balance	$ 40,000
Deposit	1,000
	$ 41,000

Customer B	
Balance	$ 30,000
Deposit	2,000
	$ 32,000

Customer C	
Balance	$ 15,000
Deposit	1,100
	$ 16,100

Customer D	
Balance	$ 10,000
Deposit	900
	$ 10,900

Customer E	
Balance	$ 5,000
Deposit	500
	$ 5,500

The new balances in the subsidiary ledger account follow:

Customer	A	$ 41,000
Customer	B	32,000
Customer	C	16,100
Customer	D	10,900
Customer	E	5,500
Total		$105,500

RECORDING WITHDRAWALS

When depositors withdraw funds, the financial institution uses the same general ledger and subsidiary ledger posting procedures. The only difference is the deposit accounts (in both the general and subsidiary ledgers) are *debited* when the withdrawals are made.

The general journal entry for withdrawals is as follows:

Debit:	Deposits	$XXX	
Credit:	Cash		$XXX

BALANCING ACCOUNTS

The total of the subsidiary ledger deposit accounts must equal the general ledger deposit account balance. The financial institution must make a daily comparison and resolve any differences. This is an *essential internal control* at every depository institution.

Single-Entry Tickets

You might ask, "How does the institution know which subsidiary ledger deposit accounts to debit or credit?" The answer is easy. Depository institutions use a single-entry ticket approach for recording all cash transactions. A *single-entry ticket* is a ticket that is used to post only one side of the entry to record a transaction.

For example, each teller accumulates debit (for withdrawal) and credit (for deposit) tickets. At the end of each day the teller adds up all the debit and all the credit tickets to get the total debit amount and total credit amount. The net change in the totals is posted to the general ledger cash account. The actual cash on hand would be counted to see if it "proves" to the cash per the general ledger account.

The individual (single-entry) tickets determine the debits and credits to the individual and general ledger customer deposit accounts. The tickets are used for single entry—not the typical double entry—to the customer accounts.

There is only one general ledger account for each specific type of deposit. The subsidiary ledgers for each type of account contain many individual accounts. The general ledger account is for *all* customers. The subsidiary ledger accounts are for specific customer Number 1, Number 2, Number 3, etc. The total of the subsidiary ledger account balances must equal the balance in the general ledger account.

In summary, the individual tickets are used for the general ledger postings to cash and deposit accounts. The same individual tickets are used for postings to the individual subsidiary ledger accounts.

In addition to deposit and withdrawal tickets, there are other tickets. Some debit and credit tickets do not involve cash (for example, waivers of charges, corrections of mispostings), and they require careful scrutiny.

Many financial institutions have easily converted the single-entry ticket approach to an electronic debit and credit approach for on-line banking. For all practical purposes, for customer accounts, the withdrawal ticket becomes the electronic debit and the deposit ticket becomes the electronic credit.

Here is a simple example of the single-entry ticket approach. Assume that the total cash on hand at the beginning of the day in all tellers' windows in a branch network is $2,000,000. By the end of the day, customers have made the following transactions:

- $50,000 in deposits to *demand deposit accounts (DDAs)* (including $20,000 in *on us checks* (checks drawn against a customer account at the financial institution where the deposit was made)
- $60,000 in deposits to *time deposit (TD)* accounts
- $2,000 to *Holiday Club (HC)* deposit accounts
- $10,000 in cash withdrawals from savings accounts at the tellers' windows
- no new loans
- no other activity

The tellers' cages all prove. Figure 3.3 summarizes the branch-level activity and the central processing activity.

FIGURE 3.3 SUMMARY OF BRANCH AND CENTRAL PROCESSING ACTIVITY

Branch-Level Activity		Central (Proof) Processing
The "net" credit of $82,000 is the result of the following:		After the individual deposit and withdrawal tickets are accumulated, the following entries are made and posted to the general ledger:

DEBIT TICKETS	CREDIT TICKETS			
$ 20,000	$ 50,000	DDA	Debit: Cash on hand	$ 82,000
$ 10,000	$ 60,000	TD	Credit: DDA Control A/C	$ 30,000
	$ 2,000	HC	Credit: TD Control A/C	$ 50,000
$ 30,000	$112,000		Credit: HC Control A/C	$ 2,000

The individual (single-entry) tickets are posted in detail to individual customers' accounts (Customer A, Customer B, Customer C) in the subsidiary ledger. Note that the $20,000 of on us checks included in the deposit is a debit.

Continuous Departmental Accountability

Because depository institutions are in the unique position of handling other people's money, they must ensure continuous departmental accountability to address the important issues of liquidity, security and control. *Continuous departmental accountability* means that one department or branch can have accounts that are affected by activity in another department or branch.

For example, customers can make deposit and withdrawal transactions at one branch for accounts at another branch. This requires daily reconciliation. To maintain the *security* of the customers' accounts, the financial institution must make sure that only authorized persons can access accounts and make transactions. Preapproved lines, limits and authority must be established.

Depository institutions also have tickets for investments and other activities (for example, federal funds buy and sell tickets, wire transfer tickets, interdepartmental debit and credit tickets). Financial institutions use the tickets to process transactions or to adjust accounts; they must account for and *control* used and unused tickets.

Additionally, various departments hold negotiable instruments such as checks and money orders. The extreme *liquidity* of such items requires individual accountability and constant balancing of transactions to avoid or immediately pinpoint errors. Continuous intraday balancing and proving demands the availability of a sufficient audit trail.

The depository institution must continuously control drafts, checks and other negotiable instruments. Due to their liquidity, maintaining the security of such negotiable items requires special controls. Continuous departmental accountability is essential to their proper handling.

Drafts, checks, cash items, clearing and exchange items, due from correspondent banks and interest bearing deposits of the financial institution in another financial institution are discussed below.

DRAFTS

A *draft* is a standard, simplified form of a letter of instruction in which one party orders the holder of a credit balance (the financial institution) to make payment to a third party. The party that executes and issues the draft is known as the *drawer*. The party that is told to make the specified payment is the *drawee* (the party on whom the draft is drawn) or the *payor financial institution*. The beneficiary who is to receive the payment is the *payee*.

CHECKS

Since banks are the primary holders of customers' credit balances, the demand drafts drawn on them are standardized, simplified and routine.

Demand drafts drawn on banks are known as *checks*. The drawer of a check gives the drawee or payor bank written instructions to make a payment of funds against an account. One party can be both the drawer and payee of a check. For example, a person can make out a check for cash, endorse it and present it to the bank for cash. This converts part or all of the demand deposit balance into coin and currency.

Every check is a type of draft; every draft is not a check. Drafts may be *time instruments* (for example, payable in 90 days). Checks must be *demand instruments* (payable upon presentation), and they must be drawn on a bank. Drafts need not be drawn on a bank.

A financial institution must record, control, sort, present for payment and collect checks it receives as deposits. This requires continuous accountability.

CERTIFIED CHECKS

Checks are claims to funds said to be on deposit; they are not legal tender. Occasionally the payee will not accept the check as a means of payment and requests a form of payment that offers greater assurance. In such instances, a certified check is often used.

A *certified check* is a draft for which the drawee financial institution assumes liability and sets aside the necessary funds. To certify a check, the drawer presents it to the drawee financial institution. The financial institution verifies that the drawer's account contains sufficient funds to cover the check. The amount of the check is immediately charged (debited) to the drawer's account and is transferred to a special account (usually called *certified checks outstanding*) on the financial institution's books.

An official financial institution stamp and an official signature on a check convert the instrument from the drawer's promise to pay into a liability. The financial institution must account for certified checks issued in order to set aside funds for eventual payment and to properly record the financial institution's liability to its depositor's payee.

Financial institutions are not legally required to certify checks. They do so as a service to customers and for the fee income. Certified checks need special internal controls.

Internal Controls

Certified checks require certain internal controls. A certified check is usually punched or otherwise marked to prevent double processing and, thus, double charges to the drawer's account. The financial institution may also use a perforated impression as part of the certification stamp to prevent alteration of the original amount.

Stop Payment

The drawer of the certified check may subsequently ask the financial institution to stop payment on the check. If the certified check has been stolen or lost, both the drawer and the financial institution are at risk. A stop payment may be used to protect the interests of the drawer and the financial institution. A financial institution is not obliged to stop payment on a certified check. However, if the drawer agrees to sign an affidavit explaining the problem and indemnifying the financial institution against claims or losses resulting from the stop payment, the financial institution generally honors the request. The financial institution charges the customer a fee for the stop payment.

CASHIER'S CHECKS

Another negotiable instrument frequently encountered is the *cashier's check*. Cashier's checks are also called *official checks* or *treasurer's checks*. They are *not* certified checks. A financial institution draws cashier's checks on itself. The financial institution is both the drawer and the drawee. Financial institutions often use cashier's checks to pay out loan proceeds to customers, to pay suppliers, vendors, etc. Cashier's checks may also be sold to customers for a fee.

Financial institutions have a unique accounting system for issued cashier's checks. When the cashier's check is issued, a liability is created. Cash is not reduced at that time. When a financial institution draws a check on itself, it records a liability for outstanding checks. It doesn't reduce the general ledger cash account until the check is paid.

When official checks are issued, they are recorded in a check register. When the items are paid, they are checked off in the register. The total of all open items in the register represents the institution's total liability for outstanding checks and should agree with the general ledger amount.

General ledger (GAAP) entries for cashier's checks follow. When an official check is drawn:

Debit:	Expense A/C	$XXX	
Credit:	Official Check A/C (liability)		$XXX

Note: At this time, an entry is made in a check register (subsidiary record). It indicates that an official check is outstanding.

When an official check is paid:

Debit:	Official Check A/C (liability)	$XXX	
Credit:	Cash		$XXX

Note: At this time, the check register entry is marked off.

The financial institution must carefully control unused cashier's checks because they are very liquid and are "near cash." Accounting for prenumbered checks, physical counts, cut-offs and similar procedures are the usual departmental controls in the draft and check areas. These procedures assure accountability over these liquid items.

CASH ITEMS

Cash items are instruments other than coin or currency that are held for conversion to cash. Examples of cash items follow.

- **FOOD STAMPS**—Customers that have retail businesses (for example, grocery stores) sometimes receive food stamps as payment. Such businesses "deposit" the stamps and the depository institution presents the stamps for cash at the appropriate government agencies.
- **MATURING BOND COUPONS**—A financial institution receives bond coupons from customers when it has agreed to collect payments for the customer for a fee.
- **INSUFFICIENT FUNDS CHECK (NSF CHECK)**—A check deposit is presented to the drawee for payment. If it is not honored, it is returned to the financial institution. The financial institution usually charges (debits) the customer's account for the amount credited at the time of deposit.

The NSF check charge back usually results in the following entry:

Debit:	Deposits (customer account)	$XXX
Credit:	Cash	$XXX

In addition, the fee the financial institution charges the customer is recorded as follows:

Debit:	Deposits (customer account)	$XXX
Credit:	Fee Income (or expense)	$XXX

A teller's cash fund may temporarily contain cash items during the day. These items should be placed in a separate general ledger account at the end of the day. For financial statement purposes, cash items are included with the balance sheet asset caption "cash and cash equivalents."

CLEARING AND EXCHANGE ITEMS

Clearing and exchange items are checks deposited at one institution that are drawn on another institution. They are the opposite of on us checks, discussed earlier. The institution that receives these checks as part of its deposits must present the checks for collection at the drawee financial institution. This can be done by using a clearinghouse, the Federal Reserve Bank, etc.

While the check is awaiting collection, it is accounted for in an account called clearings and exchanges. This account, which will have a debit balance for the one day (or few days) required for a check to be paid, is considered to be part of cash for accounting and financial purposes.

For example, assume a customer makes a $1,200 checking account deposit with the First National Bank; the deposit consists of $200 in currency and a $1,000 check drawn on another financial institution, XYZ Bank. The teller counts the currency, compares it to the deposit slip, gives the customer a receipt for the deposit and forwards the deposit ticket and checks to the Proof Department.

The journal entry to record the transaction follows:

Debit:	Cash	$ 200	
Credit:	Clearings and Exchanges	1,000	
	Deposit Account		$1,200

The Proof Department proves the amounts deposited by comparing the checks and cash total to the total amount shown on the customer's deposit ticket.

The dollar amount of each check is then encoded at the bottom of the check. The checks are mechanically endorsed on the back and sorted. Checks written on checking accounts of the institution's customers (on us checks) are charged to the appropriate customers' accounts. The remaining checks *(foreign checks)* are written on checking accounts of other institutions and must be sent to those institutions for collection. The bank sends transmittal letters, called *cash letters*, with each batch of checks to the appropriate institutions.

After cash letters are prepared, the bank sends checks and cash letters for clearing as follows.

1. The institution may send the checks directly to the other institution on which the checks are drawn. This is likely to occur between institutions in the same community.
2. A member institution may send checks drawn on other members to the clearinghouse. A *clearinghouse* is an association of local financial institutions that is used for clearing checks drawn on member institutions.
3. *Regional Federal Reserve Banks (FRBs)* and *Federal Home Loan Banks (FHLBs)* provide check clearing and collection services for their members. If the institution is a member, it may send some or all of the checks drawn on other institutions to the FRB or FHLB in that region for clearing and collection. Corporate credit unions, which are organized and owned by credit unions, provide similar check clearing and other functions for credit unions.
4. An institution may establish a correspondent relationship through one of the larger banks in its area rather than use the FRB or FHLB. The correspondent bank would provide the check clearing and collection services for the institution. Many banks are referred to as "banker's banks." These are *correspondent banks*. They act on behalf of their customers—other financial institutions. Many smaller financial institutions engage correspondent banks to provide them with services such as collecting out-of-state amounts due, buying and selling securities, providing asset/liability management services, providing investment advice, wire-transfer receipts and payments, etc.

The financial institution establishes a due from account for each of the institutions used to clear checks. The financial institution accounts for the shipment of checks to the other institutions by debiting its due from accounts for those institutions.

Assume the same facts as in the First National Bank example above. First National Bank's Proof Department proves the $1,200 deposit and prepares a cash letter for the $1,000 check. It then sends the check and cash letter to XYZ Bank.

First National Bank records the shipment of the check for clearing by making the following journal entry:

Debit:	Due from XYZ Bank	$1,000
Credit:	Clearings and Exchanges	$1,000

A similar entry would be made if the check were cleared with the FRB, the FHLB, a clearinghouse or another institution.

A financial institution will also receive cash letters for checks drawn on its customers' accounts. Assume XYZ bank sends checks totaling $800 that are drawn on First National Bank's customer accounts. First National Bank debits those checks to the customers' checking accounts and records the transactions as follows:

Debit:	Deposit Accounts	$800
Credit:	Due to XYZ	$800

DUE FROM CORRESPONDENTS

A *due from correspondents* account represents the receivable from or the payable to a correspondent bank. When the correspondent bank collects for its financial institution customer, it gets the cash and owes the financial institution customer. In such a case the financial institution customer would debit the due from correspondent account upon notification from the correspondent bank that the cash was collected. Conversely, when the correspondent bank charges its customer for various services performed, the customer would credit the due from correspondent account. Generally, the account has a debit balance, and it is considered cash for accounting and financial statement purposes. If there were a credit balance, it would be part of deposit liabilities.

Some financial institutions have a *due to* account that is a deposit account. The institution's balance sheet should present due from accounts net of due to accounts, provided that a right of setoff exists.

INTEREST BEARING DEPOSITS

Interest bearing deposits are normally certificates of deposit or other interest bearing accounts a financial institution maintains in other financial institutions. Some institutions consider such deposits a type of due from account.

Proof Function

The central unique feature in financial institution accounting is the Proof Department. It is, in effect, the central unit in a financial institution that sorts, distributes and arrives at control figures for all transactions.

The Proof Department, which is usually in the controller's office, performs routine daily functions that include

- examining all on us check *deposits* for proper account coding
- examining all checks for collection to ensure that they are eligible for posting and can be properly posted to the maker's account
- posting all debits and credits to the current customer accounts
- arriving at updated daily closing balances for all customer accounts
- creating customer statements
- producing internal reports

The Proof Department receives batches of documents (checks, deposit tickets, etc.) from various departments as well as from external sources such as clearinghouses. It verifies the accuracy of the batch totals and then sends the items to the appropriate departments for further processing.

The Proof Department is like a "traffic cop" or central controller that initiates general ledger entries and arranges data for subsidiary ledger posting. It processes most items the same day. Holdover items should be resolved and processed the next day.

Separate Ledger and Memo Accounts

For control purposes, financial institutions must carefully maintain subsidiary ledgers for various types of memorandum accounts for commitments and contingencies (for example, credit card lines authorized, letters of credit issued, loan commitments granted, unissued traveler's checks, unissued savings bonds, standby commitments).

The financial institution has a subsidiary ledger of all individual customer deposit account balances that equals the general ledger deposit account balance. In addition, financial institutions must maintain memorandum accounts. *Memorandum accounts* are not part of the general ledger; they are maintained separately. They are a current record of off-balance-sheet risk and potential risk.

For example, when a bank issues a credit card, it authorizes a customer to use the card—up to a certain limit. That limit represents a contingent liability. Should the customer use the card, the bank must honor the card charges up to the limit.

A memorandum account is more like a summary of the nonrecorded potential liabilities. For example, for credit cards issued, the memorandum account might look like Figure 3.4.

FIGURE 3.4 MEMORANDUM ACCOUNT CREDIT CARD LIMITS

Card No.	Customer Name	Maximum Line	Amount of Line Used by Customer*	Open Line of Credit
101	A	$ 10,000	$ 8,000	$ 2,000
102	B	10,000	4,000	6,000
103	C	5,000	5,000	0
104	D	5,000	1,000	4,000
105	E	2,000	1,000	1,000
106	F	2,000	1,500	500
107	G	1,000	900	100
108	H	1,000	600	400
TOTALS		$ 36,000	$ 22,000	$ 14,000

*The amount charged by the customer and due to the bank; a loan receivable on the bank's books.

Paper versus Electronic Documents

Much of this chapter refers to checks and tickets. Naturally, over the years, electronic impulses have largely replaced checks and tickets. Some community financial institutions have sophisticated computer systems; some do not. In either case, the conceptual accounting issues covered in this chapter do not change. The basic debits and credits to the accounting from typical transactions are the same, regardless of the records used—manual or electronic.

Federal legislation called the *Check Clearing for the 21st Century Act (Check 21 Act)* has been passed to authorize banks and other depository institutions to substitute an electronic check for the original hard-copy check. The substitute check is an *image replacement document (IRD)*. The Check 21 Act changed the handling of cash payments. Nevertheless, it did not change the accounting issues related to transactions that traditionally used a check. The basic accounting concepts presented in this book remain the same, regardless of the manner of processing.

This chapter presented some unique basic characteristics of financial institution accounting. Specific financial statement issues are covered in Chapter 6, which explains certain FASB Statements that are especially applicable to financial institutions.

CHAPTER 4

Basic Business Functions and Risks of Community Financial Institutions

This chapter provides an overview of the basic business functions of community financial institutions and the related business risks they face.

After studying this chapter you should be able to
- identify six typical business functions of community financial institutions
- explain the typical business risks faced by community financial institutions

Business Functions of Community Financial Institutions

An excellent way to understand the typical community financial institution is to understand its business functions, which, in summary, are (1) funding; (2) lending; (3) investing; (4) fee-based services; (5) support activities; (6) internal accounting, reporting and compliance activities. The first four functions (funding, lending, investing, fee-based services) are the line businesses of banking. The other two (support and internal accounting, reporting and compliance activities), although important, are secondary functions that service the line activities. This chapter discusses each function.

FUNDING

Funding involves obtaining cash to "carry" the assets of the community financial institution. The cash can be borrowed or bought outright in the money markets. It can come from infusions of funds or from advances from entities such as the Federal Home Loan Bank (FHLB). See Appendix A to this chapter for information about the FHLB and FHLB advances.

Most funding comes from gathering deposits from customers. The deposit base is a community financial institution's most reliable source of funds. Customers and their families and businesses usually have long-standing relationships with their financial institution, and many of the relationships result in interest bearing and non–interest bearing deposits. These ongoing deposit relationships generate core deposits.

Core deposits are the stable, relatively inexpensive (low interest cost) deposits that remain with the typical community financial institution.

Rates can go up or down, but in most cases, total core deposit amounts remain stable.

Community financial institutions try hard to maintain core deposits. Larger commercial banks generally do not have core deposits; they must buy funds at considerably higher interest cost than the no-cost demand deposits and the low-cost time deposits. Core deposits are essential to the typical community financial institution.

Community financial institutions are innovative in their search for deposits. Funding devices for gathering cash include demand deposits and time deposits. The types of demand and time deposits are described below.

Demand Deposits

Demand deposits are liabilities of the community financial institution. They represent customers' cash that is on deposit. The major types of demand deposits include checking accounts, official checks, demand CDs and escrow deposits. A description of each type of demand deposit follows.

Checking Accounts

Checking accounts are deposit accounts that depositors use for disbursements. They are substitutes for customer cash. The customer can easily order the financial institution to make payments from these accounts simply by preparing a check. They have the greatest volume of activity. Checking accounts are generally classified by type of account (for example, individual, partnership, corporation, public deposit, trust deposits, deposits due to other financial institutions). Most checking accounts do not bear interest.

The community financial institution maintains a separate deposit account for each customer. Posting to the accounts is performed daily. Automated systems identify, monitor and control all account activity. Rejected items are handled on the following day. Rejected items include checks that are missorted, lacking endorsement, subject to stop-payment orders, etc. These items are sometimes called *holdovers*.

Official Checks

Official checks (or cashier's checks, treasurer's checks, money orders, etc.) are checks issued by the institution and drawn on itself. They are generally for expense payments, loan disbursements, dividend payments, etc.

When a financial institution draws a check on itself, it records a liability for outstanding checks. It doesn't reduce the general ledger cash account until the check is paid. When official checks are issued, they are recorded in a check register. When the items are paid, they are checked off in the register. The total of all open items in the register represents the financial institution's total liability for outstanding checks. For financial statement purposes, the total is a deposit, and it should agree with the general ledger account. See Chapter 3, for a discussion of cashier's checks.

Demand CDs

Some financial institutions offer *demand CDs*, although they are not widespread. Demand CDs are certificates of deposit that the bank must honor whenever they are presented for payment—whether they are negotiable or nonnegotiable. They have no fixed maturity date. Community banks often use demand CDs for loan collateral purposes. When a time CD comes due, the interest on it is often classified as a demand CD until the financial institution receives customer instructions to roll the proceeds over or to remit them.

Escrow Deposits

Escrow deposits represent real estate taxes and insurance payments remitted to the financial institution with customer mortgage payments. Such amounts are received in advance of the date they are payable to the taxing authority or insurance company, and they are liabilities until they are paid.

Time Deposits

Time deposits are liabilities of the financial institution that represent customer deposits that will not be drawn upon for disbursement purposes; these deposits are expected to be in the financial institution for long periods. Major types of time deposits include savings accounts, time CDs, individual retirement accounts, Keogh accounts and Club accounts.

Savings Accounts

Savings accounts are time deposits that allow depositors to withdraw cash on demand. Checks cannot be drawn against these accounts. Savings accounts generally offer higher interest rates than interest bearing checking accounts, which increasingly replace them.

Time CDs

A *certificate of deposit (CD)* is also known as a *time deposit*. CDs require that the customer keep the deposit account for a minimum period of time (generally one month to five years). They may be redeemed before maturity, but the depositor usually pays a penalty for the early withdrawal.

CDs are generally denominated in large balances, and they pay higher interest rates than other deposit accounts. CD balances are volatile because CD depositors often transfer their accounts to other entities to obtain the highest interest yield.

Jumbo CDs ($100,000 or more) are the most volatile deposit accounts. These high-dollar deposits are usually from customers who are not in the financial institution's community. They are often out-of-state brokered deposits. Such depositors have little loyalty toward the institution. They are simply interested in getting the highest yield for their deposits. The institution has little or no opportunity to cross-sell other financial institution products and services to those depositors. The deposits are likely to leave the institution if rates rise; this can happen in spite of prepayment penalties. The likelihood of rolling over these deposits is uncertain. On the positive side, such large deposits do provide funds to help carry the assets, and they have lower overhead costs than other deposits because each CD contains more dollars.

Individual Retirement Accounts

Individual retirement accounts (IRAs) are tax-deferred investment accounts for retirement savings. An IRA may be maintained as a CD or as a separate form of time deposit.

Keogh Accounts

Keogh accounts are tax-deferred retirement accounts for self-employed people. A Keogh account may be maintained as a CD or as a separate form of time deposit.

Club Accounts

Club accounts are savings accounts to which the depositor makes regular weekly or monthly deposits. Christmas, Hanukkah, Holiday and other Club accounts are examples.

Recording Deposits

Most community financial institutions focus on well-defined geographic areas. Some even have networks of branches within their geographic areas. Branches, contrary to popular belief, should be raising funds; not making loans. Branches should concentrate on getting deposits. They often raise funds by offering full services in the communities they serve.

Deposits are recorded at the amount received as follows:

Debit:	Cash	$XXX
Credit:	Deposit A/C (due to Customer Liability A/C)	$XXX

Interest bearing deposits usually have daily compounded interest. The interest can be accrued daily and credited to the customer's account monthly or quarterly. The entry to record the accrued interest follows:

Debit:	Interest Expense	$XXX
Credit:	Accrued Interest Payable	$XXX

The entry to credit the customer account follows:

Debit:	Accrued Interest Payable	$XXX
Credit:	Deposit A/C (due to Customer Liability A/C)	$XXX

A withdrawal or maturity on a deposit account is recorded as follows:

Debit:	Deposit A/C	$ XXX
Credit:	Cash	$ XXX

Fed Funds Purchased and Securities Sold under Agreements to Repurchase

Other significant funding sources include federal funds purchased and repurchase agreements.

Federal Funds

Federal funds are institution-to-institution loans of excess Federal Reserve balances. A financial institution is required to maintain a legal reserve comprising (1) funds on deposit in the institution's reserve account with a Federal Reserve Bank and (2) currency and coin on hand. If an institution's legal reserve is deficient, it may borrow federal funds to increase its reserve position. The loans are generally repayable the following day and are commonly referred to as "federal funds purchased" (by the buyer) or "federal funds sold" (by the seller).

Federal funds purchased are the acquisition of another institution's excess reserve and are a *liability* on the balance sheet of the purchaser. They are a form of funding.

Federal funds sold are the sale of excess funds and represent an *asset* of the financial institution's financial statements They are a form of lending.

Repurchase Agreements

Repurchase agreements (repos) represent agreements whereby the transferor transfers a security to a transferee in exchange for cash and simultaneously agrees to re-acquire that security at a specified future date for an amount equal to the initial cash exchange plus a stipulated interest factor. In most situations the securities involved in repo agreements are U.S. Treasuries or mortgage-backed securities.

There are three major categories of repo agreements:
- Open
- Term
- Overnight

Open repo agreements have no set termination date.

Term repo agreements have a specified termination date that is set in the repurchase agreement. Term repo agreements may be either long term or short term.

Overnight repo agreements have a one-day maturity.

Open and term repurchase agreement contracts should explicitly state whether the transferor has the right and ability to redeem collateral on short notice by either substituting collateral or terminating the contract. On the other hand, overnight repurchase agreements implicitly state that the right and ability of substitution and/or termination exists due to the short-term nature of the transaction.

Recording Fed Funds Purchased

The purchase of fed funds is recorded as follows:

Debit:	Cash	$XXX
Credit:	Fed Funds Purchased	$XXX
	(a liability account)	

The amounts earned on this type of funding transaction would generate cash and interest income. The entry follows:

Debit:	Cash	$XXX
Credit:	Interest Income	$XXX

The interest cost for borrowing would be recorded as follows:

Debit:	Interest Expense	$XXX
Credit:	Cash	$XXX

Recording Repo Agreements

The funds received are recorded as follows:

Debit:	Cash	$XXX
Credit:	Securities Sold Under Agreements to Repurchase	$XXX
	(a liability account)	

Additionally the securities "sold" or used as collateral for the cash funding are earmarked with the following entry:

Debit:	Securities Pledged to Creditors	$XXX
Credit:	Securities	$XXX

The appropriate interest income and the use of borrowed funds and interest expense for the borrowing would also have to be recorded over the term of the repo agreement.

LENDING

Lending is the disbursement of funds to borrowers who agree to pay back the funds plus interest over time; it is the primary business of the community financial institution. Indeed, the financial institution is set up to loan community deposits to community members who need funds. Lending is the financial institution's most profitable activity, and it yields the best returns.

In addition to being most profitable, the credit risk related to the lending transaction can be controlled by the financial institution. The institution can set credit standards that establish the types of loans it makes, the dollar lines and limits by loan and by lending officer, when to demand collateral and the type of collateral. In short, the financial institution can control the credit or counterparty risk while at the same time earning high income.

The community financial institution must apply all lending standards to all customers in the same fashion. The institution must consistently follow fair lending practices without discriminating in any way.

Loan Types

Lending has many forms. Figure 4.1 lists common types of loans.

FIGURE 4.1 TYPES OF LOANS

- Fixed-rate, fixed-term conventional mortgages
- Government-sponsored mortgages
- Graduated payment mortgages
- Equity loans
- Adjustable-rate mortgages
- Apartment loans
- Commercial loans
- Nonresidential real estate loans
- Secured and unsecured consumer loans (mobile homes, auto, home improvements, educational, credit card purchases)
- Savings account loans
- Agricultural loans
- Other types of loans

The financial institution records loans at the amount disbursed to the customer as follows:

Debit:	Loan Receivable	$ XXX
Credit:	Cash	$ XXX

Interest income on all loans is recorded on an accrual basis. When interest is earned, the following entry is made:

Debit:	Accrued Interest Receivable	$XXX
Credit:	Interest Income	$XXX

When the customer makes a periodic payment, which includes principal and interest, the following entry is made:

Debit:	Cash	$XXX
Credit:	Accrued Interest Receivable	$XXX
Credit:	Loan Receivable	$XXX

Loans are always carried in the balance sheet at *net realizable value* (the present value of the future cash flows). If the loan is paying as scheduled, this is always the original disbursement for the loan less the principal payments.

If the loan is deemed impaired, the net realizable value must be recalculated based on the present value of the expected future cash flows in accordance with the worked out restructuring. (Chapter 10 discusses accounting for impairments.)

Fed Funds Sold and Securities Purchased Under Agreements to Resell

Lending activities include fed funds sold and securities purchased under agreements to resell (reverse repos).

Fed Funds Sold

The financial institution with excess reserve balances sells that excess to other financial institutions. This is a lending transaction that creates a "receivable" from the financial institutions that buy the excess reserves.

The entry to record that transaction is as follows:

Debit:	Fed Funds Sold (Asset A/C) *	$XXX
Credit:	Cash	$XXX

* Due from the financial institution buying the excess reserves

Reverse Repos

Sometimes the financial institution buys U.S. government securities from a borrowing financial institution (e.g., a dealer in U.S. government securities). Usually on the following day, the borrower agrees to repurchase the securities at the same price plus interest at a predetermined rate. Those transactions are referred to as *securities purchased under reverse repurchase agreements* (reverse repos—also known as resell agreements).

The novice to banking should remember that the financial institution giving up the securities has a repo; the financial institution receiving the securities has a reverse repo. The repo creates a liability; the reverse repo creates an asset.

The entry to record the reverse repo follows:

Debit:	Securities Purchased Under Agreements to Resell	$XXX
Credit:	Cash	$XXX

INVESTING

Investing represents the conversion of non-lendable funds into financial instruments that generate investment income. Figure 4.2 lists investment instruments community financial institutions commonly use.

FIGURE 4.2 INVESTMENT INSTRUMENTS

- Government securities
- Mortgage-backed and other asset-backed securities (whole or participations)
- Corporate bonds
- Other debentures
- Deposits in interest bearing accounts
- Federal agency securities
- Municipal securities
- Other securities

Placement of Excess Funds

The primary activities of depository institutions are to take deposits and make loans. Excess deposits that a financial institution cannot loan out are invested on a short-term or long-term basis.

Regulators, auditors, accountants and others closely watch investment (and/or trading) activities of depository institutions. Concerns over investment portfolio activities relate to possible material losses the financial institution could incur by investing in or trading the following:

- Junk bonds
- Derivative securities
- High-risk investments

In addition to speculative excesses with these three types of securities, abuses can occur because some institutions violate generally accepted accounting principles (GAAP).

Priority of Investments

For depository institutions, investments have a lower priority than loans—the primary banking activity. The financial institution loan involves a relationship. Loans are made to satisfy the needs of the institution's customers and community. With a loan, the financial institution is directly involved with the customer. Although interest income is earned on the loans, the primary purpose of the loan is to meet the needs of the customer base.

The investment, on the other hand, is primarily designed to generate income, although a depository institution may buy a local bond or note simply to support community needs. Depository institutions also use their investments as collateral for deposits made by federal, state and local governmental entities. The investments are segregated, and they are the backup or protection for deposits of public funds.

Risks of Investing

Depository institutions often rely on investment rating services to determine investment quality and risk; they use agencies such as *Moody's* and

Standard & Poor's to determine investment quality risk. For unrated issues (like local bond and note offerings) in-house credit analysts rate the issues before investing. Unlike the loan decision to place funds, the financial institution usually has no direct involvement with the issuer.

The investor in debt securities is primarily concerned with *credit risk*—the possibility that the issuer will not be able to pay off the entire principal and interest as scheduled. Many federal and state issues are supported by the "full faith and credit" of the issuer, which reduces credit risk.

In addition to credit risk, when investing, the financial institution is also concerned with *market risk*—the possibility that the issue will decline in value in the secondary markets (where the capital instrument is traded).

The semi-annual (usually) cash payment of interest by the issuer to the owner of the bond or note provides the financial institution with interest income, which is a large part of investment income. The increase or decrease in the value of the bonds or notes increases or decreases investment income.

As market interest rates fluctuate, the appeal of a bond or note issue paying a fixed rate of interest increases or decreases. While U.S. government obligations are believed to carry no credit risk, they do entail market risk due to changing interest rates in the market place.

If market rates rise, the value of the investment will decline until its yield reflects market conditions. The financial institution that holds such an investment has a "holding" loss. The financial institution that sells such an investment will have a "real" loss. The opposite also holds true. If market rates decline, investment values rise, and the financial institution will have either holding gains or real gains.

Chapter 10 describes the accounting required for investment gains and losses. They will be included in the income statement or on the balance sheet in the stockholders' equity section. The determining factor will be whether the investment is classified as "held-to-maturity," "trading" or "available-for-sale." The institution's intent and ability will determine the category for classifying the investment.

Investment Portfolio Instruments and Diversification

The community financial institution should create and manage its investment portfolio to continuously have a proper combination of *liquidity, safety* and *income*. This is achieved by diversification of the types of financial instruments held. Typically the types of holdings in the investment portfolio include (1) U.S. Treasury obligations; (2) U.S. government agency obligations; (3) municipal issues (state, local, etc.); (4) other issues. Each type of financial instrument is described below.

U.S. Treasury Obligations

U.S. Treasury obligations are fully guaranteed obligations of the U.S. government, including U.S. Treasury bills, notes and bonds. These are debt securities issued by the government to help finance government activities. *Bills* are short term. They mature in 13, 26 or 52 weeks and are sold on a discount basis. *Notes* are short and medium term with maturities from one to 10 years. They usually pay interest semiannually. *Bonds* are long-term instruments with 10- to 30-year maturities. All treasury obligations are safe; they have no credit risk.

U.S. Government Agency Securities

U.S. government agency securities include short-, intermediate- and long-term debt obligations of the Federal National Mortgage Association, the Federal Home Loan Bank, the Federal Farm Credit Bank, the Student Loan Marketing Association, the Government National Mortgage Association, the Tennessee Value Authority and others. They are readily marketable and generate investment income.

Municipal Issues

Muni is the term that describes bonds issued by any government or agency of government other than the federal government (for example, issues of state, city, county, town, school district, turnpike authority).

General obligation munis are backed by the full taxing power ("full faith and credit") of the issuer. Other munis, called *revenue bonds*, are not backed by the taxing power of the issuer. They are backed by the income expected from a specific project, for example, port authority, power authority, turnpike authority.

Munis involve both *credit* and *market* risk. The municipal issuer's creditworthiness is not as good as the federal government's creditworthiness. Additionally, munis are not as widely traded. Accordingly, if a financial institution wishes to sell a muni, it might have difficulty doing so, or it might take a loss. Financial institutions buy munis for two main reasons.
- Muni income is exempt from federal income taxes and may be exempt from state and local taxes.
- Muni purchases show a serious commitment to the financial institution's local community.

Other Issues

Other financial instruments the community financial institution might invest in include banker's acceptances, other financial institutions' CDs, commercial paper, asset-backed securities, corporate bonds (mortgages, credit card, receivables), foreign government securities, etc.

The investment portfolio is not only diversified among types of issues but it may also include holdings that have a range of maturity dates. The securities with the shortest maturities give the financial institution a higher degree of liquidity; at the same time, their interest rates are usually lower than those of the longer-term issues that reflect the higher risk associated with the passage of time.

Use of Collateral

Community financial institutions use collateral to borrow from a Federal Reserve Bank and to enter into repurchase agreements. Members of the

Federal Reserve Bank can borrow from the Fed. Such borrowings require collateral in the form of securities, particularly U.S. Treasury obligations. Also, an excellent funding source is the repurchase agreement, which requires the financial institution to put up government securities, usually overnight, as collateral for the cash the financial institution receives. These short-term borrowings usually require securities that are U.S. Treasury obligations.

Borrowing from a Federal Reserve Bank

U.S. government obligations are the most acceptable type of collateral when the financial institution borrows from a Federal Reserve Bank. When borrowing, the financial institution pledges the government debt securities it has in its portfolio.

Repurchase Agreements

As stated earlier in this chapter, many financial institutions enter into *repurchase* or *reverse repurchase* agreements ("repos" or "reverse repos"). Separate accounts are maintained for repos and reverse repos.

A *repo* is a sale of government securities to a counterparty with a simultaneous agreement to buy back the same security on a specific date (usually overnight) at a specific price. The repo is a *funding* transaction.

The sale of securities under repo agreement is a borrowing of cash by the selling financial institution collateralized by the government securities that must be repurchased. Financial institutions frequently use this tool for short-term financing. Depending on the prevailing cost of money (interest rates), the repo can be an excellent way to raise funds at one rate to buy securities at a higher rate—using the very securities assigned as the collateral for the funds.

For example, on a given date, a financial institution buys a $10 million U.S. government note yielding 2¼%; it enters into a repo agreement borrowing funds at 2-5/32% to buy the securities; the securities are collateral for the borrowing.

On the following day the financial institution returns the cash, gets back the security and pockets approximately $26. For a $100 million note, the "phantom" earnings would be $260 for doing virtually nothing. The calculation of the profit follows.

Calculation of Repo Profit

$$
\begin{aligned}
2\tfrac{1}{4}\%;\ \text{earned} &= .0225000 \\
\text{2-5/32\%;\ cost} &= .0215625 \\
&\quad .0009375 \times \$10{,}000{,}000 = \\
&\quad \text{Annual net earnings } \$9{,}375 \\
&\quad \text{Daily earnings} = \\
&\quad \$9{,}375\ /\ 360 = \$26.04
\end{aligned}
$$

If the security was already in the "trading" portfolio as opposed to "held-to-maturity" or "available-for-sale," the financial institution in effect helps finance the carrying of the position via the repo. (See Chapter 10 for a discussion of the unique accounting for investments.)

The *reverse repo* is the purchase of government securities from a counterparty with a simultaneous agreement to sell back the same security on a specific date at a specific price. The reverse repo is a *lending* transaction.

The financial institution might enter into a reverse repo as a lending accommodation to an important customer. The financial institution would buy the government security from the customer (that is, disburse cash to the customer) and sell it back the next day, earning the spread on the difference between the interest earned on the government security and the cost of the funds loaned out.

FEE-BASED SERVICES

Community financial institutions, like other depository institutions, have experienced difficulties sustaining growth in *net interest income*—the difference between interest income and interest expense. As a result, these entities try to cover costs via fee-based services.

Fee-based services include all activities that generate income based on service performed rather than based on funds invested or loaned. Many customer services that in the past were free to customers now require customers to pay a fee. The fee helps the financial institution pay for many of its ever-growing expenses—particularly, people-related costs such as salaries, payroll taxes and benefits. Figure 4.3 lists some of the services for which community financial institutions may charge fees.

FIGURE 4.3 FEE-BASED SERVICES

- Sale of traveler's checks
- Sale of money orders
- Payroll deduction plans
- ATM usage fees
- Telephone transfer services
- Preauthorized deposits and payments
- Debt management counseling
- Personal trust services (writing wills, estate planning, estate management)
- Discount brokerage services
- Life insurance (individual, group)
- Credit card fees
- Debit card fees
- Loan origination service fees

Customers may pay cash for fee-based services, or the financial institution may charge customers' accounts for the services.

When the customer pays cash, the accounting entry is as follows:

Debit:	Cash	XXX
Credit:	Fee-Based Income (non-interest income)	$ XXX

When the financial institution charges a customer's account, the entry is as follows:

Debit:	Deposit Account	XXX
Credit:	Fee-Based Income	$ XXX

If fees are significant, they should be credited to deferred fee income (a liability account) until they are earned. At that time they are removed from the liability account and credited to income.

SUPPORT ACTIVITIES

Support activities include all activities that are not directly related to the primary businesses of banking (funding, lending, investing, trading, fee-based services). These activities aid, assist or support the line activities. Figure 4.4 lists some common support activities.

FIGURE 4.4 SUPPORT ACTIVITIES

- Asset/liability management
- Personnel (human resources)
- Legal
- Audit
- Comptroller
- Insurance
- Data center management
- Systems Development Life Cycle*
- Payroll
- Strategic planning
- Regulatory compliance
- Facilities management

* *Systems Development Life Cycle (SDLC)* is the high-level steering group or other mechanism that assures that all automated systems developed or acquired are needed, economical and carefully planned. It is the mechanism that protects against excess spending.

INTERNAL ACCOUNTING, REPORTING AND COMPLIANCE ACTIVITIES

These activities are similar to support activities, but they are less directly related to the line activities. They deal with the necessary accounting, recording, classifying, controlling and reporting requirements of the organization. Figure 4.5 details some common activities in this category.

FIGURE 4.5 INTERNAL ACCOUNTING, REPORTING AND COMPLIANCE ACTIVITIES

- Income tax provision and accounting for deferred tax assets and liabilities
- Accounting for loans, provisions for loan losses and loan loss reserves
- Accounting for impaired loans
- Accounting for investment securities
- Pension accounting
- Computation of capital ratios
- Accounting for goodwill impairment
- Off-balance-sheet accounting and control
- Related party accounting and disclosure
- Accounting for transfers or financial instruments
- Accounting and documentation for derivatives
- Regulatory accounting and control requirements
- Depreciation, amortization and accretion

All financial institution accountants and other employees must be familiar with all aspects of the depository organization—from line activities to support activities to accounting and reporting activities.

Business Risks Faced by Community Financial Institutions

Many financial institution managers believe that a depository institution faces only credit risk and interest rate risk. To a certain extent that is true, however, that view is too simplistic. Like all other depository institutions, community financial institutions actually face *fifteen* distinct, pervasive business risks. Each of the risks is described below.

1. **CAPITAL RISK**—This is the possibility that the organization cannot attract (or internally create) adequate capital on favorable (nondilutive) terms. *Nondilutive* means new capital can be raised without reducing or watering down the value of existing capital before raising the new capital. Capital risk is the likelihood that capital will be insufficient to "carry" assets. Many poorly capitalized entities learn about this risk when it is too late.

Capital risk is increased when excessive or unnecessary costs are incurred or revenues are foregone. Anything that reduces net income reduces equity and increases capital risk.

Financial institutions have very little capital in relation to the assets they carry. The assets are carried by "other peoples money"—the deposit balances and other funding liabilities. In fact, on a regulatory, risk-weighted basis the financial institution can have a core capital ratio (capital divided by risk-weighted assets) of only 4%, and that would be considered "adequate" for capital purposes. Not much capital is available for the typical financial institution. This would never be the case for an industrial company.

The capital is so scarce, there is a risk that it can shrink or even disappear, leaving all the risk of carrying the assets with the depositors. This is the primary concern of regulators.

Capital risk cannot be over emphasized.

2. **COLLATERAL RISK**—This is exposure to losses if a security interest is not perfected, if collateral is not safeguarded, if collateral values decline, if collateral cannot be realized.

    This risk turns into hardship for the financial institution when (1) the value of foreclosed assets is not equal to the loan on the books; (2) assets thought to be collateral cannot be obtained because of defective filing of security interests in the collateral; (3) collateral cannot be located when a loan goes bad; (4) collateral cannot be sold or otherwise disposed of.

3. **CONCENTRATION RISK**—This is the possibility that losses could be sustained because the portfolio (loans, investments) is not properly diversified. This risk is assumed when there is high concentration in particular industries or geographic regions. It also occurs when the financial institution has a large number of activities with relatively few customers.

    This is the "all eggs in one basket" risk. It occurs when too many loans are due from one specific customer, customer group, region, industry, loan type, etc. It applies to fed funds sold customers and reverse repo customers. It also applies on the liability side of the balance sheet where a substantial part of the total funding might be from one person, entity, etc.

4. **COUNTRY RISK**—This type of risk exists when a particular country's conditions (political or legal) will adversely affect a U.S. organization's ability to repatriate U.S. dollars.

    Most community financial institutions do business only in the United States with U.S. customers. Therefore, country risk is nonexistent.

5. **CREDIT RISK**—This is the traditional, ongoing risk of all depository institutions. It is the risk, chance or probability that the borrower cannot, or will not, repay the original loan amount due (principal and interest). Credit risk is also a factor in trading, investing and repo transactions where the potential exists that the party on the other side of the transaction (the counterparty) will be unable or unwilling to deliver securities and/or cash when due.

    For financial institutions that use derivatives for hedging purposes, it is the risk that the entity on the other side of the derivative arrangement will not honor the commitment when it is due.

6. **FOREIGN EXCHANGE RISK**—This is the loss exposure the depository institution faces when adverse changes occur in the value of the dollar vis-à-vis other currencies. It is the risk of decline in value of "long" foreign currency positions because the dollar strengthened or "short" foreign currency positions because the dollar weakened.

    Again, most community financial institutions have transactions denominated in U.S. dollars only. Thus they would have no foreign exchange risk.

7. **FRAUD RISK**—This is the possibility that business deals, such as loans, investments and other types of transactions, are not genuine or bona fide. It is the chance that deals are not at arm's length or are not legal.

    The fraud risk takes into account the possibility that someone within or outside the organization is perpetrating a material fraud that will harm the financial institution. The fraud can be in the form of misappropriation of assets (stealing, embezzlement, kickback schemes, etc.) or in the form of fraudulent financial reporting (manipulating financial results, "cooking the books").

8. **FUNDING RISK**—This risk involves the possibility that the depository institution will not be able to renew or roll over its liabilities when they mature.

    This risk often is the result of a disgruntled depositor base because of poor customer treatment received from the institution, lack of competitiveness, services not offered, etc.

    The depositor or counterparty must be kept happy so funds will not leave the institution at maturity or prematurely. If the funding dries up, little capital is available to replace the lost funds. In such a situation, assets must be sold. When forced to sell assets, financial institutions usually sell them at a loss, which aggravates the capital risk. Because of the thin capitalization of community financial institutions, funding risk is a very serious issue.

9. **INSIDER RISK**—This is the potential that executives, directors, principal owners and related parties may obtain privileges beyond those offered to others in the normal course of business. (Insider risk is also called *Regulation O risk*.)

    This risk can cause serious regulatory problems (fines, penalties) and can lead to public embarrassment (reputation issues) that could lead to drains on deposit balances.

10. **INTEREST RATE RISK**—This is the possibility that the financial institution will sustain losses because of improper matchings of asset and liability maturities.

    Most financial institutions are "liability sensitive." This built-in, unique situation means that the items on the right-hand side of the balance sheet (deposits, borrowings, etc.) mature and reprice faster than the items on the left-hand side of the balance sheet (loans, investments). Generally, if rates in the marketplace go up, the financial institution immediately pays more for the rollover of its short-term funding but does not immediately receive more for its longer-term loans and investments. The maturities of interest-sensitive assets and liabilities must be carefully managed to avoid losses because of the built-in interest rate sensitivity.

11. **MANAGEMENT RISK**—This type of risk involves the possibility that the competency, judgment and integrity of management and their actions will jeopardize the value of net assets.

    Many financial institutions have a very liberal promotion-from-within policy with respect to employees. Employees are often promoted to higher levels of management responsibility without having the proper training or experience for the new position. This puts a number of people in positions where they could do damage to the financial institution. Without proper training and supervision of employees, management risk can create serious problems.

12. **MARKET RISK**—As previously discussed in the chapter on investing, this risk is the potential that the value of loans, investments, etc., will decline because of fluctuating markets. It is the risk that the financial institution may not be properly "hedged."

    Generally, the market risk with respect to assets is the opposite of the interest rate risk. Simplistically, as rates rise, interest-sensitive assets go down in value; as rates decline, interest-sensitive assets go up in value. Market values generally move in the opposite direction from the movement in rates.

13. **OPERATIONS RISK**—This risk involves the possibility that inadequate, ineffective or incompetent back office activities will interfere with normal business functions. It is often referred to as "internal control" risk. (For example, it is the potential that loan collectibility will be jeopardized by poor loan authorization, documentation, collateral and loan loss estimation procedures.) See Chapter 5 for discussion of internal control.

14. **REGULATORY RISK**—This is the possibility the financial institution may engage in transactions that violate laws, statutes, regulations, etc. (For example, it is the possibility the financial institution may charge usurious rates, not make full consumer disclosure or violate Bank Secrecy Act requirements regarding currency reporting.)

    Because of the many regulatory compliance requirements, this risk must be dealt with carefully and thoroughly. Often legal personnel or compliance officers working with "line" management identify compliance requirements and create controls and procedures to assure that the financial institution is in substantial compliance with all legal requirements.

15. **STRATEGY RISK**—This is the potential that the organization may not carefully establish viable plans for operations, finance and asset/liability management.

    Without careful plans the financial institution runs the risk of becoming unprofitable and even obsolete. A strategy to focus on the business plan, the business model and the corporate goal is needed, otherwise, the financial institution will lose its bearings and suffer financially.

Always keep these fifteen risks in mind. If you are involved with any banking activity in which you cannot identify some of these risks, you are involved with an activity that does not deserve your time and effort.

In summary, proper knowledge of the organization's business activities and related risks helps the community financial institution's staff and accountants better understand accounting for transactions.

APPENDIX

FHLB Borrowings—Large Funding Source for Community Financial Institutions

FHL BANK HISTORY

In 1932, Congress established the Federal Home Loan Bank (FHLB) system to create a stable source of funds for residential mortgages.

The Great Depression undermined the existing banking system, and with it, Americans who had recently purchased—or wanted to purchase—homes.

A VITAL RESOURCE FOR COMMUNITY LENDERS

Located in Atlanta, Boston, Chicago, Cincinnati, Dallas, Des Moines, Indianapolis, New York, Pittsburgh, San Francisco, Seattle and Topeka, the FHLBs help their member financial institutions meet the diverse housing-finance and economic-development needs of their communities.

ORGANIZATION

FHLBs are government-sponsored enterprises; they are federally chartered but privately capitalized and independently managed.

Each FHLB is governed by a board of directors made up of industry directors elected by member institutions and public-interest directors appointed by the system's federal regulator, the Federal Housing Finance Board.

Each FHLB is capitalized by the capital-stock investments of its members and its retained earnings.

Members purchase stock in proportion to their borrowings from the FHLB, their holdings of mortgages and mortgage securities and their assets.

No tax dollars are involved in the operation of the FHLB system.

The FHLB system raises funds by issuing debt instruments (bonds and notes) in the capital markets. Because these instruments have "AAA" credit ratings, the FHLB system can borrow at very favorable rates and terms.

FHLB debt is not guaranteed by, nor is it an the obligation of, the U.S. government.

FHLBs are not subject to federal income tax.

The FHLBs must pay 20 percent of their net earnings to fund a portion of the interest on the Resolution Funding Corporation (REFCorp) debt, which was issued to bail out insolvent savings and loans in the 1980s.

The FHLBs contribute the greater of 10 percent of their net income or $100 million toward the Affordable Housing Program, which awards grants and rate-subsidized housing loans for low-to-moderate-income families and individuals.

MEMBERSHIP

The FHLBs provide their member financial institutions with access to economical credit products and an attractive and safe stock investment.

Lenders eligible for FHLB membership include savings banks, savings and loan associations, cooperative banks, commercial banks, credit unions and insurance companies that are active in housing finance.

The system has more than 8,000 member financial institutions.

MISSION

The mission of the FHLBs is to support members' residential-mortgage and economic-development lending activities.

In a time when cash deposits in community banks are dwindling, the funds provided by the FHLBs guarantee a stable source of funds for mortgages and community lending.

Without the FHLBs, most depository institutions would not have access to medium- and long-term sources of funding.

By supporting community-based financial institutions, the FHLB system helps strengthen communities.

The system directly benefits consumers by helping to ensure competition in the housing-finance market.

FHL BANK ADVANCES

Advances are low-cost loans made by the FHLBs to their member institutions. Advances ensure that financial institutions will have sufficient funds to meet the credit needs of their communities. All member financial institutions know that FHLBs will be there for them to help them service their communities.

Benefits to Borrowers

Advances benefit member institutions and the nation's banking system in several ways:
- Advances increase the availability of residential mortgage and community investment credit, thus lowering borrowing costs for home buyers, small businesses and other community borrowers.
- Advances enable member institutions to ensure a steady flow of credit and other services for housing and community development.
- Advances provide funding to smaller lenders that lack access to funding sources available to larger entities.

Collateral

FHLB members that borrow advances must pledge collateral against them. By statute, that collateral is limited to major types of mortgage loans and mortgage-backed securities.

Community financial institutions (CFIs) with assets of less than $567 million may also pledge small business and agricultural loans.

Issues Related to Advances

The FHLB was once a regulator of the thrifts (savings and loan associations and savings institutions—the home loan banks).

About 3,000 thrifts went out of business in the 1980s, and the FSLIC (Federal Savings and Loan Insurance Corporation) funds were depleted.

Many survivors of the S&L crisis lost core deposits that took flight to safer harbors.

The FIRREA (Financial Institutions Reform, Recovery and Enforcement Act), among other things, changed the 12 FHLBs to a system of wholesale banks. FIRREA terminated the FHLB regulatory role. FHLBs simply became wholesale banks that made funds available for thrifts (their members at the time) to meet mortgage loan demand. Eventually membership was open to institutions other than thrifts.

There is some concern that many members take advances (at favorable government subsidized rates) simply because they can do so.

A borrowing at the Federal Reserve Bank is generally viewed negatively. It is considered a desperate borrowing by a bank with liquidity problems.

A borrowing from an FHLB is done routinely by banks and thrifts throughout their fiscal years, and it is not considered negative.

The funding for FHLB members is provided on a large scale by advances. Some investors and regulators are concerned about FHLB advances. For a bank that is fully "loaned out" (loan-to-deposit ratio greater than 100%), advances make sense. For others, especially those with a large available-for-sale portfolio, they don't. If the advances are not used to satisfy mortgage loan demand, they are not being used as intended, and taxpayer funds earmarked for housing may be used for other activities.

This is not a good thing for a government with a large budget deficit and lots of outstanding debt. The use of taxpayer money to subsidize non-housing activities is a growing, serious and controversial issue.

Some believe institutions without core deposits simply use tax money to finance their activities. The readily available advances have become a crutch.

Some believe the ease of inexpensive borrowing from the FHLB discourages institutions from developing core deposits. Many of the institutions that use FHLB advances as a crutch are the very ones that do not have core deposits and often have very low capital ratios. This means the government is financing weaker, riskier institutions with funds earmarked for housing. That is not good!

CHAPTER 5

Internal Controls in Community Financial Institutions

This chapter introduces and explains the importance of internal control. It emphasizes that internal control is part of the overall management process that, among other things, generates reasonably accurate GAAP financial statements.

After studying this chapter you should be able to

- explain the purpose of the Treadway Commission (the "Fraud" Commission) and its Committee of Sponsoring Organizations (COSO)
- define *internal control*
- list internal control objectives
- describe the five interrelated components of internal control defined by COSO
- explain the relationship between objectives and components
- define *effectiveness* and *adequacy*
- identify good documentation of internal control
- explain the major differences between the Federal Deposit Insurance Corporation Improvement Act of 1991 and the Sarbanes-Oxley Act of 2002
- summarize the requirements the Sarbanes-Oxley Act places upon corporations
- describe Public Company Accounting Oversight Board actions and criticisms

Recent Internal Control Initiatives

Internal controls are the procedures management puts in place to safeguard assets, to generate financial statements that are free of material misstatements and to help management achieve its objectives. Internal controls are very important for community financial institutions because they give management and the board of directors of each community financial institution the assurance that the institution is being run in a safe and sound fashion. Internal controls for the community financial institution are an important tool for the conduct of effective corporate governance.

For many years members of the private sector (professional associations, corporate leaders, academia) and government (Securities and Exchange Commission) have addressed the need for effective internal controls. In 1985 the *National Commission on Fraudulent Financial Reporting*, known as the *Treadway Commission*, was formed to identify factors that cause fraudulent financial reporting and to make recommendations to reduce the incidences of such reporting.

The five organizations that sponsored the Treadway Commission were the
1. American Institute of Certified Public Accountants (AICPA)
2. American Accounting Association (AAA)
3. Financial Executives Institute (FEI)
4. Institute of Internal Auditors (IIA)
5. Institute of Management Accountants (IMA)—formerly the National Association of Accountants (NAA)

These private sector organizations formed a *Committee of Sponsoring Organizations (COSO)* to support implementation of the Treadway recommendations. In 1992 COSO issued a report entitled *Internal Control—Integrated Framework* that provided guidance on internal control. The COSO internal control report
1. provided a *foundation* or *bedrock* for mutual understanding
2. established a *common language* to communicate internal control issues more effectively
3. enabled legislators and regulators to gain an increased *understanding* of internal control
4. provided educators with a *base* for future *research*

The COSO report provided a common reference point for companies to assess the quality of their internal control. Since most community financial institutions are corporations, they have much to learn from the recommendations of the COSO report.

The government, via the passage of the *Federal Deposit Insurance Corporation Improvement Act of 1991 (FDICIA)* and the *Sarbanes-Oxley Act of 2002 (SOX)*, embraced the internal control guidance set forth by COSO.

The beginning of this chapter summarizes aspects of the COSO report that are of interest to community financial institutions. The end of the chapter highlights the important differences between FDICIA and SOX and then details the major provisions of the Sarbanes-Oxley Act with which publicly owned community financial institutions must be familiar.

The COSO Report

The COSO report (1) defined internal control; (2) described internal control components; (3) provided criteria for management and others to assess control systems; (4) provided guidance on public reporting on internal control; (5) provided tools for conducting an evaluation of an internal control system.

This section focuses on the COSO report's internal control definition, objectives and components. It demonstrates the relationships between the objectives and components. It also explores the concepts of effectiveness and adequacy as well as documentation of internal control as presented in the COSO report.

INTERNAL CONTROL DEFINITION

The publication *Internal Control—Integrated Framework*, in its Executive Summary, defines internal control as follows.

> A process, effected by an entity's board of directors, management and other personnel, designed to provide reasonable assurance regarding the achievement of objectives in the following categories:
> - Effectiveness and efficiency of operations.
> - Reliability of financial reporting.
> - Compliance with applicable laws and regulations.[1]

Some of the terms and concepts included in the COSO internal control definition are explored in detail below.

Process

Internal control is not a separate activity; it is a series of activities. Internal control is part of a company's (community financial institution's) management process. It is most effective when it is built into the organization's infrastructure. Internal control should be "built in" rather than "built on."

People

Internal control effectiveness depends on the board of directors, management and other personnel. What the people of an organization do and say has an effect on internal control. The people establish the entity's objectives; they put control mechanisms into place and make them work.

Reasonable Assurance

Internal control provides only "reasonable assurance" that company objectives are achieved. Achieving goals is affected by inherent limitations such as the following:
- Faulty judgments in decision making
- Cost benefit considerations (some control benefits do not outweigh their costs)
- Breakdowns due to human failure (for example, simple errors or mistakes)
- Employee collusion
- Management override

---

[1] Committee of Sponsoring Organizations of the Treadway Commission, *Internal Control—Integrated Framework* (1992).

INTERNAL CONTROL OBJECTIVES

Every business must carefully set forth exactly what it wants to achieve. It must know its objectives. Then and only then can it establish strategies for achieving those objectives.

The COSO internal control objectives fall into three categories:
- **OPERATIONS**—controls related to effective and efficient use of the entity's resources
- **FINANCIAL REPORTING**—controls related to the preparation of reliable published financial statements
- **COMPLIANCE**—controls related to the entity's adherence to applicable laws and regulations

INTERNAL CONTROL COMPONENTS

The five *interrelated* COSO components of internal control are (1) control environment; (2) risk assessment; (3) control activities; (4) information and communication; (5) monitoring. A discussion of each component follows.

1. **CONTROL ENVIRONMENT**—The control environment is about people—their integrity, ethical values and competence—and the environment in which they operate. They are the key ingredients; they drive the entity forward. The people and their environment are the foundation on which everything else rests. The control environment is about the "tone at the top."
2. **RISK ASSESSMENT**—The organization must be aware of and deal with the risks it faces. It must establish and integrate objectives for all activities. It must establish mechanisms to identify, analyze and manage the related risks, and it must control the risks that could interfere with the established objectives.
3. **CONTROL ACTIVITIES**—The financial institution must establish and execute control policies and procedures to ensure that risks are managed and objectives are achieved.
4. **INFORMATION AND COMMUNICATION**—Control activities are surrounded by information and communication systems that enable people to capture and exchange the information needed to control the company's operations.
5. **MONITORING**—The entire internal control process must be monitored. The financial institution must make ongoing modifications as necessary. The system must react dynamically to changing conditions.

Internal control is a repetitive process. All five components are intrinsically linked; any one component can and will influence another component.

RELATIONSHIPS BETWEEN OBJECTIVES AND COMPONENTS

Internal control objectives and components are directly related. Each of the five *components* just discussed is directly related to each of the three *objective* categories detailed in the previous section. Figure 5.1 demonstrates the direct relationships between the objectives and the components.

FIGURE 5.1 RELATIONSHIPS BETWEEN OBJECTIVES AND COMPONENTS

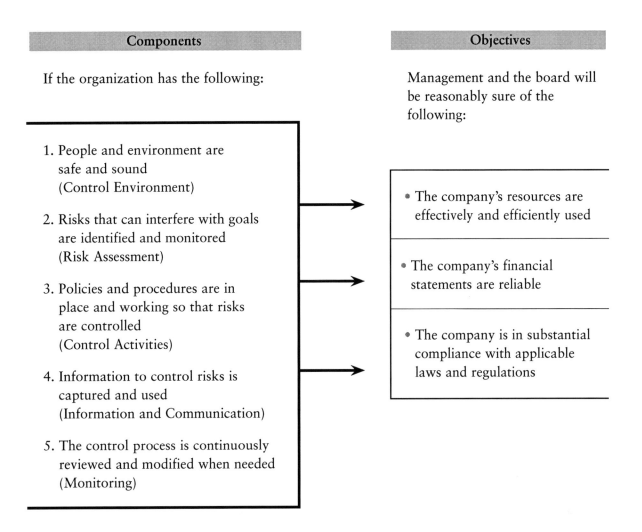

EFFECTIVENESS

Effective controls are those internal controls that work as prescribed, and they work "often enough." Internal control is effective in each of the three objective categories if the board of directors and management have reasonable assurance that the following conditions are met.
- They understand the extent to which the business is achieving its operations.
- Published financial statements are reliably prepared.
- The business complies with applicable laws and regulations.

As we mentioned earlier, internal control is a process. Internal control effectiveness is the *state* or *condition* of the process at a point in time.

"Effective" is a *subjective judgment* based on the assessment of whether the five components are present and functioning. Internal control is effective if it provides reasonable assurance that one or more of the three categories of objectives will be achieved.

Both FDICIA and SOX require management to certify that internal controls are adequate and effective. This requires careful documentation of the internal control components as well as a review and testing of the internal controls and a "call" on adequacy and effectiveness.

The call is whether the system of internal control is *adequate* (controls are designed to prevent or detect material errors or irregularities, generate reasonably accurate financial statements and help management achieve its objectives) and *effective* (controls work as prescribed by management and work often enough).

Management must conclude whether the internal controls are
- adequate (with no call about effectiveness)
- adequate and effective
- adequate but ineffective
- inadequate

Management should take care not to test the controls in systems that are *inadequate* or *adequate but ineffective*. By definition, these systems cannot be relied upon to protect assets and generate reasonably accurate financial information. For management to be comfortable with the organization's financial information, such systems would have to be ignored. *Substantive tests* (expensive, detailed tests of transactions and balances) would have to be performed to obtain satisfaction about the information generated by the inadequate or ineffective system.

ADEQUACY

The term "adequate" is a technical term. An *adequate* system of internal controls is one in which policies and procedures (control activities) are in place and are properly designed to detect material errors, irregularities (including fraud) and other risks that could interfere with management's objectives.

Errors

Errors are unintentional misstatements or omissions of amounts or disclosures in financial statements. Errors may involve
- mistakes in gathering or processing accounting data from which financial statements are prepared
- incorrect accounting estimates arising from oversight or misinterpretation of facts
- mistakes in application of accounting principles relating to amount, classification, manner of presentation or disclosure

Irregularities

Irregularities are intentional misstatements or omissions of amounts or disclosures in financial statements. Irregularities include fraudulent financial reporting undertaken to render financial statements misleading (sometimes called *management fraud*) and misappropriation of assets (sometimes called *defalcations*). Irregularities may involve acts such as the following:
- Manipulation, falsification or alteration of accounting records or supporting documents from which financial statements are prepared

- Misrepresentation or intentional omission of events, transactions or other significant information
- Intentional misapplication of accounting principles relating to amounts, classification, manner of presentation or disclosure

DOCUMENTATION

A business usually makes the call on adequacy and effectiveness (and in many cases, efficiency) after line management reviews and assesses the respective areas of responsibility and tests the controls. The basis for the assessment is usually determined after review of careful documentation. Good documentation generally identifies the area's objectives, risks and controls. It might also indicate the monitoring and/or testing done by management, internal auditors or others.

An example of the type of documentation used to help with management's internal control assessment for the conventional mortgage lending activity appears in Figure 5.2.

FIGURE 5.2. INTERNAL CONTROL DOCUMENTATION

Internal Control Matrix—Conventional Mortgage Lending

Objectives and Associated Risks	Control Activities
1. Amounts receivable will become *poor credits* (nonpayers, late payers, etc.) (Credit Risk)	1. Procedures for approving mortgage loans include • careful creditworthiness analysis • authorization guidelines • continuous monitoring • analytical overview • early warning techniques Lenders and monitors do not have incomplete duties
2. Poor credits will not be accounted for properly (Operations Risk)	2. Management carefully monitors "rules" of accounting for nonperforming loans
3. Loans are overly concentrated (Concentration Risk)	3. Procedures are in place to prepare accurately classified reports showing each type of loan and related pertinent classified data Management reviews classification of loan reports and compares to predetermined policy on concentration

Continued

FIGURE 5.2—Continued

Objectives and Associated Risks	Control Activities
4. Collection efforts for poor credits are unfavorable (Management Risk)	4. Poor credits are reviewed by a "work out" group that protects the institution and tries to get back as much as possible
5. The credit or loan review function is lax (Operation & Credit Risk)	5. The loan review function exists and has specific requirements for ongoing review of the following: • Payback ability • Collateral value • Title • Insurance • Adequate escrow balance • Unpaid taxes • Redlining issues • Misapplication of payments • Maintenance of proper documentation
6. The value of the underlying home is not continuously reviewed (Collateral Risk)	6. Home values are reviewed periodically
7. The applicant is not given proper regulatory disclosure information (Regulatory Risk)	7. Classes are held to let employees know exactly what disclosure data applicants must receive

Note: In practice, the documentation of the objectives, risks and controls might be more extensive.

Comparison of FDICIA and SOX

Both FDICIA and SOX embrace the COSO internal control framework. SOX applies to *all* public companies, while FDICIA applies only to depository institutions with $1 billion or more in total assets.

FDICIA addresses the problems that occurred during the 1980s and 1990s. It specifically regulates the banking industry. It sets forth requirements for all depository institutions (public or private) that have $1 billion or more in assets. Community financial institutions that have assets in that range are subject to FDICIA. Regulators look favorably upon FDICIA requirements with respect to internal controls. Regulators strongly encourage community financial institutions of all asset sizes to comply with FDICIA by having the COSO framework in place.

SOX addresses the serious financial irregularity problems of the 1990s. It was designed to thwart the future efforts of corporate management, external auditors and others who might consider using deceitful accounting practices to mislead investors, creditors and others and to benefit themselves. The act sets forth requirements for all publicly owned companies; it has no asset-size test. Community financial institutions that are publicly owned are subject to Sarbanes-Oxley.

Sarbanes-Oxley Provisions

As we saw in Chapter 2, SOX was signed into law by the president on July 30, 2002, following overwhelming approval by Congress. This act will have a significant, long-term impact on corporate governance, periodic disclosure, regulation of auditors, nonaudit services, SEC enforcement, securities litigation, research analysts and benefits for directors and executive officers as well as corporate responsibility for adequate and effective internal controls. The remainder of this chapter discusses provisions of SOX that are of particular importance to community financial institutions.

PROHIBITED SERVICES USED BY COMMUNITY FINANCIAL INSTITUTIONS

Many public companies, including community financial institutions, have used third-party companies to provide services. In an era of outsourcing, it is not uncommon that outsiders perform many of the corporation's tasks. The outsourcees frequently were the public company's outside auditors. The auditors were supposed to be independent with respect to the company in order to render an opinion on the company's financial statements—an output of the internal control system was in place.

A number of large financial scandals resulted from audited financial statements that were materially misstated. Those financial statements were audited by CPA firms that also performed other outsourced services such as (1) bookkeeping; (2) financial information systems design and implementation; (3) appraisal or valuation services; (4) fairness opinions, or contribution-in-kind reports; (5) actuarial services; (6) internal audit outsourcing services; (7) management or human resources services; (8) broker or dealer, investment adviser or investment banking services; (9) legal services and expert services unrelated to the audit.

SOX prohibits outside auditors from performing those nine services for public companies. However, the financial institution's board is authorized to allow the outside auditor to provide the prohibited services *if* approval is received from the Securities and Exchange Commission. For example, the board might exercise its authority to hire the outside auditors to perform a prohibited service if it would create an extreme hardship on the financial institution not to do so.

Additionally, the company's audit committee—a separate, independent group of the board—must approve all services (prohibited or otherwise) the outside auditor provides. SOX also requires periodic disclosure of all services provided by outside auditors.

AUDIT COMMITTEE RESPONSIBILITIES

The board must designate an independent audit committee to be responsible for appointing, compensating and overseeing the work of the public accounting firm. The audit committee will also be responsible for the resolution of disagreements (about financial reporting) between management and the public accounting firm.

The corporate entity must provide the audit committee with the resources it needs to perform its oversight duties. Financial institutions that have been subject to FIDICIA since 1991 already have strong boards and audit committees. Publicly owned banks that may not have been subject to FDICIA now may be subject to SOX. These financial institutions will be required to improve in the audit committee area.

MANAGEMENT INTERNAL CONTROL RESPONSIBILITIES

In its efforts to avoid any repetition of the financial irregularities of the 1990s, SOX places detailed responsibilities for internal control directly upon management.

In each annual or quarterly report filed, the financial institution's principal executive officer and principal financial officer are required to certify that (1) they have reviewed the report; (2) to their knowledge the report is true and not misleading; (3) to their knowledge the information in the report fairly presents the financial institution's operations and financial condition; (4) they are responsible for establishing and maintaining internal controls; (5) they have evaluated the effectiveness of those internal controls; (6) they have disclosed any significant deficiencies in the internal controls and any fraud whatsoever to the financial institution's auditors and the audit committee of the board of directors; (7) they have indicated whether any significant change in internal controls has materially affected or is likely to materially affect the company's internal control over financial reporting.

A signed certification from each of the financial institution's principal officers must accompany each annual or quarterly report. Figure 5.3 is an example of the required certification based on the "Final Rules Requiring Internal Control Reports in Annual Reports Pursuant to Section 302(a) of the Sarbanes-Oxley Act" issued by the SEC.

FIGURE 5.3
CERTIFICATIONS PURSUANT TO SECTION 302 OF THE
SARBANES-OXLEY ACT OF 2002

This Certification is requred by the final SEC rules for Section 302 of SOX.
CERTIFICATION

I, (Name of CEO), certify that:

1. I have reviewed this Annual Report on Form 10-K for the year ended December 31, 2008, of XYZ Financial Corporation;
2. Based on my knowledge, this report does not contain any untrue statement of a material fact or omit to state a material fact necessary to make the statements made, in light of the circumstances under which such statements were made, not misleading with respect to the period covered by this report;
3. Based on my knowledge, the financial statements, and other financial information included in this report, fairly present in all material respects the financial condition, results of operations and cash flows of the registrant as of, and for, the periods presented in this report;
4. The registrant's other certifying officers and I are responsible for establishing and maintaining disclosure controls and procedures (as defined in Exchange Act Rules 13a–15(e) and 15d–15(e)) and internal control over financial reporting (as defined in Exchange Act Rules 13a–15(f) and 15d–15(f)) for the registrant and have:

   a) Designed such disclosure controls and procedures, or caused such disclosure controls and procedures to be designed under our supervision, to ensure that material information relating to the registrant, including its consolidated subsidiaries, is made known to us by others within those entities, particularly during the period in which this annual report is being prepared;

   b) Designed such internal control over financial reporting, or caused such internal control over financial reporting to be designed under our supervision, to provide reasonable assurance regarding the reliability of financial reporting and the preparation of financial statements for external purposes in accordance with generally accepted accounting principles;

   c) Evaluated the effectiveness of the registrant's disclosure controls and procedures and presented in this report our conclusions about the effectiveness of the disclosure controls and procedures, as of the end of the period covered by this report based on such evaluation; and

Continued

FIGURE 5.3—*Continued*

> d) Disclosed in this report any change in the registrant's internal control over financial reporting that occurred during the registrant's most recent fiscal quarter (the registrant's fourth fiscal quarter in the case of an annual report) that has materially affected, or is reasonably likely to materially affect, the registrant's internal control over financial reporting; and
>
> 5. The registrant's other certifying officer(s) and I have disclosed, based on our most recent evaluation of internal control over financial reporting, to the registrant's auditors and the audit committee of the registrant's board of directors (or persons performing the equivalent functions):
>
> a) All significant deficiencies and material weaknesses in the design or operation of internal control over financial reporting which are reasonably likely to adversely affect the registrant's ability to record, process, summarize and report financial information; and
>
> b) Any fraud, whether or not material, that involves management or other employees who have a significant role in the registrant's internal control over financial reporting.
>
> Date: February 28, 2009
> /s/ (Name)
> Chief Executive Officer
>
> *Note:* Two separate certifications are required; one for the CEO and one for the CFO.

This internal control certification is especially difficult for some companies to make because it implies that the organization continuously evaluates the internal controls to ensure that they provide reasonable assurances that the company has properly collected, processed and disclosed all required information (financial and nonfinancial) in its periodic reports.

For companies that have already embraced the requirements of the Committee on Sponsoring Organizations (COSO) of the Treadway Commission and that comply with FDICIA, this requirement is not so onerous.

AUDITOR INTERNAL CONTROL RESPONSIBILITES

In addition to the management certifications, the independent CPA firm (now called "independent registered public accounting firm") must issue an attestation report on the internal control. That CPA report must be part of the annual report to stockholders. An example is in Figure 5.4.

FIGURE 5.4
REPORT OF INDEPENDENT REGISTERED PUBLIC ACCOUNTING FIRM

REPORT OF INDEPENDENT REGISTERED PUBLIC ACCOUNTING FIRM

Board of Directors and Stockholders
XYZ Financial Corporation

We have audited XYZ Financial Corporation's internal control over financial reporting as of December 31, 2008, based on criteria established in *Internal Control—Integrated Framework* issued by the Committee of Sponsoring Organizations of the Treadway Commission ("COSO"). XYZ Financial Corporation's management is responsible for maintaining effective internal control over financial reporting and for its assessment of the effectiveness of internal control over financial reporting, included in the accompanying *Management's Report on Internal Control over Financial Reporting*. Our responsibility is to express an opinion on the Company's internal control over financial reporting based on our audit.

We conducted our audit in accordance with the standards of the Public Company Accounting Oversight Board (United States). Those standards require that we plan and perform the audit to obtain reasonable assurance about whether effective internal control over financial reporting was maintained in all material respects. Our audit included obtaining an understanding of internal control over financial reporting, assessing the risk that a material weakness exists, and testing and evaluating the design and operating effectiveness of internal control based on the assessed risk. Our audit also included performing such other procedures as we considered necessary in the circumstances. We believe that our audit provides a reasonable basis for our opinion.

A company's internal control over financial reporting is a process designed to provide reasonable assurance regarding the reliability of financial reporting and the preparation of financial statements for external purposes in accordance with generally accepted accounting principles. A company's internal control over financial reporting includes those policies

Continued

FIGURE 5.4—*Continued*

and procedures that (1) pertain to the maintenance of records that, in reasonable detail, accurately and fairly reflect the transactions and dispositions of the assets of the company; (2) provide reasonable assurance that transactions are recorded as necessary to permit preparation of financial statements in accordance with generally accepted accounting principles, and that receipts and expenditures of the company are being made only in accordance with authorizations of management and directors of the company; and (3) provide reasonable assurance regarding prevention or timely detection of unauthorized acquisition, use, or disposition of the company's assets that could have a material effect on the financial statements.

Because of its inherent limitations, internal control over financial reporting may not prevent or detect misstatements. Also, projections of any evaluation of effectiveness to future periods are subject to the risk that controls may become inadequate because of changes in conditions, or that the degree of compliance with the policies or procedures may deteriorate.

In our opinion, XYZ Financial Corporation maintained, in all material respects, effective internal control over financial reporting as of December 31, 2008, based on criteria established in *Internal Control—Integrated Framework* issued by the Committee of Sponsoring Organizations of the Treadway Commission ("COSO").

We also have audited, in accordance with the standards of the Public Company Accounting Oversight Board (United States), the consolidated balance sheets of XYZ Financial Corporation as of December 31, 2008, and 2007, and the related consolidated statements of income, changes in stockholders' equity, and cash flows for each of the years in the three-year period ended December 31, 2008, and our report dated February 25, 2009, expressed an unqualified opinion on those consolidated financial statements.

Chicago, Illinois
February 25, 2009

PCAOB Actions and Criticisms

As we saw in Chapter 2, the Public Company Accounting Oversight Board is now responsible for overseeing the activities of auditors of public companies. The PCAOB, like Congress, has been especially concerned with internal controls.

EXCESSIVE COSTS RELATED TO INTERNAL CONTROL WORK

The PCAOB issued *Auditing Standard 2 (AS2)* that provided guidance to CPAs on how to audit management's internal controls for public companies. Many believe the guidance resulted in very expensive and ineffective involvement with internal controls. Management, in particular, thought the guidance was "overkill" and an overreaction to the financial irregularities that were to be cured by SOX.

Some critics of the extensive auditor involvement with internal controls were not happy. They argued that AS2 was put together haphazardly and caused unnecessary costs for corporations. They believed the arduous requirements of AS2 have led foreign companies to list their shares on stock exchanges outside the United States.

Some believed this was a false argument. They noted that SOX, Section 404, was virtually identical to section 112 of FDICIA relating to internal controls for banks. Additionally, Congress addressed internal controls in the Foreign Corrupt Practices Act in 1977. They noted that it was hard to conclude that Congress acted hastily on internal controls when passing SOX.

The controversy over internal control involvement continued to grow. The most pressure probably came from those who would have liked to see large groups of companies relieved entirely from section 404 responsibility. They wanted a complete roll back of the extensive involvement in controls.

The PCAOB, under pressure, perhaps, issued *Auditing Standard 5 (AS5)*, which superseded AS2. AS5 attempted to eliminate unnecessary requirements while preserving the key principles in AS2.

AS5 was a shorter, reorganized standard that outlined the audit process from the planning stage through the integration of the internal control audit with the audit of financial statements. AS5 provided guidance on tailoring the audit to the attributes of smaller, less complex companies. AS5 revised the AS2 definitions of material weakness and significant deficiency to encompass a "reasonable possibility" that a significant misstatement will not be prevented or detected. AS5 also refocused the auditors' multilocation testing requirements on risk rather than coverage. AS5 addressed the problem of scalability that concerned smaller companies. The standard contains a separate section on scalability with specific guidance for smaller company audits.

AS5 was approved by the SEC on July 25, 2007, and became effective for audits of fiscal years ending on or after November 15, 2007. (Auditors of companies with market capitalization of $75 million or less did not have to perform an internal control audit until fiscal years ending on or after December 15, 2008.)

LITIGATION

Additional PCAOB criticism resulted in a litigation that threatened the very survival of the PCAOB. A suit was originally filed in 2006 by a free market advocacy nonprofit organization in Washington, D.C., and a small CPA firm in Nevada. The plaintiffs claimed the creation and operation of the PCAOB under SOX violated the appointments clause (Article II, Section 2) of the U.S. Constitution—the separation of powers principles and the nondelegation principles. Plaintiffs argued that SOX did not permit adequate control over PCAOB by the President of the United States.

In September 2008 the constitutionality of the PCAOB was upheld in a two to one decision by the D.C. Circuit Court of Appeals. Plaintiffs are considering appeals—a hearing in front of the full D.C. Circuit Court or an appeal to the Supreme Court. A number of large, prestigious organizations (TIAA-CREF, AFL-CIO, pension funds, etc.) support the plaintiffs' position.

The controversy over internal controls, SOX and PCAOB will probably continue for the foreseeable future.

CHAPTER 6

Typical Financial Statements of a Community Financial Institution

This chapter presents the financial statements of the typical community financial institution. It explains key elements of the financial statements and related footnotes.

After studying this chapter you should be able to
- identify the typical GAAP financial statements of a community financial institution
- explain the purpose of the balance sheet, the income statement and the statement of cash flows
- explain the importance of the footnotes in the financial statement
- describe the purpose of the independent auditor's report
- identify typical information included with other supplemental data
- explain the purpose of management's discussion and analysis

GAAP Financial Statements

Depository institutions are required to provide regulators with quarterly financial information (the *Call Report* or the *Thrift Financial Report*). Financial institutions generally file that financial information on required forms and in the regulators' required formats.

Depository institutions usually provide owners with much information in their annual reports to shareholders. The annual report to shareholders contains the annual financial statements, which include the following:
- Balance sheet
- Income statement
- Statement of cash flows
- Statement of changes in stockholders' equity

The financial statements are *consolidated*—they include all subsidiaries, units, branches, departments, etc., of the business. Holding companies also use consolidated statements.

A *holding company* is a nonoperating corporate entity whose assets are investments in financial institutions and investments in any other operating entities (leasing companies, mortgage service companies, etc.). It consolidates all of its ownership interests (*holdings*) and prepares consolidated financial statements—much as an individual financial institution consolidates its subsidiaries, units, branches, departments, etc. Many depository organizations set up holding companies.

The consolidated financial statements and footnote disclosures in this chapter illustrate that a financial institution must present financial statements in accordance with generally accepted accounting principles (GAAP). The financial statements herein are not intended to cover all possible situations and disclosures required by GAAP.

Publicly owned depository organizations must also comply with the disclosure regulations of their securities regulatory authorities (for example, SEC). Those disclosure regulations require that financial statements be presented for more periods and contain more detailed disclosures than GAAP.

The following sections discuss each of the GAAP financial statements as well as the notes to the financial statements that are integral parts of the financial statements themselves.

BALANCE SHEET

The *balance sheet* or *statement of financial position* shows the depository institution's *assets* (the resources the business owns); its *liabilities* (the claims against its resources); *the stockholders' or owners' equity* (the residual—what is owned minus what is owed) as of a particular date.

INCOME STATEMENT

The *income statement* shows the results of the organization's operations. It demonstrates the net result of interest income less interest expense—*net interest income*. The income statement then reduces this net interest income by the *provision for loan losses*—the amount set aside for future loan losses that are probable and reasonably estimable. It also shows "other" (noninterest) income and expense that is added to or subtracted from net interest income after the provision for loan losses. The result is income before income taxes. The bottom line is net income.

STATEMENT OF CASH FLOWS

The *statement of cash flows* shows what the organization did with its cash and cash equivalents during the year. It presents gross cash flows within three distinct categories:

- Cash flows from *operating* activities
- Cash flows from *investing* activities
- Cash flows from *financing* activities

The statement of cash flows provides information about cash outflows for payment of interest and income taxes as well as information on noncash investing and financing activities.

The examples of financial statements that appear at the end of this chapter display the *indirect* method of presenting cash flows from operating activities. Although the indirect method is not the preferred method, it is widely used by financial institutions. (The FASB prefers the *direct* method, as stated in Statement of Financial Accounting Standard 95, *Statement of Cash Flows*.)

STATEMENT OF CHANGES IN STOCKHOLDERS' EQUITY

The *statement of changes in stockholders' equity* shows the activity in each of the categories in the shareholders' equity section of the balance sheet for several years (each ending on a balance sheet date). It shows number of shares issued, redeemed, etc., as well as the related dollar amounts for capital stock, paid-in capital, retained earnings, treasury stock, etc. This statement is beyond the scope of this accounting basics text and is not included herein.

NOTES TO THE FINANCIAL STATEMENTS

The *notes to the financial statements* (the "footnotes") are an integral part of the financial statements. The financial statements and footnotes together represent management's presentation of the organization's financial position as of, and results of operations for, the year ended. The financial statements and footnotes are inseparable. The footnotes to the financial statements are often extensive. For simplicity, the sample reports at the end of this chapter do not include the notes. However, the detailed discussions of the financial statements that follow in Chapters 7 and 8 give examples of notes that are appropriate.

Additional Annual Report Information

In addition to the basic financial statements and the notes, the annual report to stockholders generally contains other valuable information, including the auditor's report, other supplemental data and management's discussion and analysis. Each is discussed below.

AUDITOR'S REPORT

The *auditor's report* includes an opinion on the fair presentation of the company's financial statements. This report must be signed by the independent certified public accountant (CPA) who functions in the capacity of external auditor, and it must accompany the financial statements (including the notes).

SUPPLEMENTAL DATA

Supplemental data to the financial statements is extra data that is by definition outside the basic financial statements. It includes unaudited quarterly data along with results of operations and balance sheet data over time (several years). It also includes earnings per share data, cash dividends and book values. Financial ratios such as the following are usually also part of the supplemental data:
- Return on average assets
- Return on average shareholders' equity
- Net yield on earning assets
- Common stock dividend payout
- Average shareholders' equity to average assets
- Primary capital ratio at the balance sheet date
- Net charge-offs to average loans, net of unearned interest
- Reserve for loan losses to period end loans, net of unearned interest

Market price information for the institution's publicly traded stock and cash dividend information are also included.

MANAGEMENT'S DISCUSSION AND ANALYSIS

Management's discussion and analysis (MD & A) attempts to explain the financial results as they occurred during the period shown in the financial statements. The MD & A accompanies the financial statements, the auditor's report and the supplemental data. The MD & A provides a dialogue that covers a broad overview of what happened and a dialogue about results of operations with a focus on the following areas:

- Interest income
- Provision for loan losses
- Other income and expense
- Provision for income tax

The MD & A also contains a dialogue about the institution's financial condition with a focus on the following issues:

- Loan portfolio characteristics
- Nonperforming assets and risk elements
- Reserves for loan losses
- Composition of the securities portfolio
- Deposits
- Short-term borrowings
- Capital resources
- Liquidity and interest rate sensitivity
- The effects of inflation

Management's Report on the Effectiveness of Internal Control over Financial Reporting is included in the annual report. Publicly owned financial institutions present the CPA's Attestation Report on Management's Assertion about the Effectiveness of Internal Control over Financial Reporting.

Financial Statement Examples

The remainder of this chapter contains examples of the following financial statements for Fictitious Depository Corporation:

- Report of the independent public accountants (Figure 6.1)
- Balance sheet (Figures 6.2 and 6.3)
- Income statement (Figure 6.4)
- Statement of cash flows (Figure 6.5)

Note: For this basic accounting presentation, the statement of changes in shareholders' equity, the notes to the financial statements and the supplemental financial data are not illustrated, although they are certainly a significant part of the financial institution's annual presentation.

For your convenience, the balance sheet (Figures 6.2 and 6.3), the income statement (Figure 6.4) and the statement of cash flows (Figure 6.5) are reproduced in a perforated section in Part 3 of this book. You can remove those financial statements for easy reference as you go through the next chapters.

Chapters 7 and 8 will walk you through Fictitious Depository Corporation's financial statements. Chapter 7 addresses the assets (the left-hand side of the corporation's balance sheet). Chapter 8 details the liabilities and shareholders' equity (the right-hand side of the balance sheet) as well as the income statement and the statement of cash flows. Each chapter includes selected footnote disclosures.

Before you go on to Chapters 7 and 8, familiarize yourself with Fictitious Depository Corporation's financial statements. Notice how much you already understand, and write down questions that you want to answer in the coming chapters.

FIGURE 6.1 REPORT OF INDEPENDENT PUBLIC ACCOUNTANTS (THE AUDITOR'S REPORT)

REPORT OF INDEPENDENT PUBLIC ACCOUNTANTS

To the Board of Directors and Shareholders of Fictitious Depository Corporation:

We have audited the accompanying consolidated balance sheet of Fictitious Depository Corporation as of December 31, (current year) and (prior year) and the related consolidated statements of income, changes in shareholders' equity and cash flows for the years then ended. These consolidated financial statements are the responsibility of the Corporation's management. Our responsibility is to express an opinion on these consolidated financial statements based on our audits.

We conducted our audits in accordance with auditing standards generally accepted in the United States of America. Those standards require that we plan and perform the audit to obtain reasonable assurance about whether the consolidated financial statements are free of material misstatement. An audit includes examining, on a test basis, evidence supporting the amounts and disclosures in the consolidated financial statements. An audit also includes assessing the accounting principles used and significant estimates made by management, as well as evaluating the overall consolidated financial statement presentation. We believe that our audits provide a reasonable basis for our opinion.

In our opinion, the consolidated financial statements referred to above present fairly, in all material respects, the consolidated financial position of Fictitious Depository Corporation as of December 31, (current year) and (prior year) and the consolidated results of their operations and their cash flows for the years then ended in conformity with accounting principles generally accepted in the United States of America.

(signed)

Chicago, Illinois
(date)

Note: The language in this Auditor's Report conforms to the language required in AICPA Statement on Auditing Standards, Section 508.08, "Reports on Audited Financial Statements." (AICPA, 2007).

FIGURE 6.2 BALANCE SHEET (ASSETS)

Fictitious Depository Corporation
Consolidated Balance Sheet
(In thousands, except share data)

THE LEFT-HAND SIDE OF THE BALANCE SHEET

	Current Year	Prior Year
ASSETS		
Cash and cash equivalents	$ 21,100	$ 20,600
Money market investments:		
Interest bearing deposits with banks	18,300	12,200
Federal funds sold	21,750	9,600
Total money market investments	40,050	21,800
Securities available-for-sale	115,750	113,350
Loans	366,650	298,200
Less:		
Unearned interest	17,400	14,600
Reserve for loan losses	3,600	3,050
Net loans	345,650	280,550
Premises and equipment	11,200	9,850
Accrued interest receivable	3,450	3,600
Other assets	6,600	3,600
Total assets	$ 543,800	$ 453,350

This figure also appears in Part 3. It is perforated so it may be torn from the book and used for reference while reading.

FIGURE 6.3 BALANCE SHEET (LIABILITIES)

THE RIGHT-HAND SIDE OF THE BALANCE SHEET

LIABILITIES

Deposits:		
Non–interest bearing	$ 59,900	$ 50,450
Interest bearing	418,550	354,050
Total deposits	478,450	404,500
Federal funds purchased and securities sold under agreements to repurchase	6,200	4,450
Accrued interest payable	1,050	1,650
Other liabilities	2,900	550
Advances from Federal Home Loan Bank	9,250	4,450
Total liabilities	497,850	415,600

SHAREHOLDERS' EQUITY

Preferred stock:		
No par value; Authorized shares 2,000,000	–	–
Common stock:		
Par value, $5.00; Authorized shares 10,000,000; Shares issued: 3,390,000 for (current year) and 3,140,000 for (prior year)	9,100	7,850
Additional paid-in capital	14,550	8,200
Retained earnings	19,900	19,250
Net unrealized holding gains on securities available for sale	2,400	2,450
Total shareholders' equity	$ 45,950	$ 37,750
Total liabilities and shareholders' equity	$ 543,800	$ 453,350

This figure also appears in Part 3. It is perforated so it may be torn from the book and used for reference while reading.

FIGURE 6.4 INCOME STATEMENT

Fictitious Depository Corporation
Consolidated Statement of Income
(In thousands, except shares and per share data)

	Years Ended December 31,	
	Current Year	Prior Year
INTEREST INCOME		
Loans, including fees	$ 25,150	$ 25,050
Securities:		
Taxable	7,100	7,900
Tax-exempt	100	150
Deposits with banks	950	1,250
Federal funds sold	200	800
Total interest income	33,500	35,150
INTEREST EXPENSE		
Deposits	11,250	14,000
Federal funds purchased and securities sold under agreements to repurchase	100	250
Advances from FHLB	200	300
Total interest expense	11,550	14,550
NET INTEREST INCOME	21,950	20,600
Provision for loan losses	1,000	1,450
Net interest income after provision for loan losses	20,950	19,150
OTHER INCOME		
Trust income	850	800
Fees for other services	1,750	1,450
Security gains	–	100
Other income	600	450
Total other income	3,200	2,800

OTHER EXPENSES

Salaries and wages	7,000	6,550
Pension and other employee benefits	1,600	1,500
Net occupancy expense	1,550	1,450
Equipment expense	1,300	1,200
F.D.I.C. insurance	900	850
Amortization of intangible assets	550	400
Other operating expense	4,150	3,900
Total other expense	17,050	15,850
Income before income taxes	7,100	6,100
Provision for income taxes	2,400	1,750
NET INCOME	$ 4,700	$ 4,350
Net income per share	$ 1.39	$ 1.39

The accompanying notes* are an integral part of the consolidated financial statements.

* Extensive footnote disclosures would accompany the actual financial statement. Selected footnote disclosures are included in this book.

This figure also appears in Part 3. It is perforated so it may be torn from the book and used for reference while reading.

FIGURE 6.5 STATEMENT OF CASH FLOWS

Fictitious Depository Corporation
Consolidated Statement of Cash Flows
(In thousands)

	Years Ended December 31,	
	Current Year	**Prior Year**
CASH FLOWS FROM OPERATING ACTIVITIES:		
Net income	$ 4,700	$ 4,350
Adjustments to reconcile net income to net cash provided by operating activities:		
Provision for loan losses	1,000	1,450
Provision for depreciation and amortization	1,100	1,050
Amortization of intangible assets	550	400
Amortization of premium, net of accretion of discount on loans and investments	(50)	(100)
Deferred income taxes	(400)	(300)
Realized securities (gains) losses		(100)
Decrease (increase) in interest receivable	150	50
Decrease (increase) in interest payable	(600)	(600)
Decrease (increase) in other assets and liabilities, net	(800)	(850)
Net cash provided by operating activities	5,650	5,350
CASH FLOWS FROM INVESTING ACTIVITIES:		
Proceeds from sales of securities	18,250	8,800
Repayments and maturities of securities	27,150	18,600
Purchase of securities	(47,850)	(40,750)
Net decrease (increase) in money market investments	(18,250)	20,350
Net increase in loans	(66,050)	(3,950)
Purchases of premises and equipment	(2,450)	(2,050)
Net cash provided by (used in) investing activities	(89,200)	1,000

TYPICAL FINANCIAL STATEMENTS OF A COMMUNITY FINANCIAL INSTITUTION

CASH FLOWS FROM FINANCING ACTIVITIES:

Cash from issuance of common stock	5,250	0
Net increase in deposits	73,950	5,200
Net increase (decrease) in federal funds purchased and securities sold under agreements to repurchase	1,750	(5,700)
Cash dividends paid	(1,700)	(1,500)
Net increase (decrease) in advances from FHLB	4,800	(1,250)
Net cash provided by (used in) financing activities	84,050	(3,250)
Increase (decrease) in cash and cash equivalents	500	3,100
Cash and cash equivalents at beginning of year	20,600	17,500
Cash and cash equivalents at end of year	$ 21,100	$ 20,600

Supplemental disclosures of cash flow information:

Cash paid during the year for:

Interest on deposits and other borrowings	$ 12,200	$ 15,200
Federal income taxes, net of refunds	2,500	2,000

The accompanying notes* are an integral part of the consolidated financial statements.

* Extensive footnote disclosures would accompany the actual financial statement. Selected footnote disclosures are included in this book.

This figure also appears in Part 3. It is perforated so it may be torn from the book and used for reference while reading.

CHAPTER 7

Left-Hand Side of the Balance Sheet

This chapter examines the specific assets that appear on the left-hand side of the balance sheet (the asset side). It summarizes what the community financial institution owns and uses to earn income. Then the chapter shows how to account for what the institution owns.

After studying this chapter you should be able to

- list the assets that are on the balance sheet
- describe the basic transactions and accounting that create those asset amounts
- evaluate the adequacy of financial statement footnote disclosures
- describe the types of accounts included in the balance sheet line *cash and cash equivalents*
- determine when the right of setoff should be applied to offset corresponding assets and liabilities
- describe the balance sheet element *money market investments* and list its components
- identify the three categories of securities
- contrast the accounting treatment for each category of securities
- summarize the required footnote disclosure for securities
- identify the types of loans included in the balance sheet line loans
- distinguish among the types of loans
- identify issues related to subprime and negative amortizing loans
- calculate the fixed loan payment by reference to the Present Value of Annuity table
- prepare a loan payment schedule
- identify the journal entry to be made when loan payments are received
- identify what should by included in a loan footnote disclosure
- describe unearned interest and compute the maturity value of a loan
- determine journal entries for consumer loan activity
- describe the reserve for loan losses and identify the activity in the reserve account
- identify sound practices for determining the loan loss reserve
- list the various loan classifications used to identify loan risks
- distinguish between the loan loss reserve concerns of accountants and regulators
- identify proper footnote disclosures for the reserve for loan losses

- describe the components of *premises and equipment*
- identify and calculate *accrued interest receivable*
- list the items included in *other assets*
- describe the equity method of accounting
- explain Other Real Estate Owned

This chapter walks you through the asset side (the left-hand side) of Fictitious Depository Corporation's Consolidated Balance Sheet (Figure 6.2). When you read this chapter, have Figure 6.2 in front of you so you can easily refer to it. (Figure 6.2 is located at the end of Chapter 6 and in the removable set of financial statements in Part 3 of this book.) This chapter defines each of the terms on the asset side of the balance sheet from "cash and cash equivalents" to "other assets." It describes the accounting issues that underlie each item and gives examples of typical notes that accompany the balance sheet for each. As each item is addressed, the line from Fictitious Depository Corporation's Consolidated Balance Sheet is shown to orient you to the part of the asset side of the balance sheet addressed.

Cash and Cash Equivalents

The category *cash and cash equivalents* is sometimes called *cash and due from banks*. It generally consists of the following categories: (1) cash on hand; (2) cash items; (3) clearings and exchanges; (4) due from correspondent banks. It is the first line on the assets side of the balance sheet. On Fictitious Depository Corporation's Consolidated Balance Sheet, the item appears as follows:

Cash and cash equivalents $ 21,100 $ 20,600

Below is a brief discussion of each of the four categories that make up cash and cash equivalents.

- **CASH ON HAND**—This consists of currency and coins in the possession of tellers plus reserve cash in the financial institution's vault. Teller and reserve fund balances change on a daily basis because of cash transactions.
- **CASH ITEMS**—Cash items are items that are in the process of being recorded. Generally, the processing will be finalized the next day. Cash items include maturing coupons and bonds, petty cash vouchers, returned checks, due bills, unposted debits and other items pending disposition. They usually are not material to the overall financial statements. When finally processed, they will create debits to expense accounts, deposit accounts, etc. They are included in cash and cash equivalents until processing is finalized. If cash items are material, they should not be included in cash and cash equivalents. Instead, they should be charged to the account to which they ultimately will be charged. For example, a customer check for a material amount that was dishonored (an *NSF*—not sufficient funds—*check*) should

be charged to the customer's deposit account and *not* be included in cash items.

- **CLEARINGS AND EXCHANGES**—These are checks drawn on other financial institutions. They are usually received with deposits and are sorted, batched and totaled by the drawee institution for clearinghouse delivery or for direct settlement with the drawee. Financial institutions also clear local checks for certain out-of-town correspondents. In communities that have only a few local financial institutions, exchange of items and settlement is often handled directly between the individual institutions.

    The deposited check usually is debited to a clearings and exchanges account with a corresponding credit to the customer deposit account. The clearings and exchanges account is really a receivable from the drawee institution. For financial statement purposes this receivable (which will be cleared very quickly—usually in one day) is included in the balance sheet caption, cash and cash equivalents.

- **DUE FROM BANKS**—Correspondent bank accounts are used for check collection and other banking services between financial institutions. Due from accounts reflect transactions that create receivables from the correspondent institution (for example, correspondent collected funds for the financial institution but hasn't remitted the funds yet). Due to accounts usually reflect fees due to the correspondent for its services. It is common to find due from and due to accounts with the same financial institution. Federal Reserve member institutions include among their due from bank balances the amounts that must be deposited with the district Federal Reserve for purposes of check collection and legal reserve requirements. See "Right of Setoff" below.

BALANCE SHEET PRESENTATION

Interest bearing deposit accounts with other financial institutions are not cash. They should be disclosed separately in the balance sheet.

Due to accounts are included with deposit liabilities. Due from accounts are included with cash and cash equivalents. Reciprocal due to/from balances should be offset for balance sheet presentation if they may legally be netted in the process of collection or payment.

RIGHT OF SETOFF

Generally accepted accounting principles prohibit the offsetting of assets and liabilities in the balance sheet *except* where a "right of setoff" exists.

A *right of setoff* is a debtor's legal right, by contract or otherwise, to discharge all or a portion of the debt owed to another party by applying against the debt an amount that the other party owes to the debtor. A right of setoff exists when *all* of the following conditions are met.

1. Each of two parties owes the other determinable amounts.
2. The reporting party has the right to set off the amount owed with the amount owed by the other party.

3. The reporting party intends to set off.
4. The right of setoff is enforceable at law.

A debtor who has a valid right of setoff may offset the related asset and liability and report the net amount.

Generally, debts may be set off if they exist between mutual debtors who act in the capacity of both debtor and creditor. In some cases, state laws about the right of setoff are different from common law. Also, the U.S. Bankruptcy Code imposes restrictions on or prohibitions against the right of setoff in bankruptcy under certain circumstances. Legal constraints must be considered to determine whether the right of setoff is enforceable.

FOOTNOTE DISCLOSURE

The *significant accounting policies footnote* (the first footnote) often includes information about non–interest bearing accounts due from other banks as part of cash and cash equivalents. Footnote disclosure also includes concentration issues. A footnote example follows.

Cash Equivalents

Fictitious Depository Corporation considers all non–interest bearing amounts due from banks to be cash equivalents. At December 31, (current year) the Corporation maintained cash balances of approximately $15 million with one large financial institution located in Chicago, Illinois.

Additionally, the footnotes generally include information about how much of the cash is for Federal Reserve Bank reserve requirements. This is cash set aside and not available for use by the institution. How much cash can be *upstreamed* (sent to the parent by affiliates) is also disclosed. A sample footnote follows.

Regulatory Requirements

Reserve balances of $4,950 were required to be maintained at the Federal Reserve Bank by affiliate banks at December 31, (current year).

Dividends and loans to Fictitious Depository Corporation from banking affiliates are subject to regulatory limitations. Dividends are limited to the retained earnings of banking affiliates. Loans must be collateralized by specific obligations, and loans to a single nonbank affiliate cannot exceed 10% of any banking affiliate's capital and surplus, and the aggregate to all nonbank affiliates cannot exceed 20%. The maximum amount available to Fictitious Depository Corporation at December 31, (current year), from affiliate banks in the form of dividends and loans was $23,100 and $2,100, respectively.

Money Market Investments

The element *money market investments* usually includes interest bearing deposits with correspondent and other depository financial institutions. Some financial institutions even have large CDs (certificates of deposit) with other institutions.

This element also includes *federal funds sold*. Federal funds sold are bank-to-bank loans of excess Federal Reserve balances. A financial institution is required to maintain a legal reserve comprising (1) funds on deposit in the financial institution's reserve account with a Federal Reserve bank and (2) currency and coin on hand. If a financial institution's legal reserve is deficient, it may borrow federal funds to increase its reserve position. The loans are generally repayable the following day and are commonly referred to as "federal funds purchased" (by the buyer) or "federal funds sold" (by the seller).

Note that federal funds sold are the sale of excess funds and represent an *asset* of the financial institution's financial statements. Federal funds purchased are the acquisition of other financial institutions' excess reserve and are a *liability* on the balance sheet of the purchaser.

On Fictitious Depository Corporation's Consolidated Balance Sheet, this item appears as follows:

Interest bearing deposits with banks	$ 18,300	$ 12,200
Federal funds sold	21,750	9,600
Total money market investments	40,050	21,800

Generally no footnote disclosure is required for money market investments.

Securities Available-for-Sale

If deposited funds cannot be loaned out, they can be invested in securities. Generally, depository institutions invest in the following types of securities:
- U.S. Treasury obligations
- Federal government agency obligations
- Obligations of states, municipalities and their political subdivisions
- Corporate bonds

Regulators, who are concerned with the safety, soundness and liquidity of the investment, stipulate allowable security investments.

SECURITIES PORTFOLIO

The accounting for investments in debt or equity securities is set forth in SFAS 115, *Accounting for Certain Investments in Debt and Equity Securities*. SFAS 115 allows entities to include investments in the following three "buckets": (1) held-to-maturity securities; (2) trading securities; (3) available-for-sale securities. At each balance sheet date, the financial institution must carefully reassess the appropriateness of the classification. A discussion of each investment bucket follows.

- **HELD-TO-MATURITY SECURITIES**—These are securities that the financial institution has the positive *intent* and *ability* to hold until they mature. They should be measured at amortized cost.
- **TRADING SECURITIES**—A financial institution holds such securities principally to sell them in the near term. The financial institution seeks capital gains. They should be measured at fair value in the balance sheet with corresponding unrealized gains and losses recognized in the income statement, net of applicable taxes.
- **AVAILABLE-FOR-SALE SECURITIES**—These securities cannot be classified as held-to-maturity or trading securities. They should be measured at fair value in the balance sheet with corresponding net unrealized gains and losses recognized in the stockholders' equity section (other comprehensive income).

Fictitious Depository Corporation's Consolidated Balance Sheet shows this item as follows:

Securities available-for-sale	$ 115,750	$ 113,350

For examples of the unique accounting for securities, see Chapter 10.

FOOTNOTE DISCLOSURE

Generally, the significant accounting policies footnote includes disclosure about the accounting for investments. For example:

> **Securities**
>
> The securities portfolio consists of securities and short-term investments that are purchased by the Corporation to enhance the overall yield on earning assets and to contribute to the management of interest rate risk and liquidity.
>
> Fictitious Depository Corporation follows Statement of Financial Accounting Standard 115, *Accounting for Certain Investments in Debt and Equity Securities*. This statement requires classification of securities into three categories: held-to-maturity, trading and available-for-sale securities. Fictitious Depository Corporation categorizes all of its securities as available-for-sale. The Corporation may classify securities as held-to-maturity when it has both the ability and positive intent to hold the securities to maturity. Pursuant to Statement 115, securities available-for-sale are recorded at market value, with aggregate unrealized holding gains and losses reported net of income tax as a separate component of shareholders' equity. Securities held to maturity, if any, are stated at cost adjusted for amortization of premium and accretion of discount, computed primarily under the interest method. The Corporation's investment policy specifically prohibits the existence of a trading account portfolio.

Gains and losses are computed principally under the *specific identification method*. On a periodic basis, management evaluates each security for which amortized cost exceeds market value. If the decline is judged to be other than temporary, the cost basis of the security is written down to market value and the write-down is included in net securities gains.

· ·

Footnotes also require the following disclosures.
1. For securities classified as available-for-sale and separately for securities classified as held-to-maturity, disclose the aggregate fair value, gross unrealized holding gains, gross unrealized holding losses and amortized cost basis by major security type as of each balance sheet date presented.
2. Financial institutions must include in their disclosures the following major security types, although additional types may also be included as appropriate:
   * Equity securities
   * Debt securities issued by the U.S. Treasury and other U.S. government corporations and agencies
   * Debt securities issued by states of the United States and political subdivisions of the states
   * Debt securities issued by foreign governments
   * Corporate debt securities
   * Mortgage-backed securities
   * Other debt securities
3. For investments in debt securities classified as available-for-sale and separately for securities classified as held-to-maturity, disclose information about the contractual maturities of those securities as of the most recent balance sheet date. Maturity information may be combined in appropriate groupings.
4. Financial institutions must disclose the fair value and the amortized cost of debt securities based on at least these four maturity groupings:
   * Within 1 year
   * After 1 year through 5 years
   * After 5 years through 10 years
   * After 10 years
5. Securities not due at a single maturity date, such as mortgage-backed securities, may be disclosed separately rather than allocated over several maturity groupings. If allocated, the basis for allocations must also be disclosed.
6. For each income statement period presented, disclose the following:
   * The proceeds from sales of available-for-sale securities and the gross realized gains and gross realized losses on those sales
   * The basis on which cost was determined in computing realized gain or loss (that is, specific identification, average cost or other method used)

- The gross gains and gross losses included in earnings from transfers of securities from the available-for-sale category into the trading category
- The change in net unrealized holding gain or loss on available-for-sale securities that has been included in the separate component of shareholders' equity during the period
- The change in net unrealized holding gain or loss on trading securities that has been included in earnings during the period

7. For any sales of or transfers from securities classified as held-to-maturity, the amortized cost amount of the sold or transferred security, the related realized or unrealized gain or loss and the circumstances leading to the decision to sell or transfer the security must be disclosed in the notes to the financial statements for each period for which the results of operations are presented. Such sales or transfers should be rare.

Following is a typical example of a selected footnote disclosure that complies with SFAS 115.

Securities

The amortized cost and estimated market values of investments available-for-sale at December 31, (current year) and (prior year) were as follows.

	Current Year			
	Amortized Cost	Gross Unrealized Holding Gains	Gross Unrealized Holding Losses	Market Value
U.S. Treasury and obligations of U.S. government agencies and corporations	$ 108,250	$ 3,650	$ (250)	$ 111,650
Obligations of states and political subdivisions	1,800	50	(50)	1,800
Debt securities issued by foreign governments	50	0	0	50
Corporate securities	2,100	150	0	2,250
Totals	$ 112,200	$ 3,850	$ (300)	$ 115,750

	Prior Year			
	Amortized Cost	Gross Unrealized Holding Gains	Gross Unrealized Holding Losses	Market Value
U.S. Treasury and obligations of U.S. government agencies and corporations	$ 105,550	$ 3,550	$ (250)	$ 108,850
Obligations of states and political subdivisions	2,350	100	(50)	2,400
Debt securities issued by foreign governments	50	0	0	50
Corporate securities	1,950	100	0	2,050
Totals	$ 109,900	$ 3,750	$ (300)	$ 113,350

The market value of securities available-for-sale was based on quoted market prices or bid quotations received from securities dealers.

The amortized cost and estimated market value of securities at December 31, (current year), by contractual maturity are shown below. Expected maturities will differ from contractual maturities because borrowers may have the right to call or prepay obligations with or without call or prepayment penalties.

	Current year	
	Amortized Cost	Market Value
Due in one year or less	$ 7,650	$ 7,700
Due after one year through five years	102,050	105,400
Due after five years through ten years	950	1,000
Due after ten years	1,550	1,650
Total	$ 112,200	$ 115,750

LEFT-HAND SIDE OF THE BALANCE SHEET

Various securities were called during (current year), which resulted in gross gains of $50,000 and gross losses of $50,000. During (prior year), proceeds from sales of securities were $8.8 million with gross gains of $150,000 and gross losses of $50,000 realized on those sales. In addition, various securities were called during (prior year) which resulted in gross gains of $50,000 and gross losses of $50,000.

At December 31, (current year), securities available-for-sale carried at $37.4 million were pledged as collateral for public and trust deposits and securities sold under agreements to repurchase.

Loans

The loan section on the left-hand side of the consolidated balance sheet gives one figure for all of the types of loans the financial institution makes. The total amount of the loans is reduced by unearned interest and a reserve for loan losses to yield the financial institution's net loans.

Loans	$ 366,650	$ 298,200
Less:		
Unearned interest	17,400	14,600
Reserve for loan losses	3,600	3,050
Net loans	345,650	280,550

Loans are generally the depository institution's largest asset. This section first presents concepts that relate to the nature and types of loans; common loans community financial institutions make; loan payment and amortization; the footnotes related to loans that are an integral part of the balance sheet. Next the section discusses unearned interest and the related footnotes to the balance sheet; it ends with a presentation of the reserve for loan losses and the related notes.

TYPES OF LOANS

Community financial institution loans usually consist of (1) time and demand loans (commercial, financial, agricultural); (2) real estate mortgage loans (residential, commercial); (3) retail credit and consumer loans; (4) other consumer loans. A discussion of each type of loan follows.

Time and Demand Loans

These loans are made to individuals, industrial corporations, financial institutions, broker/dealers, farmers, nonprofit organizations, etc. *Demand loans* generally contain a provision for maturity or renewal or provide for periodic review of the loan status. They are often continued or renewed, assuming no deterioration in the borrower's credit risk. *Time loans* are generally for longer periods and contain provisions for payment in installments or at maturity. The financial institution makes a loan after careful review of the borrower's earnings potential and ability to generate cash flow to repay.

Time and demand loans may be secured by collateral (for example, negotiable securities, cash surrender values of life insurance policies, warehouse receipts, savings accounts, security interests in assets). Credit risk is reduced when collateral is pledged as security for the loan. Credit risk is also reduced, or in some cases eliminated, when loans are guaranteed by third parties or by federal agencies.

Financial institutions sometimes sell loans. Gains and losses are usually recognized at the time the loans are sold.

Many institutions use the *line-of-credit* arrangement for commercial lending. Under that plan, the financial institution gives the borrower a maximum borrowing limit for a specified period, at a stated interest rate. The credit line is often an informal expression of intent to loan funds. It is not binding. Signed formal agreements also are in use. They require the payment of fees or maintenance of deposit balances *(compensating balances)* as compensation to the financial institution for holding the line available. One common type of formal agreement, a *revolving credit agreement*, increases the amount available for subsequent borrowing when repayment of prior borrowings is made.

Real Estate Mortgage Loans

Real estate mortgage loans are secured by first mortgage liens on real property—commercial or residential. The mortgagor pays principal plus interest on an agreed periodic basis (for example, monthly). Most real estate mortgage loans are fixed-rate instruments, but many have variable interest rates. Payments for insured and guaranteed loans include escrow deposits for insurance and real estate taxes.

Real estate mortgage loans are usually of three types:
- Conventional
- Insured by Federal Housing Administration (FHA)
- Guaranteed by Department of Veterans Affairs (DVA)

Generally, the amounts of real estate mortgage loans are based on a percentage of the appraised value of the mortgaged property on the date of the loan.

Mortgage loans can be originated directly with financial institution customers or purchased from mortgage banking companies. If the financial institution originates the loan, mortgagors often make mortgage payments directly to the institution. For purchased loans, a *servicing agent*, who usually is the originator of the mortgage, may collect the mortgage payments for the financial institution.

If the borrower agrees to long-term financing at the end of a construction period, the financial institution may also provide a loan for the physical construction of real property (for example, a building).

Retail and Consumer Loans

Retail and other consumer loans include loans to individuals to buy boats, appliances, mobile homes, autos, etc. The principal form of consumer loan is the installment loan.

Installment loans may be made on either a simple interest or a discounted basis. The *discounted basis* means that interest (discount) is added to the amount loaned to the consumer to determine the loan receivable. The note is repayable in installments, usually in equal monthly amounts. The period depends on the nature of the loan and type of collateral, if any.

Unearned interest income on installment loans is normally credited to an *unearned income account*, frequently referred to as *unearned discount*. Transfers to operating income should be made using the *interest method of amortization*. This method of amortization, also called the *effective-interest method*, computes periodic interest expense based on the same effective interest rate determined at inception. The fixed rate multiplied by the ever-changing carrying amount determines the periodic interest expense. (See the section on Unearned Interest later in this chapter for an example of the interest method of amortization.)

The interest method of amortization is the opposite of the *straight-line method* of amortization, which computes interest expense evenly over the life of the obligation and results in a fixed dollar amount each period—not a fixed interest rate each period.

Other Consumer Loans

Loans that do not fall into the categories already discussed generally include the following types of loans.

- **HOME IMPROVEMENT LOANS**—These loans are made to individuals who want to expand, remodel, improve or otherwise work on their homes. They are secured by a second mortgage on the home. Like single-family residential loans, they require monthly payments, but home improvement loans have shorter maturities.
- **HOME EQUITY LINES OF CREDIT**—These loans give borrowers the ability to draw funds as needed up to a specified amount. The repayment terms are usually flexible, and interest rates are lower than those for installment loans. Home equity lines of credit are secured by liens on the equity a borrower has in the home.
- **LOANS SECURED BY DEPOSIT ACCOUNTS**—A depositor's designated deposit account balance secures this type of loan.
- **STUDENT LOANS**—Such loans are made pursuant to specific student loan programs (for example, Federal Parents Loans for Undergraduate Students—Federal PLUS Program). The college or school often handles the application processing and eligibility determination.

Credit Card Financing

Consumer loans include credit card receivables. A bank can use a national credit card plan or sponsor an independent plan. Loan transactions are initiated when the cardholder buys goods or services from a participating merchant. The merchant submits the charges electronically to the financial institution and receives credit for the transaction less a negotiated discount.

The bank processes the transactions and charges them to the cardholder's account.

The cardholder receives a monthly statement. The entire account balance may be paid without interest, or the cardholder may make a partial payment or pay a specified minimum amount on an installment basis. Interest is charged on the outstanding balance each month.

Overdraft Loans

An *overdraft loan* is a type of revolving credit loan that financial institutions offer individuals in the form of overdraft privileges. When an overdraft loan agreement is in place, if a customer issues a check in excess of his or her demand deposit balance, the financial institution sets up a loan and credits the checking account for the overdraft.

LOAN PAYMENT AND AMORTIZATION

Loans are set up at the present value of future payments using the interest rate in the agreement. As payments are made, principal and interest are recorded, and the loan principal is reduced.

To determine the annual payment, a *present value table* is used. This table provides factors for the partial payment needed to pay off (amortize) one dollar over time at certain interest rates. A portion of such a table appears in Figure 7.1.

FIGURE 7.1 PARTIAL PAYMENT TO AMORTIZE $1 WITH ANNUAL COMPOUNDING

Year	7.00% Annual Rate	8.00% Annual Rate
1	1.070000	1.080000
2	0.553092	0.560769
3	0.381052	0.388034
4	0.295228	0.301921
5	0.243891	0.250456
6	0.209796	0.216315
7	0.185553	0.192072
8	0.167468	0.174015
9	0.153486	0.160080
10	0.142378	0.149029

For a $100,000, 7%, five-year loan, the payment is determined by multiplying $100,000 by 0.243891. The payment amount each year for five years is $24,389.10. The loan payment schedule for such a loan is shown in Figure 7.2.

Note that a higher rate would require a higher payment. At 8%, the loan payment would be $25,045.60. ($100,000 x 0.250456).

FIGURE 7.2 LOAN PAYMENT SCHEDULE

Date of Payment	Payment	Interest *	Principal	Principal Amount Due
				$ 100,000.00
Payment 1 (one year later)	$ 24,389.10	$ 7,000.00	$ 17,389.10	82,610.90
Payment 2	24,389.10	5,782.76	18,606.34	64,004.56
Payment 3	24,389.10	4,480.32	19,908.78	44,095.78
Payment 4	24,389.10	3,086.70	21,302.40	22,793.38
Payment 5	24,389.10	1,595.72	22,793.38	0

* The annual interest equals 7% x the prior principal amount due (for example, 7% x $100,000 = 7,000; 7% x $82,610.00 = $5,782.76). For Payment 5, 7% x $22,793.38 = $1,595.54. Because of rounding, the interest is $1,595.72.

When payment is received, the financial institution records the principal reduction and the interest income.

For example, upon receipt of Payment 1, the following entry is made in the cash receipts journal:

Dr.	Cash		$ 24,389.10
Cr.		Loan Receivable	$ 17,389.10
Cr.		Interest Income	7,000.00

FOOTNOTE DISCLOSURE

The following disclosures for Fictitious Depository Corporation are typical of footnote disclosures for loans.

Loans ....

The composition of the loan portfolio at December 31, (current year) and (prior year) was as follows:

	Current Year	Prior Year
Commercial, financial and agricultural	$ 65,050	$ 63,050
Real estate:		
Residential	123,950	83,350
Commercial	61,000	62,000
Consumer	116,650	89,800
Total	$ 366,650	$ 298,200

Commercial real estate, residential real estate and other loans held by the Corporation are primarily located in Northern and Central Illinois. The Corporation evaluates each customer's creditworthiness on a case-by-case basis. Collateral held includes mortgages on residential and income-producing properties. Included in consumer loans are education loans held-for-sale that totaled $4.6 and $3.9 million at December 31, (current year) and (prior year), respectively.

A summary of loans to executive officers and directors, including associates of such persons, follows:

	Current Year	Prior Year
Loans at beginning of year	$ 7,100	$ 6,600
New loans	4,800	3,900
Loan payments	(3,850)	(3,400)
Loans at end of year	$ 8,050	$ 7,100

UNEARNED INTEREST

Unearned interest is interest the financial institution has not yet earned that is charged to a customer for a loan. Unearned interest is not credited to income. Instead, it is a credit used to reduce the carrying value of the loan receivable. When earned, it is removed from the unearned interest account on the balance sheet and transferred to the interest earned account on the income statement.

Fictitious Depository Corporation's Consolidated Balance Sheet had the following unearned interest:

Unearned interest	17,400	14,600

Some financial institutions charge simple interest. They only have unearned interest if a customer specifically pays ahead of schedule and requests that the excess *not* be applied to principal.

Some states do not allow excessive unearned interest on loans because they have a maximum rate that can be charged.

Unearned interest is generally associated with consumer financing where interest is compounded. This means periodic interest is added to the amount due, and each period's interest is based on the amount due. The next section gives an example of unearned interest on an installment consumer loan.

Unearned Interest on Installment Consumer Loan

Assume the financial institution makes a consumer loan to finance a $2,000 purchase of an appliance. The institution will pay the $2,000 and make a loan at 12% annual compounded interest payable in equal monthly installments over 24 months.

To compute the maturity value of the loan, the financial institution multiplies the principal by a PV factor for the future amount of one dollar. A *PV factor* is a statistic that (given an established interest rate) allows one to easily compute, among other things:

- The future value of $1.00 (what a dollar today invested at a fixed rate will be worth in the future)
- The future value of $1.00 per period (what a dollar continuously invested over fixed periods at a fixed rate will be worth in the future)
- The present value of $1.00 (what a dollar in the future is worth today at a given interest rate)
- The present value of $1.00 per period (what a dollar continuously invested each period at a given interest rate is worth today)

PV factors come from carefully designed, mathematically accurate tables based on mathematical formulae.

Using the table for the present value of a future amount of $1 per period for 24 periods at 1% per period, the factor is 1.2697. The principal amount of $2,000 x 1.2697= 2,539.40, the maturity value or future amount.

Principal =	$ 2,000.00
Interest =	
1% per month for 24 months	539.40
Maturity Value ($2,000 x 1.2697*)	$ 2,539.40

*PV Factor for future amount of $1

The entry in the cash disbursement journal at the inception of the loan would be as follows:

Dr.	Consumer Loan Receivable	$2,539.40
Cr.	Unearned Interest (discount)	$ 539.40
Cr.	Cash	2,000.00

To determine the monthly payment, the institution divides the amount of the obligation ($2,539.40) by a PV of Annuity Factor. *A PV of annuity factor* is the statistic that when multiplied by the periodic payment will result in the future amount. Conversely, the future amount divided by that factor will result in the amount of periodic payment. In our example, the PV of annuity factor is 21.2435.

Monthly Payment = Obligation/PV of Annuity Factor

$$\frac{\$2{,}539.40}{21.2435} = \$119.54$$

When the financial institution has calculated the loan's maturity value and the monthly payment, it uses an amortization table to determine the amount of interest and the amount of principal that each payment represents. Figure 7.3 shows the loan's amortization schedule.

FIGURE 7.3 AMORTIZATION SCHEDULE
Loan Amortization Schedule

Annual Interest Rate = 12.00%
Payment = $119.54
Obligation = $2,539.40

Payment Number	Payment	Interest	Reduction of Obligation	Obligation	Payment Number
				$2,539.40	
1	$119.54	$25.39	$94.15	$2,445.25	1
2	$119.54	$24.45	$95.09	$2,350.16	2
3	$119.54	$23.50	$96.04	$2,254.12	3
4	$119.54	$22.54	$97.00	$2,157.12	4
5	$119.54	$21.57	$97.97	$2,059.15	5
6	$119.54	$20.59	$98.95	$1,960.20	6
7	$119.54	$19.60	$99.94	$1,860.26	7
8	$119.54	$18.60	$100.94	$1,759.32	8
9	$119.54	$17.59	$101.95	$1,657.37	9
10	$119.54	$16.57	$102.97	$1,554.40	10
11	$119.54	$15.54	$104.00	$1,450.40	11
12	$119.54	$14.50	$105.04	$1,345.36	12
13	$119.54	$13.45	$106.09	$1,239.27	13
14	$119.54	$12.39	$107.15	$1,132.12	14
15	$119.54	$11.32	$108.22	$1,023.90	15
16	$119.54	$10.24	$109.30	$914.60	16
17	$119.54	$9.15	$110.39	$804.21	17
18	$119.54	$8.04	$111.50	$692.71	18
19	$119.54	$6.93	$112.61	$580.10	19
20	$119.54	$5.80	$113.74	$466.36	20
21	$119.54	$4.66	$114.88	$351.48	21
22	$119.54	$3.52	$116.02	$235.46	22
23	$119.54	$2.35	$117.19	$118.27	23
24	$119.54	*$1.27	$118.27	$0.00	24
Total	$2,868.96	$329.56	$2,539.40		

*The last interest amount has been adjusted to balance due to rounding.

The entry in the cash receipts journal after the first payment would be as follows:

Dr.	Cash	$ 119.54	
Cr.	Consumer Loan Receivable		$ 94.15
Cr.	Interest Income		25.39

The entry in the general journal would be as follows:

Dr.	Unearned Interest (discount)	20.00	
Cr.	Interest Income		20.00

The amount of unearned interest to be transferred to current earnings is based on the effective-interest method using the appropriate rates and factors. Although the financial institution collected the extra $539.40, it did not earn it. The income statement should not reflect any of the amount collected until it is earned. It is earned over the life of the loan. When each principal payment is received, some part of the deferred amount (the unearned interest), which initially was put on the balance sheet, is now put into the income statement. The financial institution would use the unearned interest amortization schedule shown in Figure 7.4 throughout the life of the consumer loan.

The entry in the cash receipts journal after the second payment follows:

Dr.	Cash	$ 119.54	
Cr.	Consumer Loan Receivable		$ 95.09
Cr.	Interest Income		24.45

The entry in the general journal would be as follows:

Dr.	Unearned Interest (discount)	$ 20.20	
Cr.	Interest Income		20.20

FIGURE 7.4 UNEARNED INTEREST AMORTIZATION TABLE
Unearned Discount Amortization

Annual Interest Rate = 12.00%
Original Discount = $539.40

Payment Number	PV Factor*	Earned Interest	Unearned Discount**	Payment Number
			$539.40	
1	26.9735	$20.00	$519.40	1
2	25.7163	$20.20	$499.20	2
3	24.4716	$20.40	$478.80	3
4	23.2392	$20.60	$458.20	4
5	22.0190	$20.81	$437.39	5
6	20.8190	$21.01	$416.38	6
7	19.6147	$21.23	$395.15	7
8	18.4304	$21.44	$373.71	8
9	17.2579	$21.65	$352.06	9
10	16.0969	$21.87	$330.19	10
11	14.9474	$22.09	$308.10	11
12	13.8093	$22.31	$285.79	12
13	12.6825	$22.53	$263.26	13
14	11.5668	$22.76	$240.50	14
15	10.4622	$22.99	$217.51	15
16	9.3685	$23.22	$194.29	16
17	8.2857	$23.45	$170.84	17
18	7.2135	$23.68	$147.16	18
19	6.1520	$23.92	$123.24	19
20	5.1010	$24.16	$99.08	20
21	4.0604	$24.40	$74.68	21
22	3.0301	$24.65	$50.03	22
23	2.0100	$24.89	$25.14	23
24	1.0000	$25.14	$0.00	24
Total		$539.40		

* PV Factor = Factor for amount of ordinary annuity of $1 per period at 1% for 24 periods
** Unearned discount of prior period divided by PV factor for current period (for example $539.40 / 26.9735 = $20.00; $519.40 / 25.7163 = $20.20)

The amortization transfers the deferred income from the balance sheet to the income statement because after each payment, some portion of the "up front" collected discount is earned. It is recorded using the effective-interest method.

Footnote Disclosure

A typical footnote disclosure for unearned interest in the Significant Accounting Policies footnote follows.

Unearned Interest ··

Unearned interest represents interest deducted from the proceeds of consumer loans. Income is recognized over the life of the loan as payments become due.

···

Reserve for Loan Losses

Financial institutions must establish a *reserve for loan losses* (or *allowance for loan losses*). This account is similar to the allowance for bad debts account for an industrial company. The balance in such an account at a particular balance sheet date is management's best estimate of the amount of probable losses that exist in the loan portfolio. The following was Fictitious Depository Corporation's reserve for loan losses:

Reserve for loan losses	3,600	3,050

This section first presents the concept of net realizable value as it relates to GAAP requirements for the reserve for loan losses. Next the section describes how a community financial institution establishes and maintains a reserve for loan losses as well as policies and procedures related to the reserve. The end of the section covers loan classifications, a controversy over amounts that should be maintained in the account and examples of footnote disclosures for reserves for loan losses.

NET REALIZABLE VALUE

GAAP require that receivables be carried at *net realizable value (NRV)*. A depository institution's receivables are its loans. The institution must reduce its loans to NRV. To accomplish that, the institution establishes a valuation or "contra" account—the reserve for loan losses.

ACTIVITY IN THE RESERVE ACCOUNT

The financial institution initially establishes the reserve for loan losses account by a charge to the provision for loan losses (an income statement account). The balance in the account is reduced by actual loan write-offs. It is increased by estimated future loan losses and recoveries of loan amounts previously written off.

The allowance should cover losses on specifically identified loans and on likely losses that cannot yet be associated with specific loans.

SFAS 5 and SFAS 114

Each financial institution is responsible for maintaining an allowance at a level that is appropriate to cover estimated credit losses in its entire portfolio of loans held for investment. FASB Statement 114, *Accounting by Creditors for Impairment of a Loan—an Amendment of FASB Statements*

5 and 15 (SFAS 114) sets forth measurement methods for estimating the portion of the overall allowance for loan and lease losses attributable to individually impaired loans (troubled debt restructures). For the remainder of the loan portfolio, an appropriate allowance must be maintained in accordance with *SFAS 5, Accounting for Contingencies*. For comprehensive guidance on the maintenance of an appropriate allowance, financial institutions should refer to the FFIEC Interagency Policy Statement on the Allowance for Loan and Lease Losses dated December 13, 2006.

Quarterly Determination

At the end of each quarter, or more frequently, if warranted, the management of each financial institution must evaluate, subject to examiner review, the collectibility of the loan portfolio, including any recorded accrued and unpaid interest.

In addition, management must maintain reasonable records in support of its evaluations and entries.

Each financial institution is responsible for ensuring that controls are in place to consistently determine the allowance for loan losses in accordance with GAAP, the institution's stated policies and procedures, management's best judgment and relevant supervisory guidance.

Increases and Decreases in the Account Balance

Additions to, or reductions of, the allowance account resulting from such evaluations are to be made through charges or credits to the provision for loan and lease losses in the income statement. All charge-offs of loans and leases shall be charged directly to the allowance. Under no circumstances can loan losses be charged directly to retained earnings. Recoveries on loans represent collections on amounts that were previously charged off against the allowance. Recoveries shall be credited to the allowance, provided, however, that the total amount credited to the allowance as recoveries on an individual loan (which may include amounts representing principal, interest and fees) is limited to the amount previously charged off against the allowance on that loan. Any amounts collected in excess of this limit should be recognized as income.

When a financial institution makes a full or partial direct write-down of a loan that is uncollectible, the financial institution establishes a new cost basis for the asset. Once a new cost basis has been established for a loan through a direct write-down, this cost basis may *not* be "written up" at a later date. Reversing the previous write-down and "re-booking" the charged-off asset after the financial institution concludes that the prospects for recovering the charge-off have improved is not an acceptable accounting practice, even if the financial institution assigns a new account number or the customer signs a new note.

The allowance account must *never* have a debit balance. If losses charged off exceed the amount of the allowance, a provision sufficient to restore the allowance to an adequate level must *immediately* be charged to expense on the income statement.

APPROACH TO DETERMINING THE ALLOWANCE

After deducting all confirmed losses on loans, the allowance should include amounts for the following components based on *all relevant facts and circumstances as of the evaluation date.*

1. For loans within the scope of SFAS 114 that are individually evaluated and found to be impaired, the allowance should be based upon one of the three impairment measurement methods specified in SFAS 114 (PV of future cash flows, the loan's observable market value and the FV of the collateral).
2. For all other loans, including individually evaluated loans determined not to be impaired under SFAS 114, the allowance should be measured under SFAS 5 and should provide for all estimated credit losses that have been incurred on groups of loans with similar risk characteristics.
3. For estimated credit losses on accrued interest and fees on loans that have been reported as part of the respective loan balances on the institution's balance sheet, the allowance should be evaluated under SFAS 114 or SFAS 5 as appropriate, if not already included in one of the preceding components.

Because deposit accounts that are overdrawn (that is, overdrafts) must be reclassified as loans on the balance sheet, overdrawn accounts should be included in one of the first two components and evaluated for estimated credit losses.

Whether loans are evaluated individually or as a group, the allowance is ultimately determined by management's judgment. Management is responsible for estimating credit losses inherent in the portfolio of loans. Judgments are made about collectibility and estimates of losses.

Judgments require the careful consideration of the following:
* Economic factors (micro and macro)
* Past events
* Current events
* Anticipated events based on current evidence on the loan evaluation date
* Realistic action carefully planned to be taken by the depository institution

Factors that influence management's estimates of credit losses inherent in the loan portfolio are included in Figure 7.5.

FIGURE 7.5 FACTORS THAT INFLUENCE MANAGEMENT'S ESTIMATES OF CREDIT LOSSES

- Company size
- Organizational structure
- Risk temperament
- Business strategies and plans
- Business environment
- Management style (tone at the top)
- Loan portfolio characteristics
- Loan administration procedures and controls
- Information technology

Different institutions use different methods to arrive at a reasonable estimate. Whatever methodology is used, it should include the following elements:

- Detailed and regular analysis of the loan portfolio and off-balance-sheet instruments with credit risk
- Procedures for timely identification of problem credits
- Consistent usage of the methodology
- Consideration of all known relevant internal and external factors that may affect collectibility
- Consideration of all loans (whether on an individual or pool-of-loans basis) and other relevant credit exposures
- Consideration of the particular risks inherent in the different kinds of lending (residential versus commercial lending)
- Consideration of current collateral fair values, where applicable
- Performance of procedures by competent and well-trained personnel
- Use of current and reliable data
- Documentation of decisions with clear explanations of the supporting analyses and rationale for the same

The financial institution should select individual loans for the SFAS 114 "impairment review" based on a board-approved policy that should require, at a minimum, management review of the information listed in Figure 7.6.

FIGURE 7.6 INFORMATION TO REVIEW TO DETERMINE SPECIFIC LOANS FOR SFAS 114 IMPAIRMENT REVIEW

1. Specific materiality criterion (dollars)
2. Regulatory report of examiners
3. Internally generated watch lists, overdraft listings, listings of loans to insiders
4. Reports of total loans by borrower
5. Historical loss experience by type of loan
6. Loan files lacking financial data related to borrowers or guarantors
7. Borrowers with operating problems (losses, working capital deficiencies, inadequate cash flows, business interruptions)
8. Loan collateral not readily marketable
9. Loan collateral subject to deterioration in NRV
10. Loans to borrowers in industries or countries with unstable economic experience
11. Loan documentation (or lack thereof)
12. Compliance exception reports

The total allowance for loan losses generally consists of the following individual allowances:
- Allowances for specifically identified loans
- Allowances relating to classified loans
- Allowances relating to loans that are evaluated in homogeneous pools (such as consumer loans and single-family residential loans)

The total allowance is designed to absorb credit losses incurred by the institution. The allowances for each category may be reallocated as needed. For example, if the estimated loss for a specific loan decreases, the related allowance may be reallocated to a component with increased losses. At all times, the institution must have a sufficient total in the allowance for the loan losses account to equal the reasonable estimate of probable total losses in the loan portfolio.

Management's estimate of an adequate balance must be a sound estimate based on reliable current information. Management must document the determination of the estimate. Regulatory examiners and external auditors carefully review the balance. Failure to have an adequate balance is an unsafe and unsound banking practice.

For more information about determining the allowance account balance, see Appendix A to this chapter.

LOAN CLASSIFICATIONS

Loan classifications describe the amount of risk particular loans represent to the institution and indicate the likelihood that the institution can recover loaned funds. They generally consist of the following four categories: (1) unclassified; (2) substandard; (3) doubtful; (4) loss. Figure 7.7 presents a description and examples of each loan classification.

FIGURE 7.7 LOAN CLASSIFICATIONS

Classification	Description
1. Unclassified	Unclassified loans are not considered a greater-than-normal risk. (This rating may also be referred to as "pass" or "good.") **Examples** Performing loans for which the borrower appears to have the ability to repay its obligations and the collateral value exceeds the loan amount.
2. Substandard	Loans are classified as substandard where they are inadequately protected by (a) the current financial condition and paying capacity of the borrower or (b) the value of the collateral. Substandard assets have a well-defined weakness or weaknesses that jeopardize the collectibility of the loan. There is a distinct possibility that the lender will incur some loss if the deficiencies are not corrected. A loan may be classified substandard even though no specific losses can be identified. However, losses are assumed to exist in substandard loans as a group. **Examples** Loans with one of the following conditions: • The borrower is unable to generate enough cash flow to make debt payments, but collateral value may be sufficient to cover amounts due. • The value of the collateral has declined significantly. • Flaws in documentation or inability to control collateral may impair the lender's access to the collateral upon default. • A loss may not be readily apparent, but sufficient problems have arisen to cause the lender to go to abnormal lengths to protect its position. • The loan has been restructured in a troubled debt restructuring, and the value of the collateral approximates the loan balance.

Continued

FIGURE 7.7—Continued

Classification	Description
3. Doubtful	A doubtful loan has the same weaknesses as a substandard loan. However, the weaknesses of doubtful loans are so severe that collection in full is highly questionable or unlikely, given current facts, conditions and values. The likelihood of some loss is high, but enough mitigating factors are present to warrant postponing a loss classification until management can evaluate those factors further. Examples of such factors include proposed merger, acquisition or liquidation procedures, proposed capital inclusions or perfecting liens on additional collateral and refinancing plans. (Entire loans generally are not classified as doubtful. Only the portion of the loan that exceeds the value of the collateral is considered doubtful.)

Examples
Loans with one of the following conditions:
- The borrower is having financial difficulties, and the collateral value does not cover the loan balance. (The collateral shortfall amount should be classified as doubtful.)
- The loan is unsecured, and repayment is highly questionable. (The loan balance, less any amounts that are probable of collection, may be classified as doubtful.)
- The borrower is having financial difficulties, and the lender's access or rights to the collateral are unclear, for example, because the lender's lien is subordinate to other substantial liens or a dispute exists over title to the collateral or the lender's lien position. (The loan balance, less any amounts that are probable of collection, may be classified as doubtful.)

4. Loss	Loans classified as loss are considered uncollectible with little or no recovery or salvage value. (Loss classifications typically cover only portions of loans rather than entire loan balances. Amounts classified as loss should be charged off or fully covered by a specific allowance or allocation.)

Continued

FIGURE 7.7—*Continued*

Classification	Description
4. Loss (cont.)	**Examples** Loans with the following conditions: • Borrower has defaulted, foreclosure is imminent and the collateral value does not cover the loan balance. (The collateral shortfall amount should be classified as loss.) • The loan is an in-substance foreclosure, and the collateral value does not cover the loan balance. (The collateral shortfall amount should be classified as loss.) • Repayment of the loan is unlikely, and the loan is unsecured. (The loan balance, less any amounts that are probable of collection, should be classified as loss.)

Regulators also have a category of assets known as *special mention* or *OLEM (Other Loans Especially Mentioned)*. OLEM applies to assets with special weaknesses that deserve management's attention. Special mention assets are not considered "classified" and need not be considered in determining the allowance for classified loans.

A portion of the loan allowance might be determined in the following fashion using a classification system. Assume a bank has the following:

Substandard loans	=	$ 500,000
Doubtful loans	=	250,000
Loss loans	=	50,000
		$ 800,000

The bank's experience for substandard and doubtful loans has been 20% and 60%, respectively, and trends and circumstances indicate that those percentages are still appropriate. The portion of the allowance for classified loans would be computed as follows:

Substandard	$ 500,000 x 20% =	$ 100,000
Doubtful	250,000 x 60% =	150,000
Loss	50,000 x 100% =	50,000
		$ 300,000

CONTROVERSY

The allowance for loan and lease losses has always been a misunderstood and confusing balance sheet account. It has been a difficult and often abused estimate of the amount needed to reduce the gross loans to their estimated NRV. The confusion over the years has been caused, in part, by the following mistaken beliefs:

- Many believe the allowance should be based on a percentage of loans within peer groups. This quantitative approach is not acceptable.
- Some believe the allowance is a "free credit" to be used when needed to smooth earnings.
- Some believe the allowance should reflect all future losses that can be anticipated. They believe this is a conservative approach to estimating.

Over the years accounting rule makers have always insisted that the reserve balance should reflect management's best estimate of *inherent* credit losses that exist in the loan portfolio that are *probable* and *reasonably estimatable*.

The accounting approach is now the regulatory approach (see **FFIEC Interagency Policy Statement on the *Allowance for Loan and Lease Losses* dated December 13, 2006**). GAAP and RAP (regulatory accounting principles) are now the same.

Some believe financial institution management has not done well in estimating the amount of cushion needed in the allowance account. The 2007–2008 credit crisis was an example of poor estimating. The credit losses, particularly in real estate lending—the "bread and butter" of most banks—seemed to have come as a surprise for those estimating the allowances.

Deteriorating asset quality concentrated in real estate loan portfolios took a toll on the earnings performance of many insured institutions in 2008. Higher loan loss provisions were the primary reason that industry earnings collapsed. How could financial institution management have been so wrong? The allowance estimates weren't even close to reality. Better focus in this area will be required in the future. Perhaps, with the "marriage" of the GAAP and the RAP approaches, the estimates will get better and the allowance will become less confusing and less controversial.

FOOTNOTE DISCLOSURE

Generally, the Significant Accounting Policies footnote for the reserve for loan losses would be as follows.

Reserve for Loan Losses

The reserve for loan losses is maintained at levels that are adequate to absorb probable losses inherent in the loan portfolio as of the date of the consolidated financial statements. The Company has developed policies and procedures for assessing the adequacy of the reserve for loan losses that reflect the assessment of credit risk considering all available information. Where appropriate, this assessment includes monitoring qualitative and quantitative trends including changes in the levels of past due, criticized and nonperforming loans. In developing this assessment, the Company must rely on estimates and exercise judgment in assessing credit risk. Depending on changes in circumstances, future assessments of credit risk may yield materially different results from the estimates, which may require an increase or a decrease in the reserve for loan losses.

The Company employs a variety of modeling and estimation tools for measuring credit risk that are used in developing an appropriate reserve for loan losses. The reserve for loan losses consists of components for both the commercial and consumer portfolios, each of which includes an adjustment for historical loss variability, a reserve for impaired loans and an unallocated component. The factors supporting the reserve for loan losses do not diminish the fact that the entire reserve for loan losses is available to absorb losses in the loan portfolio.

The Company's principal focus, therefore, is on the adequacy of the total reserve for loan losses. The reserve for loan losses is subject to review by banking regulators. The Company's primary bank regulators regularly conduct examinations of the reserve for loan losses and make assessments regarding the adequacy and the methodology employed.

In addition, the financial institution must disclose the activity in the account. An example follows.

Reserve for Loan Losses

Transactions in the reserve for loan losses account were as follows:

	Current Year	Prior Year
Balance at beginning of year	$ 3,050	$ 2,550
Additions:		
Provisions for loan losses	1,000	1,450
Recoveries of loans charged off	150	150
Deductions:		
Loans charged off	(600)	(1,100)
Balance at end of year	$ 3,600	$ 3,050

Premises and Equipment

Premises and equipment refers to fixed assets, including office buildings, equipment, leasehold improvements, furniture and fixtures, that are required for use in operating the financial institution. Accounting for fixed assets must follow GAAP—that is, capitalize the historical cost of the fixed asset and depreciate it over the estimated useful life.

Premises and equipment $ 11,200 $ 9,850

ALL COSTS INCLUDED

Fixed assets should contain all costs related to acquisition, including transportation and installation costs. For property being constructed for financial institution use, costs should include direct construction costs, architect fees, excavation costs, interest costs, etc.

DEPRECIATION

Depreciation is the systematic allocation of fixed asset costs from the balance sheet to the income statement over the estimated useful life of the fixed assets.

Financial statement depreciation should follow acceptable methods (straight line, double-declining balance, sum-of-the-years' digits). Tax depreciation usually differs, which creates a temporary difference when accounting for income taxes. Generally, straight-line depreciation (same amount each year) is used in the GAAP financial statements, while an accelerated method is used for the tax return. This produces net income (on the books) that is greater than taxable income (on the tax return).

FOOTNOTE DISCLOSURE

The Significant Accounting Policies footnote for premises and equipment is usually similar to the following note.

> **Premises and Equipment**
>
> Premises and equipment, including leasehold improvements, are stated at cost less accumulated depreciation and amortization. Depreciation is computed by both straight-line and accelerated methods used over the estimated useful lives of the assets. Leasehold improvements are amortized over the terms of leases or estimated useful lives of improvements, whichever is shorter.
>
> Maintenance, repairs and minor renewals are charged to expense as incurred. Expenditures for betterments and major renewals are capitalized and depreciated over their estimated useful lives.
>
> When premises and equipment are removed or otherwise disposed of, the cost and related accumulated depreciation or

amortization are removed from the accounts, and any resulting gain or loss is credited or charged to income.

Additionally, GAAP disclosures require listing the composition of the fixed assets and the accumulated depreciation. An example follows.

Premises and Equipment

Major classes of premises and equipment at December 31 current year and prior year were as follows:

	Current Year	Prior Year
Land	$ 1,650	$ 1,500
Buildings	10,150	8,900
Leasehold improvements	400	350
Equipment	8,450	7,450
	20,650	18,200
Less: Accumulated depreciation	9,450	8,350
Premises and equipment, net	$ 11,200	$ 9,850

Accrued Interest Receivable

Accrued interest receivable represents interest earned but not yet received on interest bearing deposits and investments. GAAP require that interest earned be accrued at the balance sheet date. When the interest is actually received in the subsequent period, it will be credited to this asset account.

Accrued Interest Receivable	$ 3,450	$ 3,600

An example of accrued interest receivable follows. The financial institution owns a $100,000 held-to-maturity debt security that was bought at par. The bond pays 6% interest on February 1 and August 1. On December 31, (current year), the financial institution has recorded earned interest up to the last payment on August 1. The interest earned from August 1 to December 31 (five months) is $2,500 (6% x 100,000 = $6,000 / 12 = $500 per month; $500 x 5 months = $2,500).

The journal entry required to record the accrued interest at December 31 of the current year follows:

Dr.	Accrued Interest Receivable	$2,500	
Cr.	Interest Income		$2,500

Other Assets

Other assets do not fit into any of the preceding categories. They include items such as (1) customer acceptance liability; (2) investments accounted for under the equity method of accounting; (3) nonmarketable securities; (4) Other Real Estate Owned (OREO); (5) accounts receivable; (6) prepaid items. This section explores each of those items.

Other assets	$ 6,600	$ 3,600

CUSTOMER ACCEPTANCE LIABILITY

Customer acceptance liability is the receivable from the institution's customers for outstanding drafts and bills of exchange that have been accepted by the institution *(banker's acceptances)*. The acceptance stamp indicates the institution's agreement to pay, and at the same time it establishes the receivable from the customer. Thus, an amount equal to the customer acceptance liability in the other assets section is normally included in the other liabilities section as "acceptance outstanding."

INVESTMENTS ACCOUNTED FOR UNDER THE EQUITY METHOD OF ACCOUNTING

When the financial institution owns 50% or more of the voting common stock of another entity, the other entity's financial statements should be consolidated with the institution's financial statements. When the ownership is less than 50% (usually 20% to 50%), but the owner can exercise significant influence (board representation, policy making, etc.), the equity method must be used.

The *equity method* refers to the recording of an investment on the books of an investor at the cost of acquisition; an increase or decrease in carrying value of the investment and income thereon is recognized based on accrual of the investor's share of the investee's post-acquisition net income or loss. Dividends received reduce the carrying value of the investment.

For example, the bank buys a 25% interest in a financing company. The bank pays $42,500 for the interest in the company's equity, which is $170,000 on the acquisition date. The bank pays book value for its 25% share. The bank can exercise significant influence. The financing company has net income of $20,000 and pays a cash dividend of $12,000. The following entries are made on the bank's records under the equity method.

To record the 25% investment in the financing company (25% x $170,000 = $42,500; acquisition made at book value; no goodwill) in the bank's cash disbursements journal:

Dr.	Investment in Financing Company	$42,500
Cr.	Cash	$42,500

To record the 25% share of the reported net income of the investee (25% x $20,000) in the bank's general journal:

Dr.	Investment in Financing Company $5,000	
Cr.	Income—Equity Method	$5,000

To record the 25% share of the cash dividend declared and paid (25% x $12,000) in the bank's cash receipts journal:

Dr.	Cash	$3,000
Cr.	Investment in Financing Company	$3,000

The bank carries the investment account balance of $44,500 ($42,500 + $5,000 - $3,000) on the balance sheet as part of other assets.

NONMARKETABLE SECURITIES

The *nonmarketable securities* category includes securities that cannot immediately be converted to cash by sale in the open market. Generally, this includes the stock that represents the financial institution's investment to become a member of the Federal Reserve Bank or the Federal Home Loan Bank. The nonmarketable securities are carried in other assets at cost unless there is a permanent impairment.

OTHER REAL ESTATE OWNED

Generally, *Other Real Estate Owned (OREO)* is real property (other than premises the financial institution uses) that was acquired through a foreclosure.

Other real estate is carried at the lower of estimated market value, less selling costs, or the value of the outstanding loan balance. Costs to maintain the assets and subsequent gains and losses attributable to their disposal are included in other expense.

Financial institutions do not want OREO. It is an undesirable asset that is the result of a loan failure and that requires the maintenance of substantial capital to carry the asset. OREO is carried in other assets on the balance sheet.

ACCOUNTS RECEIVABLE

Accounts receivable are receivables other than loan receivables. They include utility, space rental and other required deposits. Also included are advances made to trusts for conducting trust business.

PREPAID ITEMS

Prepaid items were paid for in advance; they include insurance, taxes, FDIC assessments, etc. They are carried in other assets on the financial institution's balance sheet.

This chapter explored the assets on the left-hand side of the balance sheet. The next chapter takes you through the liabilities and shareholders' equity on the right-hand side of the balance sheet.

APPENDIX A

Determining the Allowance Account

1. The reserve should not be "layered" so that all loans selected for impairment review and evaluations have some amount set aside or reserved. If the selected loan requires no reserve, so be it.

2. The allowance should not include an amount for unfunded commitments.

3. Adjustments to historical charge-off experience for current environmental factors need not result in an increase in the allowance.

4. Adjustments for current environmental factors should rarely include arbitrary percentages, and all adjustments and reasons for such adjustments must be documented.

5. "Substandard" loans are not automatically "impaired" loans.

6. Financial institutions should consider using ratio analysis as a supplemental tool to validate the directional consistency of both the allowance and the provision. This may help identify additional issues or factors that previously had not been considered. Such analysis alone is not a sufficient basis for determining loss allowances. It is inappropriate for management to adjust the loss allowance to match any targeted or budgeted ratio.

7. When determining the allowance, financial institutions should not take into account any events that occur after the balance sheet date.

8. Adequate policies and procedures must be in place. Management is responsible for adopting and adhering to written loss-allowance policies that include an effective loan review system, adequate data capture and reporting systems and a periodic validation of the allowance methodology.

9. The board of directors is responsible for reviewing and approving on an annual basis the institution's written loss-allowance policies. The board must review management's assessment that the loan review system is sound and appropriate as well as the results of management's quarterly assessment of loss allowances.

10. Documentation must be maintained to support the identified range and the rationale used for determining the best estimate from within the range.

11. While financial institutions usually already have historical loss data, they must evaluate conditions as of the financial statement date to determine what qualitative and environmental factors have changed. The overall effect of these factors should be reflected as an increase or decrease to the historical loss rate for each loan group.

12. Financial institutions should be aggressive about commercial real estate loan portfolios. For such loans, management should:

    a. Indicate which borrowers might require workout strategies

    b. Identify borrowers who probably will go out of business

    c. Reward loan officers who bring collection problems to the attention of management

    d. Classify loans properly

    e. Quickly identify losses and nonaccruals

    f. Analyze current significant issues of concern in the commercial loan real estate portfolio such as troublesome commercial real estate ARMs.

APPENDIX B

Subprime and Negative Amortizing Loans

At the time of the printing of this edition of this book, the country was in crisis because of the credit problems in the financial services industry. Although there are a number of reasons for the credit crisis, they all seem to be related to credit or counterparty risk. This appendix has a few words about some of the credit risk problems created by subprime and negative amortizing loans.

SUBPRIME LOANS

Many lenders engaged in the practice of making loans to borrowers whose credit risk had been "spotty." The borrowers had past payment and/or default problems. The lenders, nevertheless, to achieve a bigger portion of their markets or to supply "bundlers" of loans with "product" for the asset-backed security business (securitizations), took a chance with the poor credit risk borrowers. In fact, many lenders acted like predators and aggressively sought this type of borrower. The lenders made the loans with higher rates or with adjustable rates. Many of the loans were "no income verification" loans or "stated income" loans. The borrower never had to verify that he or she had enough income to pay back the loan. These loans are referred to as *subprime loans*.

NEGATIVE AMORTIZING LOANS

Additionally, some lenders engaged in *2/28 loans* or *3/27 loans*. These 30-year loans had a relatively low fixed interest rate for the first two years (or three years) and then were adjusted to a much higher adjustable rate for the subsequent twenty-eight (or twenty-seven) years. These loans allowed a borrower to make a fixed payment for the early years (presumably when the borrower was hard-pressed financially) then to start paying a higher amount when the borrower was better off financially.

If rates increased significantly in the early years, the fixed payment might not have been enough to cover the current interest cost. Thus, the lender would have to loan more funds to the borrower to cover the interest. The additional loan would increase the outstanding balance on the original loan. The outstanding balance, which was supposed to go down, would go up. Thus, the loan had *negative amortization*.

THE PROBLEM

These types of loans are beyond the normal credit risk on the first day the loan is granted. If rates rise they become even more risky. The hard-pressed borrower may not be able to pay the higher current rate and may default. The borrower's equity interest in the property underlying the loan declines, and it is easier for the borrower to walk away from the loan. The borrower would have little to lose. Additionally, if the property value declines, the loan-to-value ratio rises and the financial institution has more to lose than the borrower.

An example follows that shows how dangerous these loans were.

EXAMPLE

On September 1, 2007, a bank loans $100,000 to a customer. The loan is an adjustable rate mortgage. The bank allows the customer to pay $600 per month for the first two years. Thereafter, the customer will make payments based on the current rate at the time of each payment.

The loan is at 6% on the day it is granted, and the rate resets monthly, although the payment is fixed for two years.

Assume the rates for such a loan change dramatically as follows:

01/07	-	6%
02/07	-	6.5%
03/07	-	7%
04/07	-	7.5%
05/07	-	8%
06/07	-	8.5%

The payment activity and amortization of principal would be as follows:

Month	Payment	Interest	Principal	Outstanding Balance
1st Day				$100,000
01/07	$600	$500 (1)	$100	99,900
02/07	600	541 (2)	59	99,841
03/07	600	582 (3)	18	99,823
04/07	600	624 (4)	(24)	99,847
05/07	600	666 (5)	(66)	99,913
06/07	600	708 (6)	(108)	100,021

(1) $100,000 x 6% = $6,000 ÷ 12 = $500
(2) $99,900 x 6.5% = $6,494 ÷ 12 = $541
(3) $99,841 x 7% = $6,98 ÷ 12 = $582
(4) $99,823 x 7.5% = $7,486 ÷ 12 = $624
(5) $99,847 x 8% = $7,988 ÷ 12 = $666
(6) $99,913 x 8.5% = $8,493 ÷ 12 = $708

· ·

In this exaggerated example it is clear that the outstanding amount due to the bank goes down in the first three months. However, as rates in the market place rise, it is also clear that the fixed payment is not enough to cover the interest cost of the loan.

Accordingly the loan balance goes up instead of down (which is the way it should go). In fact by June 2007 the loan balance after six payments is higher than the balance on day one.

When borrowers could not continue to pay the stipulated reset amount, the loan became suspect. On top of that, real estate values started to plunge and the loan balance, in many cases, was greater than the value of the property. Borrowers walked away from the loans, and lenders were stuck with a nonperforming loan or real estate that had dropped significantly in value. In addition, many of these loans were packaged and sold or were sliced and diced and sold as interest-only securities or principal-only securities throughout the globe. All of this contributed greatly to the credit collapse in world markets.

The essential issue is to always have prudent credit risk. It makes no sense to make a loan to someone who clearly is unable to pay—even if the underlying collateral has good value at the time of the loan. At the time subprime and negative amortizing loans were booming, many said the situation was an accident waiting to happen. They were correct.

CHAPTER 8

Right-Hand Side of the Balance Sheet, Income Statement and Statement of Cash Flows

This chapter examines the right-hand side of the balance sheet (the liabilities and equity). It explains the types of funds a community financial institution obtains to carry assets and earn income. The chapter also explains how to account for the funds the institution uses.

After studying this chapter you should be able to
- list the liabilities on the balance sheet
- explain the basic transactions and accounting that create the liability amounts
- list the shareholders' equity on the balance sheet
- explain the basic transactions and accounting that create the equity amounts
- identify the purpose of the income statement and its elements
- describe the transactions that create the income statement elements and the applicable accounting and disclosure issues
- explain the purpose of the statement of cash flows and its elements

• •

This chapter continues our study of Fictitious Depository Corporation's Consolidated Balance Sheet. The beginning of the chapter takes you through the liabilities side (the right-hand side) of the balance sheet. The end of the chapter presents two important financial statements: the income statement and the statement of cash flows. As in Chapter 7, the appropriate section from Fictitious Depository Corporation's Consolidated Balance Sheet is shown as each item is addressed.

Right-Hand Side of the Balance Sheet

This section defines each of the terms on the right-hand side of the balance sheet (Figure 6.3), including liabilities and shareholders' equity and all the categories related to each. It also describes the accounting issues that underlie each item and gives examples of typical balance sheet notes. Make sure you have Figure 6.3 where you can easily refer to it. Figure 6.3 is located at the end of Chapter 6 and in the removable set of financial statements in Part 3 of this book.

LIABILITIES

Liabilities are claims against the resources of a business. On the balance sheet, they include (1) deposits; (2) federal funds purchased and securities sold under agreement to repurchase; (3) accrued interest payable; (4) other liabilities; (5) advances from Federal Home Loan Banks. Each type of liability is discussed below.

Deposits

Deposits are the largest liability of the institution. They are the result of funding activities. Without deposits, the other activities of the institution (lending, investing, etc.) cannot happen. Deposits consist of demand and time deposits. (See Chapter 4 for details about the types of deposits used as funding devices.) The deposits on Fictitious Depository Corporation's Consolidated Balance Sheet follow:

Deposits:		
Non–interest bearing	$ 59,900	$ 50,450
Interest bearing	418,550	354,050
Total deposits	478,450	404,500

Financial Statement Disclosures

In GAAP financial statements, depository institutions generally disclose separately the following components of the deposit liability: (1) domestic demand; (2) domestic time; (3) foreign demand; (4) foreign time; (5) jumbo CDs.

The financial institution must disclose deposits it receives on terms other than those available in the normal course of business. Material deposits received from related parties must also be disclosed.

A typical footnote disclosure for deposits follows:

Footnote Disclosure

	December 31	
	Current Year	**Prior Year**
Transactions accounts:		
Non–interest bearing accounts	$ 8,200	$ 8,600
Interest bearing accounts		
Checking accounts	26,100	25,100
Money market accounts	14,800	13,200
Passbook and statement savings accounts	27,300	28,100
Certificates of deposit	157,700	160,700
Total	234,100	235,700

At December 31, current year, the scheduled maturities of certificate accounts were as follows:

Year ending:
1st subsequent year	$ 130,700
2nd subsequent year	15,400
3rd subsequent year	4,500
4th subsequent year	4,500
5th subsequent year	2,600
	$ 157,700

Interest expense on deposit accounts is summarized as follows:

	Current Year	Prior Year
Interest bearing transaction accounts	$ 1,000	$ 1,000
Passbook and statement savings accounts	900	800
Certificates of deposit accounts	7,700	8,500
Total	9,600	10,300

Federal Funds Purchased and Securities Sold

Federal funds sold (the asset) was part of the discussion about the left-hand side of the balance sheet. When a depository institution needs funds and buys them from another institution, fed funds are purchased, and a liability is created.

Federal funds purchased and securities sold under agreements to repurchase	$ 6,200	$ 4,450

Sometimes the financial institution buys U.S. government securities from a borrowing financial institution or dealer in U.S. securities. The borrower agrees to repurchase the securities (usually on the following day) at the same price plus interest at a predetermined rate. Those transactions are referred to as *securities sold under agreements to repurchase (repos)* by the borrowing financial institution and as *securities purchased under reverse repurchase agreements (reverse repos—*also known as *resell agreements)* by the lending financial institution. The institution that gives up the securities has a repo;

the repo creates a liability. The institution that receives the securities has a reverse repo; the reverse repo creates an asset.

The sale of securities under a repo agreement is a cash loan (liability) to the financial institution that sells the security. The securities collateralize the loan. The reverse repo is a lending accommodation the financial institution makes to its corporate customer.

Fed Funds Examples

When a financial institution sells fed funds, the entry is as follows:

Dr.	Fed Funds Sold (asset)	$ XXX
Cr.	Cash	$ XXX

When a financial institution buys fed funds, the entry is as follows:

Dr.	Cash	$ XXX
Cr.	Fed Funds Purchased (liability)	$ XXX

Repo and Reverse Repo Examples

When a financial institution sells its securities under agreement to repurchase, the entry is as follows:

Dr.	Cash	$ XXX
Cr.	Securities Sold under Repo Agreement (liability)	$ XXX

When a financial institution buys government securities under an agreement to resell, the entry is as follows:

Dr.	Securities Purchased under Repo Agreement (asset)	$ XXX
Cr.	Cash	$ XXX

Note that the underlying securities are simply the collateral for these funding or lending arrangements.

Accrued Interest Payable

Accrued interest payable represents interest earned by depositors and others to whom the institution owes money. The amount is the interest expense incurred through the balance sheet date—even though such amounts are not payable until after that date.

Accrued interest payable	$ 1,050	$ 1,650

For example, a customer may have a $100,000 six-month CD that pays annual interest of 4%. The CD was created on September 1, current year. It will be worth $102,000 on March 1, next year ($100,000 x 4% x ½ = $2,000). At December 31, current year, a journal entry is needed to record the customer interest earned through December 31, current year.

To record interest expense incurred from September 1 to December 31 ($100,000 x 4% x 4 months), the entry would be as follows:

Dr.	Interest Expense	$ 1,333.33	
Cr.		Accrued Interest Payable	$1,333.33

Other Liabilities

Other liabilities generally include items such as the following:
- Acceptances outstanding
- Accrued expenses payable
- Accrued income taxes currently payable
- Deferred income taxes
- Undistributed payroll deductions (taxes payable)
- Accounts payable

If material, each of these accounts should be stated separately in the balance sheet or in the related notes.

Other liabilities $ 2,900 $ 550

Advances from the Federal Home Loan Bank

Depository institutions that are members of an FHLB often avail themselves of the borrowing facilities offered to members by the bank. Generally, the cost of FHLB borrowings is less expensive than other sources of borrowing. Borrowings from FHLB are referred to as *advances from the FHLB*. See the appendix to Chapter 4 for information about FHLB and FHLB advances.

Advances from Federal Home
Loan Bank 9,250 4,450

Appropriate GAAP disclosure requires the following:
- Amount of the advances
- Interest rate on the advances
- Maturity date(s) for the advances
- Type of interest (fixed or variable)
- Benchmark rate if the advance is at a variable rate
- Additional credit availability in excess of the advances outstanding
- Collateral pledged for the advances and potential advances (usually the financial institution's stock in the FHLB and a floating lien on the institution's real property)
- Collateral arrangement (for example, 100% of the FHLB advances must be covered by the unencumbered collateral discounted at 75%)

Advances have become a larger and ever-growing source of funds for community financial institutions. The institution must disclose its use of advances with all pertinent details. Hopefully, the advances from the FHLB are taken by the financial institution to satisfy mortgage loan demand.

SHAREHOLDERS' EQUITY

Shareholders' equity is the carrying amount of the assets less the carrying amount of the liabilities. It represents the book value of the company. The shareholders' equity section of the balance sheet generally includes the following:

- Capital stock (common or preferred at par or stated value)
- Surplus (amounts paid in excess of par or stated value)
- Retained earnings (accumulated earnings available for distribution as dividends)

The equity section can also contain amounts (debits or credits) that relate to the holding gains and losses for investments in available-for-sale debt and equity securities and foreign currency translation gains or losses.

Generally, for each class of stock the equity section shows the number of shares authorized, issued and outstanding and any previously issued shares currently held as treasury stock.

Fictitious Depository Corporation has a simple capital structure with only common shares outstanding. Preferred shares, although authorized, have not been issued. Fictitious Depository Corporation has a holding gain on the securities it holds.

Preferred stock:		
No par value;		
Authorized shares 2,000,000		
Common stock:		
Par value, $5.00; Authorized shares 10,000,000; Shares issued: 3,640,000 for (current year) and 3,140,000 for (prior year)	9,100	7,850
Additional paid-in capital	14,550	8,200
Retained earnings	19,900	19,250
Net unrealized holding gains on securities available-for-sale	2,400	2,450
Total shareholders' equity	$ 45,950	$ 37,750
Total liabilities and shareholders' equity	$ 543,800	$ 453,350

The difference between fair value and cost of all available-for-sale securities, adjusted for income tax effects, is the amount that appears as an increase (gain) or decrease (loss) in the stockholders' equity section. The net holding gain or loss is part of other comprehensive income. Other items could include foreign currency translation gains or losses, holding gains or losses from derivatives designated as cash flow hedges and a certain portion of the minimum liability under unfunded defined benefit pension plans.

Fictitious Depository Corporation only has available-for-sale (AFS) holding gains and losses. See Chapter 10 for the unique accounting aspects related to AFS holding gains and losses.

The Income Statement

The *income statement* shows the results of the financial institution's operations. As you read this section, refer to Fictitious Depository Corporation's Consolidated Statement of Income (Figure 6.4). Figure 6.4 is located at the end of Chapter 6 and in the removable set of financial statements in Part 3 of this book.

INTEREST INCOME

Interest income is the top line on the income statement. It is the principal source of revenue for the institution. Interest income has several sources:
- Loans (including fees)
- Securities (taxable and tax-exempt)
- Deposits with others
- Federal funds sold
- Securities bought under agreement to resell (reverse repos)

(Note that Fictitious Depository Corporation only has interest income from federal funds sold. It does not engage in reverse repos. If it did it would have interest income from securities purchased under agreement to resell. See Chapter 7 for an explanation of federal funds sold, federal funds purchased, reverse repos and repos. Like most small community financial institutions, Fictitious Depository Corporation is a net seller of federal funds—its excess deposits.)

INTEREST EXPENSE

Interest expense is the amount the institution incurred for use of other people's money (OPM). Interest expense is incurred on the following:
- Deposits
- Federal funds purchased
- Securities sold under agreement to repurchase (repos)
- Advances from FHLB

NET INTEREST INCOME

Net interest income is the difference between interest income and interest expense. This is the institution's *margin* (gross profit) from deposit, lending and investing activities.

The provision for loan losses (the amount the financial institution needs in the current period to establish the adequate reserve for loan losses that it will need at year-end) subtracted from the net interest income yields the net interest income after the provision for loan losses. (See the section "Reserve for Loan Losses" in Chapter 7.)

OTHER INCOME

This category includes fee-based income items such as the following:
- Trust (corporate and personal) fees
- Miscellaneous fees
- Security gains
- Trading gains (currency, etc.)

The fee-based income categories are of great concern. They represent income the financial institution can generate without having to put assets at risk. Thus, they increase the return on assets ratio.

OTHER EXPENSES

This category, generally a large one, includes expenses such as the following:
- Salaries and wages
- Employee benefit costs
- Occupancy costs
- Equipment costs
- FDIC insurance costs
- Amortization of intangibles

In recent years this category has received much attention. Institutions that can control their other expenses will have a better bottom line.

PROVISION FOR INCOME TAXES

This is the GAAP income tax expense based on the balance sheet approach required by SFAS 109, *Accounting for Income Taxes*. It consists of a current provision and a deferred provision.

The *deferred provision* takes into account those temporary differences between GAAP income (book net income) and taxable income that will theoretically reverse or turn around in the future. For example, the depreciation expense or amortization expense on the books in a given year may not be allowed as a tax return deduction in that year (straight line per books, accelerated per tax return). The provision for loan losses may not be completely deductible on the tax return in the year it is expensed on the books. Unrealized security gains on trading securities are recorded as income on the GAAP financial statements, but they are deferred until the security is sold for tax purposes.

SFAS 109 Example

Suppose a financial institution has a net recorded income of $1,000,000 and the following activity for the year:

- Provision for loan loss $ 75,000
- Loans written off against the reserve 25,000
- Depreciation Expense on the GAAP Financial Statements 130,000
- Depreciation Expense on the Federal Income Tax Return 210,000
- Unrealized Gain on Trading Account Securities 100,000

Figure 8.1 demonstrates the calculation of the provision for income taxes the financial institution must make to conform to the requirements of SFAS 109.

FIGURE 8.1 CALCULATION OF TAXABLE INCOME
Taxable Income Worksheet

Net Income (GAAP) in the Income Statement	$ 1,000,000
BASIS FOR DEFERRED TAX ASSET	
Amounts deducted on books but not allowed on tax return:	
• Loan Loss Provision Less Write-offs ($75,000 - $25,000)	50,000
BASIS FOR DEFERRED TAX LIABILITY	
Amounts included in net income but not included in taxable income:	
• Trading Account Security Gains	(100,000)
Amount deducted on tax return but not on books:	
• Depreciation (extra—beyond straight-line amount) ($210,000 - $130,000)	(80,000)
Taxable Income on Tax Return	$ 870,000

The financial institution would make the following entries in the general journal to record the calculations in Figure 8.1:

Current Provision

For this example, assume a 40% tax rate for all forms of income.
Taxable income of $ 870,000 x 40%:

Dr.	Income Tax Expense—Current	$ 348,000
Cr.	Income Taxes Payable—Current	$ 348,000

Deferred Provision

To record the deferred provision at the year-end enacted rate:

Dr.	Deferred Tax Asset ($50,000 x 40%) $ 20,000	
Cr.	Deferred Tax Liability	
	($100,000 + 80,000 = 180,000 x 40%)	$ 72,000
Dr.	Deferred Income Tax Expense 52,000	

This is a simple example. It does not consider loss carrybacks, etc. Also, if the financial institution considers the probability that it will *not* realize the deferred tax asset to be high (more likely than not), it must establish a valuation account (allowance or contra account). In this example, the $20,000 asset could be offset against the $72,000 liability. Thus, no valuation account is needed. If a net asset existed, a careful analysis of its future realization would be made. If the probability were great (more likely than not) that the net asset would *not* be realized, a valuation account would be needed.

The financial institution can net the deferred tax asset and deferred tax liability if each represents an asset and a liability with the same taxing jurisdiction (federal, state, city). If the assets and liabilities have different jurisdictions, they cannot be netted.

Advanced treatments of accounting for income taxes are not covered in this book.

Footnote Disclosure

A typical income tax footnote disclosure follows:

Federal Income Taxes

The Corporation follows Statement of Financial Accounting Standard 109, *Accounting for Income Taxes*. This statement requires a liability approach for measuring deferred taxes based on temporary differences between the financial statement and the tax basis of assets and liabilities existing at each balance sheet date using enacted tax rates.

The components of the provision for income taxes from operations are as follows:

	Current Year	Prior Year
Current	$ 2,800	$ 2,050
Deferred	(400)	(300)
Total	$ 2,400	$ 1,750

The significant components of temporary differences for current year and prior year are as follows:

	Current Year	Prior Year
Provision for loan losses	$ (50)	$ (150)
Leasing transactions	(50)	(50)
Depreciation	(75)	(100)
Other	(225)	0
Total	$ (400)	$ (300)

A reconciliation of the federal statutory tax rate to the effective tax rate applicable to income before income taxes follows:

	Current Year	Prior Year
Federal statutory tax rate	35.0%	35.0%
Add (deduct) the tax effect of		
tax-exempt interest	(5.0)	(8.0)
Interest expense limitation	.5	.7
Other, net	3.7	1.4
Effective tax rate	34.2%	29.1%

The deferred tax assets and deferred tax liabilities recorded on the balance sheet as of December 31, current year, are as follows:

	Deferred Tax Assets	Deferred Tax Liabilities
Provision for loan losses	$ 1,250	$ 0
Net unrealized holding gains on securities	0	1,150
Depreciation	150	0
Deferred loan fees, net	150	0
Adjustment due to acquisition	0	1,400
Other	250	350
	$ 1,800	$ 2,900

No valuation allowance was established at December 31, current year, in view of the Corporation's ability to carry back deferred tax assets to taxes paid in previous years and certain tax strategies available to the Corporation such as realization of the appreciation in the Corporation's securities portfolio.

CURRENT INCOME STATEMENT DEFICIENCIES—
NO SEGMENT INFORMATION

The typical income statement of a depository institution (including the income statement of Fictitious Depository Corporation) leaves a lot to be desired. It simply is not very meaningful.

Many larger depository institutions have been involved in many aspects of funding, lending, trading, investing, etc. Over the years they have striven to develop, internally, a management information system (MIS) that reports the profitability of various "segments" of the businesses they are involved in. In addition to financial profitability, the MIS provides valuable data for analyzing customer relationships (profiles) and developing marketing strategies (for example, cross selling).

Companies generally use a management reporting model that includes methodologies for funds transfer pricing, allocation of economic capital, expected losses and cost transfers to measure business segment results. Various estimates and allocation methodologies are used in preparing business segment financial information.

In order to remove interest rate risk from each core business segment, the management reporting model employs a funds transfer pricing system that matches the duration of the funding used by each segment to the duration of the assets and liabilities contained in each segment. Matching the *duration*, or the effective period until an instrument can be repriced, allocates interest income and/or interest expense to each segment so its resulting net interest income is insulated from interest rate risk.

A risk-based methodology is used to allocate capital based on the credit, market and operational risks associated with each business segment.

A provision for credit losses is allocated to each core business segment based on net charge-offs.

Intersegment revenues, or referral fees, are paid by a segment to the segment that distributes or services the product. The amount of the referral fee is based on comparable fees paid in the market or negotiated amounts that approximate the value provided by the selling segment. Cost transfers are made for services provided by one segment to another. Activity-based costing studies are continually being refined to better align expenses with products and their revenues. Income tax expense or benefit is generally allocated to each core business segment based on a statutory tax rate adjusted for items unique to each business segment.

Profitability reporting helps the company make judgments about the profitability of market segments organized according to product, business partner and bank transaction or even according to business units such as company code or operating concern.

The main goal of MIS is to provide the different areas—management, marketing, product management and customer relations—with controlling and decision-making information. The data generally is displayed by period or by transactions.

The internally generated MIS that reports profitability is needed for the financial statements given to the stockholders.

As it is now, all interest income and interest expense on the GAAP income statement are not separated by type of business. Additionally, other income and, more important, other expense are lumped together as if there were only one line of business. The expenses are never allocated to the various businesses. The reader cannot know which segments are most profitable, which are least profitable and which are not profitable at all. A new income statement with transparency about segment or function or lines of business information with carefully thought-out income and expense allocations is needed. The new financial institution accountants of today will be the architects of a new, informative, segment-type income statement tomorrow.

The new segment-based income statement will be beneficial for investors, regulators and, most important, those who are paid to efficiently and profitably manage the financial institution.

Statement of Cash Flows

The *statement of cash flows* is a summary of the institution's cash flows from all sources: operating activities, investing activities and financing activities. The concept seems self-explanatory, however putting this statement together is easier said than done. Accounting records are not set up to allow the financial institution to easily obtain the generic gross cash inflows and outflows. A trained accountant (usually a CPA) must carefully create this statement. For an example of this statement, review Fictitious Depository Corporation's Consolidated Statement of Cash Flows (Figure 6.5). Figure 6.5 is located at the end of Chapter 6 and in the removable set of financial statements in Part 3 of this book.

This statement is important for readers of financial statements because the information provided, if used in connection with other financial statements, is helpful to investors, creditors and others in assessing the following:
- The financial institution's ability to generate positive future net cash flows
- The financial institution's ability to meet its obligations and pay dividends as well as its needs for external financing

- The reasons for differences between net income and associated cash receipts and cash payments
- The effects on a business's financial position of its cash investing and financing transactions during a given period

Chapters 6, 7 and 8 have presented detailed descriptions of the typical financial statements a community financial institution uses. The next chapter discusses ratios financial institutions use to analyze the information the financial statements present.

CHAPTER 9

Ratio Analysis

This chapter explains how to analyze financial statements. It emphasizes classic ratio analysis and examines ratios that community financial institutions often use.

After studying this chapter you should be able to
- explain the importance of key financial statement ratios
- calculate key ratios
- identify and use certain profitability, capital, asset quality, liquidity and productivity ratios

• •

As mentioned in Chapter 6, financial statements generally are accompanied by other supplemental data that are useful for investors, regulators and others who analyze financial activity. The other supplemental data, along with the basic financial statements, are valuable sources of information to conduct financial institution ratio analysis. The beginning of this chapter presents ratios that financial institutions commonly use. The end of the chapter uses Fictitious Depository Corporation's supplemental financial data and the financial statements we examined in Chapter 6 to illustrate the calculation of those ratios.

Ratio Analysis for Financial Institutions

Ratio analysis is an analytical review technique that uses financial statement information to study plausible relationships among data. Ratio analysis helps investors, regulators, auditors, controllers and others focus on the following occurrences that can interfere with expected results:
- Unusual transactions
- Unexpected events
- Accounting changes
- Business changes, reorganizations, curtailments, expansions, etc.
- Misstated financial statements

It is a valuable tool for detecting past occurrences and for predicting future happenings. Some common ratio areas that annual reports frequently provide include (1) profitability ratios; (2) capital ratios; (3) asset quality ratios; (4) liquidity ratios; (5) productivity ratios. Explanations of the ratios, their meanings and their uses follow. Some of these ratios are prominently displayed in financial institutions' annual reports to stockholders.

PROFITABILITY RATIOS

Profitability ratios are relationships that help explain to what extent the company is generating income, given the assets and equity that are available. Some of the most common are explained below.

1. **RETURN ON AVERAGE ASSETS (ROA) =**

    Net Income (NI) ÷ Avg. Total Assets

    Basic profitability measure. The relationship of net income after taxes—the bottom line—to average total assets. Shows how profitably the total assets have been employed. High is good. Low is bad.

2. **RETURN ON AVERAGE EQUITY (ROE) =**

    NI ÷ Avg. Total Stockholders' Equity (SE)

    Basic profitability measure. Shows how profitably the net assets (equity) have been employed. High is good. Low is bad.

3. **INTEREST ROA =**

    Net Interest Income after Loan Loss Provision ÷ Avg. Total Assets

    Shows the portion of ROA produced from *net interest margin* (interest income less interest expense less provision for loan losses). High is good. Low is bad.

4. **INTEREST INCOME RATIO =**

    Interest Income ÷ Avg. Earning Assets

    Shows the yield on earning assets for the year. *Earning assets* generate a monetary return, generally in the form of interest income. Earning assets include loans, investments, federal funds sold, etc. High is good. Low is bad.

5. **INTEREST EXPENSE RATIO =**

    Interest Expense ÷ Avg. Interest Bearing Liabilities

    Shows the average rate paid for the use of interest bearing liabilities. *Interest bearing liabilities* are funds the financial institution uses for its operations for which interest costs are incurred. They represent the liabilities that must be paid for. They generally are all the liabilities other than demand deposits that are interest free. The ratio shows the cost of funding. High is bad. Low is good.

6. **NET INTEREST MARGIN =**

    Interest Income Ratio - Interest Expense Ratio

    Shows the institution's gross profit for the period. *Net interest margin* is the company's spread. High is good. Low is bad.

7. **NON–INTEREST ROA =**
   Non-interest Income ÷ Avg. Total Assets

   Shows the portion of ROA from sources of income other than interest income. Unusual transactions can result in significant fluctuations in this ratio from period to period. It measures fee-based income as a percentage of assets. High is good. Low is bad.

8. **OVERHEAD BURDEN RATIO =**
   Non-interest Expense ÷ Avg. Total Assets

   Shows overhead expenses as a percentage of assets. Increases can be influenced by unusual transactions. Decreases can be the result of unrecorded expenses. Low is good. High is bad.

CAPITAL RATIOS

Capital ratios are relationships between assets and equity. They measure the adequacy of equity levels in light of the assets carried by the limited amounts of equity of depository institutions.

1. **CAPITAL ADEQUACY =**
   Total Equity ÷ Total Assets

   Basic measure of an institution's capital adequacy. A measure of financial condition. High is good. Low is bad. (Note that this is not the regulatory risk-weighted capital ratio.)

2. **REGULATORY CAPITAL RATIO =**
   Regulatory Capital ÷ Minimum Regulatory Capital

   Shows the amount by which the institution exceeds minimum requirements. If this is less than 1.0, the institution is not properly capitalized. More than 1.0 is good, but a very high number might indicate overcapitalization and possible underutilization of capital.

3. **ASSET LEVERAGE RATIO =**
   Average Total Assets ÷ Average Shareholders' Equity

   A basic measure of leverage. Shows how far equity is stretched. It shows to what extent dollar amounts of assets are carried by limited equity levels. All depository institutions are leveraged. This ratio shows how much.

4. **INTERNAL CAPITAL GENERATION RATE =**
   ROE x Earnings Retention Rate

   Shows to what extent earnings on invested equity are retained in the business. For expansion-minded entities, high is good. For entities that pay a large portion of earnings to owners, low is good. (Note that net income after dividend declaration divided by net income is the retention rate.)

ASSET QUALITY RATIOS

Asset quality ratios are relationships between "good" assets, "bad" assets, write-offs and resources. They provide a measure of how good the assets are. That is, they measure the quality of the assets.

1. **ASSET QUALITY RATIO =**

    Classified Assets ÷ Risk-Based Capital + Loan Loss Allowance Not Counted as Risk-Based Capital

    This ratio measures the quality of the assets. It is a standard ratio used by federal regulators. A ratio of 1.0 or more requires immediate corrective action. A low ratio is good. High is bad.

2. **NET CHARGE-OFF RATIO =**

    Net Loan Charge-offs ÷ Average Loans before Reserve for Loan Losses

    Shows the portion of the loans that have gone sour during the period. It measures the collectibility of loans. It is an indication of credit standards and/or economic conditions. High is bad. Low is good.

3. **NONPERFORMING RATIO =**

    Nonperforming Assets (Nonaccrual Loans + Renegotiated Loans + OREO) ÷ Total Loans

    Shows how much of the total loans is tied up in bad loans (nonperformers). An indicator of overall loan portfolio quality. High is bad. Low is good.

4. **NONPERFORMING ASSETS RESERVED RATIO =**

    Loan Loss Reserve ÷ Nonperforming Loans

    Shows the portion of the overall loan loss cushion reserved for nonperformers. High is generally good, but an excess amount could be reserved for nonperformers. Low is bad.

LIQUIDITY RATIOS

Liquidity ratios are relationships between the assets and liabilities and among the types of assets. They measure the degree to which the assets can readily be converted to cash—the most liquid asset.

1. **LOAN TO DEPOSIT RATIO =**

    Total Loans ÷ Total Deposits

    Shows the extent to which funds from deposits are invested in loans. A high ratio indicates liquidity risk. A low ratio indicates ample (perhaps, excess) availability of funds for loans.

2. **JUMBO DEPOSIT RATIO =**

    Jumbo Deposits and Brokered Deposits ÷ Total Deposits

    Measures volatility of the deposit base. Jumbos and brokered deposits are not desirable. They are the least stable funding sources. They are subject to flight and often do not renew. High is bad. High ratio indicates high liquidity risk.

3. **LOANS TO EARNING ASSETS RATIO =**

    Average Loans ÷ Average Earning Assets

    Shows the portion of earning assets invested in loans—the organization's primary business. Since loans are most profitable if properly controlled for credit quality, high is good. Low is bad.

4. **SHORT-TERM INVESTMENT RATIO =**

    Short-Term Investments ÷ Total Investment Portfolio

    This measures the liquidity of the investment portfolio. Short-term investments generally are more liquid. Thus, a high ratio is good. A low ratio is bad.

PRODUCTIVITY RATIOS

Productivity ratios are relationships between expenses and assets and expenses and revenue. They show how well or how poorly funds are spent.

1. **NON-INTEREST EXPENSE RATIO =**

    Non-interest Expense ÷ Average Total Assets

    This ratio is a basic measure of expenses from sources other than the basic business of the financial institution—lending. Low is good. High is bad.

2. **REVENUE PER EMPLOYEE RATIO =**

    Total Revenue ÷ No. of Employees

    Shows how much the institution grosses per employee. The more revenue each employee generates, the more funds will be available to cover operating costs. That is, the more productive the entity will be. High is good. Low is bad.

3. **OVERALL EFFICIENCY RATIO =**

    Total non-interest expense ÷ (net interest income before provision for loan losses + non-interest income)

    Non-interest expense used up by margin plus fees. The more efficient banks have low total expenses as a percentage of assets and employees. Low is good. High is bad.

Limitations of Ratio Analysis

While ratio analysis can provide much information about an institution's financial status, it has limitations. Readers of financial statements must be aware of those limitations and avoid overreliance on ratios. Important limitations of ratio analysis follow.

- **AVERAGES**—The ratio calculations in this chapter use a simple average of the beginning and ending balances divided by two. This is not appropriate in practice. To eliminate unusual occurrences, transactions, events, etc., that cause unusual fluctuations in financial data, averages should be based on many observations.

    Quarterly averages are better than annual averages. Twelve-month averages are better than quarterly averages. A 52-week average is still better. Of course, a 360-day moving average is best.

- **INCONSISTENCIES**—Different financial institutions use different averages when presenting their ratios. The inconsistency in presentation creates analysis problems for anyone comparing one financial institution to another.

- **UNAUDITED NUMBERS**—In many cases, the ratio data is based on numbers that have not been audited. The numbers may not be accurate and can therefore cause analysis difficulties.

- **UNDERLYING MANAGEMENT**—The ratios do not, and cannot, show policies, changes, shifts in thinking, reorganizations, new management, etc. Ratios are historical; they are not prospective.

- **BEST FOOT FORWARD**—Managers, like other people, always like to put their best foot forward. To highlight what is best and in some cases to stretch or favorably spin a particular situation are natural tendencies. Management may tend to overemphasize or embellish a particular ratio while playing down or not even presenting a ratio that shows something negative. In fact, the type of information presented as part of supplemental data is entirely up to management. Nothing requires the presentation of any particular ratios, so the presentation of different sets of ratios from year to year is not uncommon.

Peer Group Analysis

In spite of the limitations, the ratios are a good source of industry-wide comparisons. Many private companies (RMA, formerly Robert Morris Associates, Sheshunoff and others) tally the ratios and present them by peer group, showing results within various sections and quartiles. This allows company analysis and comparisons to others in the industry and peer group.

Each quarter the government issues the *Uniform Bank Performance Report (UBPR)* that shows a host of ratios for banks within various peer groups. This free service for banks and thrifts uses the actual numbers filed by depository institutions on their quarterly Call Reports and their Thrift Financial Reports.

Ratio analysis is second nature in the financial services industry. Much analytical data is available and is widely used—especially by accountants.

Fictitious Depository Corporation Ratios

This section applies the ratio information just discussed to the example of Fictitious Depository Corporation we examined in Chapter 6. Figures 9.1 and 9.2 show the corporation's supplemental financial data. Figure 9.1 includes the selected data and per share data; Figure 9.2 contains the financial ratios. Review those figures.

Have Fictitious Corporation's financial statements available for easy reference. Copies of those financial statements are located at the end of Chapter 6. For your convenience, copies of the financial statements from Chapter 6 as well as copies of Figures 9.1 and 9.2 can be found in the removable set of financial statements at the end of this book.

After you have reviewed Fictitious Depository Corporation's supplemental financial data, use the ratio descriptions from the beginning of this chapter to determine the corporation's ratios based on the supplemental financial data in this chapter and the financial statements in Chapter 6. Calculating those ratios will provide a review of this book.

The ratios below were calculated using Fictitious Depository Corporation's information. Use the ratios to help you learn to calculate the ratios—or to check your ratios.

PROFITABILITY RATIOS

Below are Fictitious Depository Corporation's profitability ratios.

1. **ROA**
   NI / Average Total Assets
   $4,700 / .5 ($543,800 + $453,350) =
   $4,700 / $498,575 = 0.94%

2. **ROE**
   NI / Average Total Stockholders' Equity
   $4,700 / .5 ($45,950 + $37,750) =
   $4,700 / $41,850 = 11.23%

3. **INTEREST ROA**
   NII after Provision for Loan Losses / Average Total Assets
   $20,950 / $498,575 = 4.20%

FIGURE 9.1 SELECTED SUPPLEMENTAL DATA

Fictitious Depository Corporation
Supplemental Financial Data
(in thousands, except per share data)
Years Ended December 31

	Current*	Prior*	2nd Prior	3rd Prior	4th Prior
SELECTED DATA					
Total assets	$543,800	$453,350	$450,000	$449,000	$446,500
Loans, net of unearned interest	349,250	283,600	279,000	275,000	270,000
Securities available-for-sale	115,750	113,350	110,000	109,500	108,000
Total deposits	478,450	404,500	401,600	400,900	398,900
FHLB advances	9,250	4,450	4,000	3,900	3,800
Total shareholders' equity	45,950	37,750	36,500	36,300	35,100
Net loans charged off[1]	450	950	770	700	730
Dividends	1,700	1,500	1,400	1,400	1,300
Net income (after tax)	4,700	4,350	4,100	4,000	3,900
Average shares outstanding	3,390	3,140	3,140	3,140	3,140

	Current	Prior	2nd Prior	3rd Prior	4th Prior
PER SHARE DATA					
Net income[2]	$1.39	$1.39	$1.30	$1.27	$1.25
Cash dividends declared[3]	0.50	0.48	0.45	0.45	0.41
Year-end book value[4]	13.55	12.02	11.62	11.56	11.18

* Readers should be able to locate these amounts in the financial statements in Chapter 6.
(1) See the Footnote Disclosure in the Reserve for Loan Losses section in Chapter 7.
(2) $4,700 ÷ 3,390 shares = $1.39 current; $4,350 ÷ 3,140 shares = $1.39
(3) $1,700 ÷ 3,390 shares = $0.50; $1,500 ÷ 3,140 shares = $0.48
(4) $45,950 ÷ 3,390 shares = $13.55; $37,750 ÷ 3,140 shares = $12.02

This figure also appears in Section 3. It is perforated so it may be torn from the book and used for reference while reading.

FIGURE 9.2 FINANCIAL RATIOS

Fictitious Depository Corporation
Supplemental Financial Data
Financial Ratios
Years Ended December 31

	Current	Prior	2nd Prior	3rd Prior	4th Prior
Return on average assets	0.94%	0.96%	0.91%	0.89%	0.87%
Return on average shareholders' equity	11.23%	11.72%	11.26%	11.20%	11.11%
Net yield on earning assets (Interest Income Ratio)	7.31%	6.90%	6.60%	6.55%	6.50%
Common stock dividend payout %	36.17%	34.48%	34.15%	35.00%	33.33%
Average shareholders' equity to average assets	8.39%	8.22%	8.10%	8.01%	7.86%
Net charge-offs to average loans, net of unearned interest (Net Charge-off Ratio)	0.14%	0.33%	0.28%	0.26%	0.26%
Reserve for loan losses to period-end loans, net of unearned interest	1.03%	1.08%	0.92%	0.99%	1.02%

Note: The reader should try to calculate ratios based on the Supplemental Financial Data in this chapter and the financial statements in Chapter 6.

This figure also appears in Section 3. It is perforated so it may be torn from the book and used for reference while reading.

4. **INTEREST INCOME RATIO**
   Int. Income / Average Earning Assets
   $33,500 / .5 ($501,450 + $415,700)
   $33,500 / $458,575 = 7.31%

	CY	PY
Money Mkt. Invest.	$ 40,050	$ 21,800
AFS	$ 115,750	$ 113,350
Loans	$ 345,650	$ 280,550
	$ 501,450	$ 415,700

5. **INTEREST EXPENSE RATIO**
   Int. Expense / Average Interest Bearing Liabilities
   $11,550 / .5 ($434,000 + $362,950)
   $11,550 / 398,475 = 2.90%

	CY	PY
Deposit	$ 418,550	$ 354,050
Fed funds & repos	$ 6,200	$ 4,450
FHLB advances	$ 9,250	$ 4,450
	$ 434,000	$ 362,950

6. **NET INTEREST MARGIN**
   Int. Income Ratio - Int. Expense Ratio
      7.31%   Int. Income Ratio (#4)
    (2.90%) Int. Expense Ratio (#5)
      4.41%

7. **NON-INTEREST ROA**
   Non-interest Income / Average Total Assets
   $3,200 / $498,575 = 0.64%

8. **OVERHEAD BURDEN RATIO**
   Non-Interest Expense / Average Total Assets
   $17,050 / $498,575 = 3.42%

   Note the following:

Interest ROA (#3)	4.20%
Non-interest ROA (#7)	+0.64%
	4.84%
Efficiency Ratio (#8)	−3.42%
ROA (before Income Taxes) (#1)	1.42%

RATIO ANALYSIS

See the first profitability ratio (ROA). If it were calculated before taxes ($7,100 ÷ $498,575 = 1.42%), it would reconcile to the efficiency ratio.

CAPITAL RATIOS

Below are Fictitious Depository Corporation's capital adequacy ratios.

1. **CAPITAL ADEQUACY**
   Total Equity / Total Assets
   $45,950 / $543,800 = 8.45%

   Note: Without OCI the ratio is as follows:
   $43,550 / $543,800 = 8.01%

2. **REGULATORY CAPITAL RATIO**
   Not enough information to compute. Need Call Report Schedule RC-R. The *Call Report* is a very detailed government form that must be filed by each depository institution with the institution's primary regulator (FDIC, Federal Reserve Bank, etc.) each calendar quarter. The form is a detailed balance sheet and a detailed income statement with supporting schedules for many items on the financial statements. The Call Report is beyond the scope of this book.

3. **ASSET LEVERAGE RATIO**
   Average Total Assets / Average Shareholders' Equity
   $498,575 / $41,850 = 11.91 times

   Note that this is *not* expressed as a percentage. The ratio says that the assets are stretched to almost twelve times the equity in the business. Each $1 of equity carries $11.91 of gross assets. That's leverage.

4. **INTERNAL CAPITAL GENERATION RATE**

Net income	$ 4,700
Dividends	$ 1,700
Retained	$ 3,000

   $3,000 / $4,700   =   63.83% Earnings Retention Rate

   11.23% x 63.83%   =   7.17% ROE x Earnings Retention Rate

ASSET QUALITY RATIOS

Below are Fictitious Depository Corporation's asset quality ratios.

1. **ASSET QUALITY RATIO**
   Not enough data to calculate.

2. **NET CHARGE-OFF RATIO**
   Net Loan Charge-offs / Average Loans before Reserve for Loan Losses
   450 / .5($345,650 + $3,600 + $280,550 + $3,050)
   450 / $316,425 = 0.14%

3. **NONPERFORMING RATIO**
   Not enough data to calculate.

4. **NONPERFORMING ASSETS RESERVED**
   Not enough data to calculate.

LIQUIDITY RATIOS
Below are Fictitious Depository Corporation's liquidity ratios.

1. **LOAN TO DEPOSIT RATIO**
   Total Loans / Total Deposits
   $345,650 + 3,600 / $478,450 =
   $349,250 / $478,450 = 73.00%

2. **JUMBO DEPOSIT RATIO**
   Not enough data to calculate.

3. **LOANS TO EARNING ASSET RATIO**
   Average Loans / Average Earning Assets
   .5 ($345,650 + $3,600 + $280,550 + $3,050) / .5 ($461,400 + $394,300)
   $316,425 / $427,850 = 73.96%

4. **SHORT-TERM INVESTMENT RATIO**
   Not enough data to calculate.

PRODUCTIVITY RATIOS
Below are Fictitious Depository Corporation's productivity ratios.

1. **NON-INTEREST EXPENSE RATIO**
   Non-interest Expense / Average Total Assets
   $17,050 / $498,575 = 3.42%

2. **REVENUE PER EMPLOYEE RATIO**
   Not enough data to calculate.

3. **OVERALL EFFICIENCY RATIO**
   Total non-interest expense ÷ (net interest income before provision + non-interest income)
   $17,050 ($21,950 + $3,200) =
   $17,050 $25,150 = 67.79%

CHAPTER 10

Unique Accounting Issues for Community Financial Institutions

This chapter clarifies unique accounting issues for community financial institutions, such as accounting for nonrefundable fees, loan impairments, securities, loan losses, derivatives, sales of financial assets and sales of Other Real Estate Owned.

After studying this chapter you should be able to
- account for nonrefundable fees in accordance with SFAS 91
- account for marketable securities (held-to-maturity, trading and available-for-sale) in accordance with SFAS 115
- account for held-to-maturity securities bought at a discount and/or a premium, and account for the amortization of the related discount or premium
- account for loan impairments in accordance with SFAS 118
- account for derivatives acquired as a speculation, as a fair value hedge or as a cash flow hedge
- account for the transfer of financial assets as a sale or as a collateralized borrowing in accordance with SFAS 140
- account for Other Real Estate Owned (OREO) sold

A community financial institution's financial statements require the application of many specific accounting techniques. This chapter presents accounting issues that are unique for community financial institutions.

Accounting for Nonrefundable Fees

One of the areas that included abusive accounting in past years was the timing of recognition of revenue related to nonrefundable fees on loans. Many institutions recorded the entire nonrefundable fee as income at the time of the loan. Others, more appropriately, recorded the fee as income over the life of the loan.

SFAS 91, *Accounting for Nonrefundable Fees and Costs Associated with Originating or Acquiring Loans and Initial Direct Costs of Leases*, settled the issue by requiring the recognition of net fees (fees less origination costs) over the life of the loan using the effective interest method. The *effective-interest method* is an amortization approach that computes periodic interest (expense or income) based on the same effective interest rate determined at the inception of the related transaction. (See Chapter 7, which explains the method in view of unearned interest income.) An example of the recognition of net fees using the effective interest method follows.

On January 1, Year 1, XYZ Bank originates a 10-year $50,000 loan with a 10% stated interest rate. The loan agreement requires equal annual payments of $8,137.10 through December 31, Year 10. No penalty will be charged for prepayments of the loan. XYZ Bank charged 3.0% ($1,500) nonrefundable fees to the borrower and incurred $500 in direct loan origination costs (attorney fees, appraisal, title insurance, wages and payroll-related fringe benefits of employees performing origination activities, outside broker's fee).

The *carrying amount* (the net amount) of the loan on January 1, Year 1, is computed as follows:

Loan principal	$ 50,000
Origination fees	(1,500)
Direct loan origination costs	500
Net amount of loan (cash disbursed)	$ 49,000

XYZ Bank accounts for this loan using the effective interest method of amortization. In calculating the effective rate to apply the interest method, the discount rate necessary to equate 10 annual payments of $8,137.10 to the initial carrying amount of $49,000 is approximately 10.472971 percent. This can easily be calculated using an appropriate calculator or computer program. The amortization, if no prepayment occurs, is shown in Figure 10.1.

FIGURE 10.1 AMORTIZATION TABLE

Yr	(1) Cash (Out) Inflow	(2) Stated Interest	(3) Amortization	(4) "Real" Interest Income (4) - (2)	(5) Principal Payment	(6) Remaining Principal	(7) Net Fees	(8) Carrying Amount
	$49,000.00					$50,000.00	$1,000.00	$49,000.00
1	$8,137.10	$5,000.00	$131.76	$5,131.76	$3,137.10	$46,862.90	$868.24	$45,994.66
2	$8,137.10	$4,686.29	$130.72	$4,817.01	$3,450.81	$43,412.09	$737.53	$42,674.56
3	$8,137.10	$4,341.21	$128.09	$4,469.29	$3,795.89	$39,616.20	$609.44	$39,006.76
4	$8,137.10	$3,961.62	$123.55	$4,085.17	$4,175.48	$35,440.72	$485.89	$34,954.83
5	$8,137.10	$3,544.07	$116.74	$3,660.81	$4,593.03	$30,847.69	$369.16	$30,478.53
6	$8,137.10	$3,084.77	$107.24	$3,192.01	$5,052.33	$25,795.36	$261.92	$25,533.44
7	$8,137.10	$2,579.54	$94.57	$2,674.11	$5,557.56	$20,237.80	$167.34	$20,070.45
8	$8,137.10	$2,023.78	$78.19	$2,101.97	$6,113.32	$14,124.48	$89.15	$14,035.33
9	$8,137.10	$1,412.45	$57.47	$1,469.92	$6,724.65	$7,399.82	$31.68	$7,368.14
10	$8,137.10	$739.98	$31.68	$771.66	$7,397.12	$2.71*	$0.00	$2.70*
	$81,371.00	$31,373.71	$1,000.00	$32,373.70	$49,997.29			

* These amounts should be zero. They are the result of rounding.

Computations:
Column (1)—Contractual payments
Column (2)—Column (6) for prior year x the loan's stated interest rate (10%)
Column (3)—Column (4) - Column (2)
Column (4)—Column (8) for prior year x the effective interest rate (10.472971%)
Column (5)—Column (1) – Column (2)
Column (6)—Column (6) for prior year - (Column (1) - Column (2))
Column (7)—Initial net fees - amortization to date
Column (8)—Column (6) - Column (7)

XYZ Bank would make the following entry to make the loan in its cash disbursements journal:

Dr.	Loan Receivable	$ 50,000.00	
Cr.	Deferred Loan Fees		$ 1,000.00
Cr.	Cash		$49,000.00

XYZ Bank would make the following entry to receive the first payment in its cash receipts journal:

Dr.	Cash	$ 8,137.10	
Cr.		Loan Receivable	$3,137.10
Cr.		Interest Income	$5,000.00

XYZ Bank would make the following entry to record deferred fees now earned in the general journal:

Dr.	Deferred Loan Fees	$ 131.76	
Cr.		Loan Fee Income	$ 131.76

Year 2— Entry in cash receipts journal:

Dr.	Cash	$ 8,137.10	
Cr.		Loan Receivable	$ 3,450.81
Cr.		Interest Income	$ 4,686.29

Year 2—Entry in general journal:

Dr.	Deferred Loan Fees	$ 130.72	
Cr.		Loan Fee Income	$ 130.72

Accounting for Investments

For years, accounting for investments in marketable securities was not clear. The various accounting approaches were controversial.

The old accounting rules required that all investments be carried at historical costs, never written up and only written down when there was a permanent impairment. However, what constituted a permanent impairment was not clear.

In the 1970s, the Financial Accounting Standards Board (FASB) attempted a fair value approach for marketable *equity* securities in which those securities in a current status were *marked-to-market* (carried at fair value) based on the lower of cost or market rule. This meant investment securities could be written down, but they could not be written up. The write-down was charged to earnings.

Noncurrent investments were also marked-to-market—lower of cost or market—but the unrealized holding loss was charged to stockholders' equity on the balance sheet.

The 1970s approach was not very useful. With the movement by depository institutions toward more assets in the form of investments, and with the need to fix the rather poor accounting for investments, in the mid-1990s the FASB issued SFAS 115.

Under SFAS 115, *Accounting for Certain Investments in Debt and Equity Securities*, when a financial institution acquires debt and equity securities, it puts them into one of the following three categories: (1) held-to-maturity; (2) available-for-sale; (3) trading. At each balance sheet date, the financial institution must carefully reassess the appropriateness of the classification. Below is a description of each category.

1. **HELD-TO-MATURITY (HTM) SECURITIES**—These are securities the company has positive *intent* and *ability* to hold until they mature. They should be measured at amortized cost.
2. **TRADING SECURITIES (TRADING)**—These securities are held principally for sale in the near term. They should be measured at fair value in the balance sheet with corresponding unrealized gains and losses recognized in the income statement.
3. **AVAILABLE-FOR-SALE (AFS) SECURITIES**—These securities cannot be classified as held-to-maturity or trading securities. They should be measured at fair value in the balance sheet with corresponding unrealized gains and losses recognized in the stockholders' equity section.

The securities are placed in each bucket based on the entity's intent and ability with respect to the investment. For example, a security cannot be in the held-to-maturity category if the bank intends to hold it until it matures but can't do so because it needs funds and must sell the securities. An example of how to comply with SFAS 115 follows.

RECORDING MARKETABLE SECURITIES TRANSACTIONS

PQR Community Bank has an investment portfolio that includes all three types of securities. This example describes the bank's portfolio and shows its year-end journal and balance sheet entries. It then gives a summary of the following year's transactions and the interim journal entries, general ledger account balances and fair market values related to those transactions. The example ends with PQR's year-end journal entries. Throughout this section, you can follow PQR's reclassification of some of its securities and the journal entries it makes to document the changes.

Portfolio Summary for December 31, Year 1

For illustrative purposes, this example assumes that all of PQR's December 31, Year 1, holdings were bought during Year 1.

12/31/Year 1

Category	Cost	MKT	MKT>Cost
Trading	$ 200	$ 223	$ 23
AFS	750	625	(125)
HTM	1,050	1,025	(25)
	$ 2,000	$ 1,873	$ (127)

Composition of 12/31/Year 1 Portfolios

	Trading			AFS			HTM	
	C	FMV		C	FMV		C	FMV
Sec A	75	98	Sec D	250	213	Sec G	375	338
Sec B	75	72	Sec E	250	212	Sec H	375	387
Sec C	50	53	Sec F	250	200	Sec I	300	300
	200	223		750	625		1,050	1,025

Year-End Entries for December 31, Year 1

What journal entries are needed at December 31, Year 1, and what would PQR's balance sheet investment assets look like on that date?

Journal Entries

PQR would make the following journal entries at *year-end (Y/E)*, December 31, Year 1, to record the Trading and AFS securities at *fair market value (FMV)*:

Dr.	Trading A/C Securities (net)	$23	
Cr.	Unrealized Gain on Trading A/C Securities (I/S)		$23

Sec A + $ 23
Sec B − 3
Sec C + 3
 + $ 23

Dr.	Unrealized Loss on AFS Securities (S/E)	$125	
Cr.	AFS Securities		$125

Sec D − $ 37
Sec E − 38
Sec F − 50
 − $125

Balance Sheet

As a result of the mark-to-market of the Trading and AFS securities, PQR's balance sheet assets at December 31, Year 1, would be as follows:

Trading account securities (at FMV)	$ 223
Available-for-sale securities (at FMV)	$ 625
Held-to-maturity securities (at cost with FMV of $1,025 disclosed, usually parenthetically)	$ 1,050

Transaction Summary for Year 2

The following transactions occurred in Year 2:
- Sold Security A for $100 cash
- Sold Security B for $80 cash
- Bought Security J for $175 (Trading account security) for cash
- Transferred Security F from AFS to Trading when the fair market value (FMV) of Security F was $225
- Transferred Security E from AFS to HTM when the FMV of Security E was $188

Interim Figures for Year 2

What entries are needed for the Year 2 activity? PQR makes entries throughout the year as it makes securities transactions. This section includes the journal entries for all the interim transactions and shows the general ledger account balances and fair market values at the end of the year—prior to year-end adjustments.

Interim Journal Entries

Below are the journal entries for each of PQR's securities transactions made during Year 2. The transactions include sales, purchases and category transfers.

1. Sold Security A for $100
   At date of sale in Year 2, the following entry would be made:

Dr.	Cash	$100	
Dr.	Unrealized Gain on Trading Securities (I/S)	23	
Cr.	Trading A/C Securities (net)		$ 98
Cr.	Realized Gain on Trading Securities (I/S)		25

2. Sold Security B for $80
   At date of sale in Year 2, the following entry would be made:

Dr.	Cash	$ 80	
Cr.	Trading A/C Securities (net)		$ 72
Cr.	Unrealized Loss on Trading Securities (I/S)		3
Cr.	Realized Gain on Trading Securities (I/S)		5

3. Bought Security J for $175
   At date of purchase in Year 2, the following entry would be made:

Dr.	Trading A/C (net)	$ 175	
Cr.	Cash		$ 175

4. Transferred Security F from available-for-sale to trading with $225 FMV
   At the transfer date in Year 2, the following entry would be made:

Dr.	Trading A/C Securities (net)	$ 225	
Cr.	AFS Securities (net)		$ 200
Cr.	Unrealized Loss on AFS Securities (S/E)		50
Dr.	Unrealized Loss on Trading Securities (I/S)	25	

5. Transferred Security E from available-for-sale to held-to-maturity with $188 FMV
   At the transfer date in Year 2, the following entry would be made:

Dr.	HTM Securities (cost)	$ 188	
Cr.	AFS Securities (net)		$ 212
Cr.	Unrealized Loss on AFS Securities (S/E)		38
Dr.	S/E – Discount on HTM Securities (to be amortized until maturity)	62	

General Ledger Account Balances

After recording all the Year 2 transaction entries, but before year-end adjustments, PQR's general ledger securities account balances would be as follows:

TRADING (AT FMV)

Sec A	0
Sec B	0
Sec C	53
Sec J	175
Sec F	225
	453

AFS (AT FMV)

Sec D	213
Sec E	0
Sec F	0
	213

HTM (AT COST)

Sec G	375
Sec H	375
Sec I	300
Sec E	188
	1,238

Fair Market Values

If available, quoted market value should be used for fair market value estimates. *Quoted market value* is the number of trading units times the market price per trading unit in the financial instrument's most active market.

If quoted market prices are not available, management's best estimate of fair market value may be based on the quoted market price of a financial instrument with similar characteristics. If no similar instrument exists, valuation techniques (for example, the present value of estimated future cash flows using an appropriate discount rate or mathematical pricing models) should be used. A number of mathematical models based on regression analysis, probability theory and other techniques have become popular, particularly for derivative securities and others not actively traded. These models are easily obtainable from consultants, CPA firms and others. They provide reasonably accurate estimates of fair market value. Details about such models are beyond the scope of this book.

Assume the following fair market values for PQR's securities at December 31, Year 2:

TRADING

	Sec A	$ 0
	Sec B	0
	Sec C	48
	Sec J	170
	Sec F	200
		$ 418

AFS

	Sec D	$ 200
	Sec E	0
	Sec F	0
		$ 200

HTM

	Sec G	$ 325
	Sec H	375
	Sec I	288
	Sec E	175
		$ 1,163

Year-End Entries for December 31, Year 2

What entries must PQR Community Bank make at December 31, Year 2? The entries required for trading, available-for-sale and held-to-maturity securities are detailed below.

Trading and Available-for-Sale Securities

The following entries would be made at December 31, Year 2, to record the Trading and AFS securities at FMV.

1. Trading
   To enter the unrealized loss:

Dr.	Unrealized Loss on Trading A/C Securities (I/S)	$ 35	
Cr.	Trading A/C Securities		$ 35

$ 453 Carrying value (general ledger balance)
 418 FMV
$ 35 Unrealized loss

2. Available-for-Sale
   To enter the unrealized loss:

Dr.	Unrealized Loss on AFS Securities (S/E)	$13	
Cr.	AFS Securities		$13

$ 213 Carrying value (general ledger balance)
 200 FMV
$ 13 Unrealized loss

Note that the trading and AFS securities are always carried at fair market value. The unrealized holding gains or losses from trading securities are charged or credited to the income statement. The unrealized holding gains or losses for AFS securities, on the other hand, are charged or credited to stockholders' equity. They are part of other comprehensive income (OCI).

Held-to-Maturity Securities

PQR's transfer of Security E out of AFS to HTM (entry 5 in Interim Journal Entries above) creates a stockholders' equity debit that is treated like a discount on the new HTM securities.

The discount, in this case $62, is really the amount of unrealized holding loss on the old AFS securities at the time of transfer. The discount is amortized to income over the life of the bonds as a yield adjustment as follows:

Dr.	Interest Expense	$62	
Cr.	S/E – Discount on HTM Securities		$62

In addition, each year the HTM securities are adjusted so they are at face amount at maturity. Over the life of the transferred bond, the entry would be as follows:

Dr.	HTM Securities	$62	
Cr.	Interest Expenses		$62

The loss never appears in PQR's income statement. Depository institutions often avail themselves of this loophole when they have an unrealized holding loss on AFS securities. This occurs when market interest rates, in general, rise.

ACCOUNTING FOR PREMIUMS AND DISCOUNTS ON HTM SECURITIES

Held-to-maturity securities are carried at cost plus or minus the unamortized premium or discount.

Obligations (bonds) are bought at a market price in excess of face value *(premiums)* or at a market price less than face value *(discounts)*. A premium represents a downward adjustment of the stated rate of interest to reflect the market yield at purchase. A discount represents an upward adjustment of the stated rate of interest to the market yield at purchase.

The book or carrying amount of the bond during the holding period should be adjusted so that it equals the maturity value at the maturity date.

Amortization of premium or accretion of discount results in the recognition in the income statement of a yield that approximates the market yield at purchase date. The entry to record the amortization of premium requires a debit to interest income with a corresponding credit to the investment account. To record discount accretion, debit the investment account and credit interest income. The amortization or accretion period is from the purchase date to the maturity date. Below is an example of the purchase of a bond at a discount.

ABC Bank bought a 9%, $200,000 bond with semiannual interest payments. The bond matures five years from the purchase date and was bought when the market yield for such an instrument was 10% annually.

Purchase Price

Present value of $200,000 payable in 10 interest-paying periods (5 yrs. x 2) at 5% (10% x 1/2) = $200,000 x .614* =	$ 122,800
Present value of stream of payments of $9,000 (200,000 x 9% x 1/2) at 5% for 10 interest-paying periods = $ 9,000 x 7.722* =	69,498
Total cost of the bond	$ 192,298
Maturity Value	$ 200,000
Cost	192,298
Discount	$ 7,702

* PV Factors are readily available in computer programs, in hand calculators and in accounting and statistics books.

The journal entry to record the purchase follows:

Dr.	HTM Securities	$200,000	
Cr.	Discount on HTM Securities		$ 7,702
Cr.	Cash		$192,298

Each year the discount is amortized. The following entry would be made in Year 1:

Dr.	Discount on HTM Securities	$614	
Cr.	Interest Income		$614

The amount of amortization for each year is based on the amortization schedule in Figure 10.2. By the end of the 10th year, the discount will be zero—fully amortized.

FIGURE 10.2 AMORTIZATION SCHEDULE FOR DISCOUNT BOND PURCHASE
Amortization Table

Year	Stated Interest Income at 4½%	Effective Interest Income at 5%	Amortization	Discount	Carrying Value
				7,702	192,298
1	9,000	9,614	614	7,088	192,912
2	9,000	9,645	645	6,443	193,557
3	9,000	9,677	677	5,766	194,234
4	9,000	9,712	712	5,054	194,946
5	9,000	9,747	747	4,307	195,693
6	9,000	9,784	784	3,523	196,477
7	9,000	9,823	823	2,700	197,300
8	9,000	9,865	865	1,835	198,165
9	9,000	9,908	908	927	199,073
10	9,000	9,953	927	–	200,000
			7,702		

Accounting for Loan Impairments

Chapter 7 discussed the reserve for loan losses and how to determine the amount needed in the reserve. The accounting is simple enough. When the reserve is set up or added to, a general journal entry such as the following is made:

Dr.	Provision for Loan Losses (expense A/C)	$XXX	
Cr.	Reserve for Loan Losses		$XXX

The entry is based specifically on those loans (identified or in homogeneous groups) where a loss is probable and the amount is reasonably estimable. When the financial institution gives up on a loan for which it maintains a reserve, the general journal entry is as follows:

Dr.	Reserve for Loan Losses	$XXX	
Cr.	Loan Receivable		$XXX

This takes the loan off the books.

If the loan (or part of it) is eventually paid (recovered), the reserve is reinstated and the cash receipts journal entry is as follows:

Dr.	Cash	$XXX	
Cr.	Reserve for Loan Losses		$XXX

Since only those loans that are written off are deductible on the tax returns, the GAAP entries create deferred tax accounts. When the provision is made, since it is not tax deductible, a deferred tax asset (due from taxing authority) is created by the following general journal entry:

Dr.	Deferred Tax Asset	$XXX	
Cr.	Income Tax Expense—Deferred		$XXX

This sets up a receivable in the amount that the tax benefit is expected to be when the receivable is eventually written off on the tax return. When the receivable is taken off the books, the tax benefit is realized, and the general journal entry is as follows:

Dr.	Income Taxes Payable	$XXX	
Cr.	Deferred Tax Asset		$XXX

The reserve for loan losses deals with loans that are probable of loss and the amount of loss is a reasonable estimate.

Sometimes loans that are expected to be fully collected are impaired. Generally no reserve is set aside for these good loans. They are unclassified loans that suddenly become impaired.

A loan is *impaired* when, based on current information, it is probable that the financial institution will be unable to collect all amounts due based on the original loan agreement. *Probable* means the future event (failure to collect) is *likely* to occur.

In accordance with SFAS 114, *Accounting by Creditors for Impairment of a Loan*, impaired loans must be measured based on the present value of the expected cash flows discounted at the loan's effective interest rate (or, if practical, at the loan's observable market price or the fair value of the loan collateral, if any).

If a loan is impaired, proper accounting requires immediate use of standard present value techniques to recognize the loss. The present value of the new loan arrangement must be determined using the Standard Present Value of $1 table. An impaired loan example follows.

The financial institution has on its books a loan receivable for $120,100 payable in three annual payments of $50,000, including interest at 12%. Total payments will be $150,000. (See Figure 10.3.)

FIGURE 10.3 ORIGINAL LOAN CONTRACT
Original Contractual Arrangement

Amount Due (PV of original Cash Flows) $ 120,100

Year	Payment	12% Interest	Principal	Outstanding Principal after Payment
1	$ 50,000	$ 14,410	$ 35,590	$ 84,510
2	50,000	10,140	39,860	44,650
3	50,000	5,350	44,650	0
	$ 150,000	$ 29,900	$ 120,100	

The loan is deemed impaired (that is, it will not be paid off as specified in the original loan agreement). The debtor, it is believed, can pay only $25,000 per year for the next six years to discharge the obligation. The present value of an annuity of $25,000 per year for six years at 12% is $102,775 ($25,000 x 4.111). The factor 4.111 is the statistic for the present value of $1 per year for six years at 12%. In other words, the receipt of $1 each year for six years with annual interest of 12% has a value today of $4.11. This factor, like other present value and future value factors, is readily available. The financial institution would have to immediately recognize a loss of $17,325 ($120,100 - $102,775). (See Figure 10.4.) The journal entries and balances for this impaired loan follow.

FIGURE 10.4 RECOGNITION OF IMPAIRMENT
Immediate Recognition of Impairment

Amount Due (PV of Revised Cash Flows) $ 102,775

Year	Payment	12% Interest	Principal	Outstanding Principal after Payment
1	$ 25,000	$ 12,335	$ 12,665	$ 90,110
2	25,000	10,815	14,185	75,925
3	25,000	9,110	15,890	60,035
4	25,000	7,205	17,795	42,240
5	25,000	5,070	19,930	22,310
6	25,000	2,690	22,310	0
	$ 150,000	$ 47,225	$ 102,775	

$25,000 x 4.111* = $ 102,775
Allowance   17,325

Original loan $ 120,100

* PV Factor

Journal Entries

Dr.	Loss Impairment Expense	$ 17,325	
Cr.	Valuation Allowance for Impaired Loan		$ 17,325

Dr.	Cash	$ 25,000	
Cr.	Loan Receivable		$ 12,665
Cr.	Interest Income		$ 12,335

Balances for These Balance Sheet Accounts

Loan Receivable (Dr. balance)	$ 107,435	($120,100 - $12,665)
Valuation Allowance (Cr. balance)	(17,325)	
Net	$ 90,110	

Assume that the borrower honors the revised cash flow arrangement over the remaining life of the loan. If the loan is paid off in accordance with the agreement, the journal entries will be as follows:

		Yr. 1	Yr. 2	Yr. 3	Yr. 4	Yr. 5	Yr. 6	Total
Dr.	Cash	$25,000	$25,000	$25,000	$25,000	$25,000	$25,000	$150,000
Cr.	Loan Receivable	(12,665)	(14,185)	(15,890)	(17,795)	(19,930)	(22,310)	(102,775)
Cr.	Interest Income	(12,335)	(10,815)	(9,110)	(7,205)	(5,070)	(2,690)	(47,225)

The final balance in each of these balance sheet accounts would be

Loan Receivable (Dr. balance) $120,100 less $102,775 or	$ 17,325
Valuation Allowance (Cr. balance)	(17,325)
	0

The two remaining balances (Loan Receivable and Valuation Allowance) would be "paired off" to reach the zero balance.

Note in the example that the receivable is always carried at the present value of its estimated future cash flows—based on the current estimate of how the loan will be paid down.

Also, note that the impairment creates a loss—a debit to the income statement. There is no reduction of the loan loss reserve since, in most cases, the impaired loan was not classified and no reserve was made for it. Most impairments are for loans presumed to be good loans.

If the agreement in the example were further revised to attempt to recapture the original terms, the impairment revenue would be reduced. That would create income. The income would be recorded in the income statement. Nevertheless, the balance sheet carrying value of the loan would be accurate. It would always be the present value of the future cash flows.

Accounting for Derivatives

Derivatives are financial instruments that have no value in and of themselves. They derive their value from elsewhere—from outside themselves—for example, from the performance of underlying assets, interest rates, currency rates, various indices, etc.

Community financial institutions sometimes (but not very often) engage in derivative transactions for the following reasons:
- To substitute for cash market investments
- To help interest rate risk management (A/LM use)
- To reduce or modify the financial institution's risk profile

The first part of this section presents types of derivatives. The section ends with a discussion and examples of the use of derivatives as hedges to manage interest rate risk.

TYPES OF DERIVATIVES

Derivatives include but are not limited to (1) swaps; (2) futures; (3) forwards; (4) forward rate agreements; (5) options; (6) caps; (7) floors; (8) collars. A discussion of each of those derivatives follows.

Interest Rate Swaps

Swaps are private agreements between two counterparties to exchange cash flows in the future according to a prearranged formula.

Many financial institutions use *plain vanilla* interest rate swaps to lock in fixed rate funding (for example, pay fixed/receive variable). On a predetermined amount *(notional amount)* the financial institution will pay a counterparty a predetermined fixed rate and will receive a variable rate based on some independent benchmark, for example, *LIBOR (London Interbank Offered Rate)*. Two checks will not change hands. Only the net amount will be paid one way or the other. For the typical *liability-sensitive financial institution* (a financial institution that has liabilities maturing at a faster rate than the maturing assets, which creates sensitivity to higher interest rates) that expects higher rates, the swap will lock in a fixed rate. These first-generation swaps are used to hedge interest rate risk. They cannot solve funding risk problems. (See Chapter 4 for a discussion of business risks.)

The swap, itself, introduces the risk that the counterparty will not perform in accordance with the swap agreement. This counterparty or credit risk must be carefully assessed. It is essential to know your counterparty and know how much is at risk with the counterparty.

Futures Contracts

Futures contracts are binding agreements to deliver or accept delivery of a standard quantity of securities, currencies, commodities, etc., on a certain date and place at a price established at the time the agreement is made. An institution can use financial futures to match the maturities of assets and liabilities by locking in the cost of funds or by locking in a current yield for future investments.

Futures are exchange-traded contracts. Futures contracts are traded on exchanges such as the Chicago Board of Trade and the New York Futures Exchange. The futures contracts in Treasury securities include the following:
- Three-month T-bill
- Two-year T-note
- Five-year T-note
- Ten-year T-note
- T-bond future contract

The bill contract has a face value of $1 million per contract, while the others have a value of $100,000. Futures contracts do not require an initial investment and are marked to market daily.

Forward Contracts

A *forward contract* is an agreement to buy or sell an asset at a specified future time for a specific price. The contract is usually written by a financial institution and is not normally traded on an exchange. (It is an over-the-counter financial instrument.)

One of the parties to a forward contract assumes a long position and agrees to buy the underlying asset on a specified date at a specified price. The other party assumes a *short* position and agrees to sell the asset on the same date for the same price. The specified price in a forward contract is referred to as the *delivery price*. At the signing date when the contract is entered into, the delivery price is chosen so that the value of the forward contract to both parties is zero. This means that there is no initial cost to take either a long or a short position. Accordingly, cash is not normally exchanged on the signing date.

A forward contract is generally settled at maturity. The holder of the short position delivers the asset to the holder of the long position in return for a cash amount equal to the delivery price.

Forward contracts are used for hedging odd amounts at odd maturity dates that don't correspond to the standardized terms offered by exchange-traded futures contracts.

Forward Rate Agreements

Forward rate agreements (FRAs) are forward contracts on interest rates. The buyers and sellers in FRAs are referred to as counterparties. FRAs are like a one-period interest rate swap in which the fixed rate is set at the signing date and the floating rate is set at a specified forward date, called the *reset date*.

The FRA seller will receive a fixed interest payment and will pay a floating interest payment. The FRA seller, also referred to as the *receive fixed counterparty*, expects interest rates to fall.

The FRA buyer will receive a floating interest payment and pay a fixed interest payment. The FRA buyer, also referred to as the *receive floating counterparty*, expects interest rates to rise.

The FRA floating rate is usually LIBOR (London Interbank Offered Rate). It could be the federal funds rate, the 90-day Treasury-bill rate, the prime rate or some other rate.

Options

A *call (put) option* is an agreement granting the right to buy (sell) a fixed quantity of a bond or a bond future, at a specified price, for a specified period. The predetermined sale or purchase price of the underlying security is known as the *strike price* or the *exercise price*. An option contract is good only until its expiration date. If the buyer of the call (put) option can exercise his or her right to buy (sell) the underlying security on any date up to the expiration date, the option is said to be an *American option*. If it can be exercised only on the expiration date, it is said to be a *European option*.

The buyer of a call option has limited loss potential but unlimited gain potential. Buying a call option is similar to buying the underlying security—it is a *bullish* strategy.

The buyer of a put option has limited loss potential and limited gain potential. For example, if the price of the bond falls to zero, the buyer of a put option has the right to sell the bond at the strike price. Thus, the potential gain to the buyer of a put option is limited to an amount equal to the strike price. The potential loss to the buyer of a put option cannot exceed the cost of the option. Buying a put option is similar to shorting the underlying security—it is a *bearish* strategy.

The seller (or writer) of a call option is exposed to unlimited loss potential because of the obligation to sell the underlying security at the strike price—regardless of its market price—if and when the option is exercised. A call seller (or writer) that holds the underlying security on which the option is written is said to have written a *covered call*. A call seller that does not hold the underlying security on which the option is written is said to have written a *naked call*.

The seller (or writer) of a put option is exposed to limited loss potential because if the price of the bond falls to zero, the seller of the put option is obligated to buy the bond at the strike price. Thus, the potential loss to the seller of a put option cannot exceed an amount equal to the strike price.

Interest Rate Caps

An *interest rate cap* is an off-balance-sheet financial instrument that pays the holder of the cap the difference between the cap (or strike) rate and an index (that is, rate to be capped) rate. For example, a financial institution with a variable interest rate bond payable that believes rates will rise sharply might buy a cap from a dealer in derivatives. The cap will specify that the financial institution will pay a maximum rate on the bond interest. If the bond interest amount is determined by a changing market rate (T-bill, T-note, LIBOR, etc.), the financial institution may have to pay interest well in excess of the cap rate. The financial institution pays the high interest rate, but the dealer reimburses the financial institution for the amount paid in excess of the cap rate. An interest rate cap is valid for a specific term and is sold for an up-front fee expressed in basis points as a percentage of the notional principal to be capped.

An interest rate cap is designed to provide borrowers with protection against the cap rate rising above the index rate. If the cap rate goes above the index rate, the seller of the cap pays the buyer the difference between the cap rate and the index rate. Interest rate caps are a type of over-the-counter interest rate option. They are appropriate for liability-sensitive financial institutions that wish to hedge against rising interest rates.

Interest Rate Floors

An *interest rate floor* is designed to provide lenders (investors) with protection against the interest rate on a floating rate loan going below a specified rate level. If the rate of interest on the loan does go below the floor rate, the seller of the floor pays the buyer (lender or investor) the difference between the interest on the loan and the interest that would be required if the floor rate applied. Floors are useful to asset-sensitive financial institutions that want protection from falling interest rates.

Interest Rate Collars

An *interest rate collar* specifies both the upper and lower limits for the rate that would be charged. An interest rate collar, which is sometimes referred to as a *floor-ceiling agreement* or a *range swap* is initially like an out-of-the-money interest rate swap because the collar agreement is activated only if rates move up or down by a predetermined level.

A collar is a combination of a long position in a cap and a short position in a floor. It is usually constructed so the price of the cap equals the price of the floor. The net cost of the collar is then zero.

USE OF DERIVATIVES TO MANAGE INTEREST RATE RISK

Derivatives are used for hedging purposes. *Hedging* is the act of taking a temporary position in the futures market that is equal to and opposite to the cash market position. The purpose of hedging is to protect the cash position against loss due to price fluctuations.

Hedging is a very useful tool for the management of interest rate risk. It can be used for specific assets or liabilities *(micro hedges)* or for the entire balance sheet *(macro hedges)*.

During a period of rising interest rates, the following hedging strategies can be used.

1. **BUY A PUT OPTION**—If interest rates rise, securities held will decline in value. The increase in the value of the put option will offset the decrease in value of the hedged securities. If interest rates do not rise, the loss is limited to the cost of the put option.
2. **BUY AN INTEREST RATE CAP**—If rates rise above the cap rate, the seller of the cap pays the buyer its obligation under the cap agreement.
3. **BUY AN OPTION TO BUY A CAP**—Buy a *caption*, or an option to buy a cap. This would reduce the cost because the option would be cheaper than the actual cap.

4. **SELL (OR WRITE) A COVERED CALL OPTION**—Premiums from selling covered call options can partially offset losses or decline in value of the underlying security.

Accounting for derivatives has clearly been a problem. Standardized accounting was not put into place until the 1990s. SFAS 133, *Accounting for Derivative Instruments and Hedging Activities*, standardized the accounting of derivatives. It requires that all derivative financial instruments be recognized as assets or liabilities in the balance sheet.

Measurement is at fair value, and if the derivative is not designated as a hedging instrument, changes in fair value are to be recognized in earnings in the period of change. If certain conditions are met, a derivative may be designated as a hedge, in which case the accounting for changes in fair value will depend on the specific exposure being hedged. Examples of hedges for three types of exposure follow.

1. **HEDGE OF EXPOSURE TO CHANGES IN THE FAIR VALUE OF A RECOGNIZED ASSET OR LIABILITY OR FIRM COMMITMENT** (referred to as a *fair value hedge*)

    Gain or loss is recognized in earnings in the period of the change in fair value, together with the offsetting gain or loss on the hedged item that is attributable to the risk being hedged. The result is to reflect in earnings the extent to which the hedge is not effective in achieving an exact offset in changes in fair value. This accounting also applies to a derivative designated as a hedge of the foreign currency exposure of an unrecognized firm commitment or available-for-sale security. (Figure 10.5 summarizes fair value hedges.)

2. **HEDGE OF EXPOSURE TO VARIABLE CASH FLOWS OF A FORECASTED TRANSACTION** (referred to as a *cash flow hedge*)

    The effective portion of the derivative's gain or loss is initially reported as a component of other comprehensive income and subsequently reclassified into earnings when the forecasted transaction affects earnings. The ineffective portion of the derivative's gain or loss is reported in earnings in the period of the change in fair value. This accounting should also be used for a derivative that is designated as a hedge of the foreign currency exposure of a foreign-currency-denominated forecasted transaction. (Figure 10.5 summarizes cash flow hedges.)

3. **HEDGE OF FOREIGN CURRENCY EXPOSURE OF A NET INVESTMENT IN A FOREIGN OPERATION**

    Gains or losses from changes in fair value are reported in other comprehensive income as part of the cumulative translation adjustment.

Under SFAS 133, the method that will be used for assessing the effectiveness of a hedging derivative, as well as the measurement approach for determining the ineffective aspects of the hedge, *must be established at the inception of the hedge*. The methods must be consistent with the financial institution's approach to managing risk.

FIGURE 10.5 SUMMARY OF CASH FLOW AND FAIR VALUE HEDGES
Cash Flow and Fair Value Hedges
(Non–Foreign Exchange)

	Derivative Use	Example	Accounting
1	To hedge the exposure to changes in *fair value* of a recognized asset or liability or a firm commitment	A pay variable/receive fixed swap used to hedge the interest rate risk of fixed-rate debt	Change in fair value of derivative and item being hedged recognized in earnings
2	To hedge the exposure to changes in *fair value* of a recognized asset carried at fair value with changes reported in other comprehensive income	A purchased put option used to hedge an available-for-sale equity security	Change in fair value of derivative and item being hedged recognized in earnings
3	To hedge the exposure to variability in the *cash flows* of a recognized asset, liability or forecasted transaction	A pay fixed/receive variable interest rate swap used to hedge the cash flow risk of floating rate debt	Change in fair value allocated between other comprehensive income (effective portion) and earnings (ineffective portion)

The following sections contain examples of accounting for nonhedging, fair value hedging and cash flow hedging.

Accounting for a Derivative Not Designated as a Hedge

XYZ Bank believes interest rates will fall and as a result bond prices will rise. On July 1, Year 1, XYZ Bank buys a call option to acquire a 10-year Treasury bond, face amount $100,000, at par. The call costs $1,000. On December 31, Year 1, the call is selling for $800. Rates went up.

Journal Entries

The accounting entries for this speculative use of a derivative follow.

On July 1, Year 1, the initial cash disbursement journal entry to record the purchase of the call option is as follows:

Dr.	Trading Account Securities	$ 1,000
Cr.	Cash	$ 1,000

On December 31, Year 1, the general journal entry to mark to market the derivative is as follows:

Dr.	Trading Loss (I/S)	$ 200	
Cr.		Trading Account Securities	$ 200

Financial Statement Effect

The trading account balance of $800 (assuming no other trading account financial instruments are held) will be included in other assets on the balance sheet.

The holding loss will be on the income statement as part of noninterest income.

Accounting for a Fair Value Hedge

On September 1, Year 1, a financial institution purchases a two-year U.S. Treasury note that pays 3% interest and sells at par for $1,000,000. It classifies the note as an available-for-sale security. It simultaneously buys a put option (an option to sell the **exact** two-year note within the period up to maturity). The put option costs $500.

The put option is expected to provide an effective hedge. Its value is anticipated to move in the opposite direction as the value of the two-year note, as shown in Figure 10.6.

FIGURE 10.6 VALUE OF DERIVATIVE AND VALUE OF NOTE

Value of Note	Intrinsic Value of Derivative	Note Holding Gain or Loss	Total Gain or Loss
$ 1,005,000	0	$ 5,000	$ 5,000
$ 1,004,000	0	4,000	4,000
$ 1,003,000	0	3,000	3,000
$ 1,002,000	0	2,000	2,000
$ 1,001,000	0	1,000	1,000
$ 1,000,000	0	0	0
$ 999,000	$ 1,000	-1,000	0
$ 998,000	2,000	-2,000	0
$ 997,000	3,000	-3,000	0
$ 996,000	4,000	-4,000	0
$ 995,000	5,000	-5,000	0

If the note declines in value over the two-year period, the put option is expected to be an effective hedge.

Intrinsic value and time value are reflected in the option's selling price. As the option approaches maturity, its time value diminishes. At maturity, the option value is its intrinsic value—which is zero.

The note and the option should both be marked to market, and the holding gain or loss on both should be included in income. Theoretically, the income would reflect only the change in the time value of the option.

Assume on December 31, Year 1 (four months after it was bought and still having 20 months of remaining life), the option was trading for $2,300 and the note was trading for $998,000 (interest rates rose).

Journal Entries

On September 1, Year 1, the initial cash disbursements journal entry to record the acquisition of the put and the note was as follows:

Dr.	AFS Securities	$1,000,000	
Dr.	Trading Account Securities	$ 500	
Cr.	Cash		$1,000,500

On December 31, Year 1, the entries to record the mark-to-market of the note and the put were as follows:

Dr.	Trading Account Securities	$1,800	
Cr.	Unrealized Holding Gain or Loss on Derivative Securities (I/S)		$1,800

Dr.	Unrealized Holding Gain or Loss on Hedged AFS Securities (I/S)	$2,000	
Cr.	AFS Securities		$2,000

Note that the unrealized holding loss on the AFS security, which is normally charged to stockholders' equity, is charged to the income statement in this case because it is an item hedged by a derivative. Because the derivative is used as a fair value hedge, the normal accounting for the AFS security is changed.

Financial Statement Effect

The put in the trading account would be carried at its fair value of $2,300 ($500 cost plus increase in value of $1,800).

The AFS security would also be carried at its fair value of $998,000 ($1,000,000 cost less the decrease in value of $2,000).

The income statement holding loss of $200 (the gain on the increase in the value of the derivative less the loss on the decrease in the value of the note) would be shown on the income statement as part of noninterest expense.

Accounting for Cash Flow Hedges

ABC Bank enters into an interest rate swap with a dealer in derivative securities. ABC agrees to pay a fixed rate and receive a variable rate for the notional amount of $100 million. The swap's fixed rate is 3% and the variable rate is the one-year Treasury rate, which on the date of the swap is also 3%.

ABC just issued a $100 million variable interest rate bond. The bond pays interest based on the one-year Treasury rate.

ABC uses the swap as a hedge of the exposure to variability in the cash flows related to the liability.

The bond will pay interest four times per year. If the one-year Treasury rate rises, the interest cost for the bond rises. However, the increased cost would be offset by the receipt of the difference between the pay fixed/receive variable amounts calculated in accordance with the swap agreement.

If the one-year Treasury rate goes up, the financial institution pays more interest on the bond but is reimbursed because it receives the Treasury rate from the counterparty of the swap. The financial institution in effect locks in a 3% fixed-rate interest cost by using the swap.

The journal entries for the interest rate swap follow.

1. When the swap is entered into:
   No entry (the swap is costless)

2. At the end of the quarter:
   Assume the swap was entered into before the issuance of the bond and the Treasury rates went to 4%. The general journal entry would be

Dr.	Interest Rate Swap (Trading A/C) $250,000	
Cr.	Stockholders' Equity (OCI)	$250,000

   ($100,000,000 x 1% = $1,000,000 x ¼ = $250,000)

   This records the gain on the derivative, which is kept on the balance sheet until the actual bond interest cost is incurred.

3. When bond interest cost is incurred, the general journal entry would be

Dr.	Interest Expense	$1,000,000
Cr.	Interest Payable	$1,000,000

   ($100,000,000 x 4% = $4,000,000 x ¼ = $1,000,000)
   This records interest expense on the bond at 4%.

4. To transfer the gain on the swap from the balance sheet to the income statement, reducing interest expense to 3% ($100,000,000 x 3% = $3,000,000 x ¼ = $750,000):

Dr.	OCI	$250,000
Cr.	Interest Expense	$250,000

Accounting for Transfers of Financial Assets

Accounting principles for transfers of financial assets were developed years ago in many industries. The accounting practices developed were inconsistent. There was no one generally accepted way to account for transfers of financial assets. Practices were complex and not consistent with present-day transactions that use financial instruments. Additionally, off-balance-sheet financing and arbitrage transactions were not booked, and the financial reporting for such items was inconsistent.

The FASB's basic solution to the problem of accounting for transfers of financial assets in SFAS 140, *Accounting for Transfers and Servicing of Financial Assets, and Extinguishments of Liabilities,* focuses on three issues: (1) control over assets; (2) financial components approach; (3) accounting for a sale (as opposed to a secured borrowing). A summary of each issue follows.

1. **CONTROL OVER ASSETS**—The basic issue is whether the transferor has lost control (not ownership) of the financial assets.
    - If control is lost, the transfer is a sale (or a securitization).
    - If control is *not* lost, the transfer is a secured borrowing.
2. **FINANCIAL COMPONENTS APPROACH**—This conceptual approach considers the following:
    - Transfers break up assets into components.
    - Components created by the transfers are assets or liabilities like any other assets or liabilities.
    - Components are just like all other freestanding instruments.
    - Components should be recognized as assets and liabilities just as other freestanding instruments are recognized.
3. **ACCOUNTING FOR A SALE**—When the transfer is a sale (loss of control), the accounting is as follows:
    - Continue to recognize what has *not* been transferred and recognize it at the previous carrying amount.
    - Recognize whatever proceeds were received (asset) or assumed (liability) at fair value.
    - *Derecognize* (take off the books) what the transferor lost control of (sold), and book all related profit or loss.

    The transfer is a sale when the following statements apply:
    - Assets are isolated (that is, beyond the reach of creditors, even in bankruptcy).
    - The transferee can sell or pledge the assets free of constraint (or the transferee is a qualifying special-purpose entity).
    - The transferor does not maintain effective control through agreement to repurchase.

The transferee must recognize all assets obtained and liabilities incurred and measure them at fair value.

If the criteria for a sale are not met, the transfer must be accounted for as a secured borrowing with a pledge of collateral.

Securitizations

Most small community financial institutions were not in the securitization business. Given that that business has dried up, it is not likely they will be in that business in the foreseeable future. Even larger community financial institutions have departed from the securitization business as a result of chaos in the credit markets. In light of the situation, no SFAS 140 accounting examples are included herein.

Accounting for Other Real Estate Owned and Its Sale

Other Real Estate Owned (OREO) is real property that was acquired through a foreclosure. Real estate acquired in settlement of loans by foreclosure or by deed (in lieu of foreclosure) is initially recorded at the lower of cost (unpaid loan balance plus costs of obtaining title and possession) or fair value less estimated costs to sell at the time of acquisition.

Subsequent costs directly related to development and improvement of property are capitalized. Costs relating to holding the property are expensed.

When the carrying value of real estate exceeds its fair value less cost to sell, an allowance for loss on real estate is established and a provision for loss on real estate is charged to other expenses.

The overriding accounting question is when should the OREO be removed from the books and records? Generally, OREO is removed from the books and records when it is sold. The methods of sale of OREO follow.

BOOKING OREO

Before we look at the accounting for removal of OREO, we must first review how it got on the books in the first place. The OREO is the result of foreclosure. When a financial institution gives up trying to collect on a loan, it goes through the legal procedures to take title to the underlying real estate collateral.

Lower of Cost or Market

When a bank receives a long-lived asset, such as real estate, from a borrower in full satisfaction of a loan, the long-lived asset is held for sale and the bank must account for this asset at its fair value less cost to sell—an amount that is usually less than the carrying value of the loan receivable. This fair value less cost to sell becomes the "cost" of the foreclosed asset. In accounting terminology this is the lower of cost or market (LOCOM). The amount, if any, by which the net recorded loan amount exceeds the fair value less cost to sell is a loss which must be charged to the reserve for loan losses account at the time of foreclosure or repossession.

Foreclosed assets include loans for which the bank, as creditor, has physically received possession of a borrower's assets, regardless of whether formal foreclosure proceedings take place.

The amount of any senior debt (principal and accrued interest) to which foreclosed real estate is subject at the time of foreclosure must be reported as a liability.

LOCOM Determination

After foreclosure, each foreclosed real estate asset (including any real estate for which the bank receives physical possession, regardless of whether formal foreclosure proceedings take place) must continue to be carried at the lower of the following:

1. The fair value of the asset minus the estimated costs to sell the asset
2. The cost of the asset (as defined in the preceding paragraphs)

This LOCOM determination must be made on an asset-by-asset basis.

If the fair value of a foreclosed real estate asset minus the estimated costs to sell the asset is less than the asset's cost, the deficiency must be recognized as a valuation allowance against the asset that is created through a charge to expense. The valuation allowance should thereafter be increased or decreased (but not below zero) through charges or credits to expense for changes in the asset's LOCOM amount. An example of the accounting follows.

Assume a bank has a mortgage loan for $500,000. The borrower runs into financial difficulties and it is clear the loan is impaired. A "work out" is not possible, and the bank forecloses on the property.

At foreclosure the property is worth $400,000 (estimated fair value) and the bank estimates it will cost $50,000 to dispose of the property.

The pertinent entries follow:

Dr.	OREO ($400,000 - $50,000)	$350,000	
Cr.	Loan Receivable		$500,000
Dr.	Allowance for Loan and Lease Losses	$150,000*	

Assume in the following quarter the value of the property declines another 10% to $360,000, and the cost to dispose is estimated to be $46,000. The LOCOM rule now requires the OREO to be carried at $314,000 necessitating the following entry:

Dr.	Loss on Foreclosure (Schedule RI, line 5j)	36,000
Cr.	OREO ($350,000 - $314,000)	36,000

* If the proper amount is not set aside in the allowance account, an additional provision for loan losses must be recorded.

METHODS OF SALE OF OREO

SFAS 66, *Accounting for Sales of Real Estate*, addresses the sale of OREO. Three of the methods SFAS 66 prescribes for the sale of OREO are (1) full accrual; (2) cost recovery; (3) deposit method. A discussion of each method follows.

Full Accrual Method

Full accrual accounting (accounting for the OREO "sale" as a genuine, bona fide sale) is permitted when the following criteria are met:
1. A sale is consummated.
2. The buyer's initial and continuing investments are adequate to demonstrate a commitment to pay for the property.
3. The seller's receivable is not subject to future subordination.
4. The seller has transferred to the buyer the usual risks and rewards of ownership in a transaction that is, in substance, a sale and does not have a substantial continuing involvement with the property.

Under these circumstances, the bank can legitimately sell the OREO. It can book the sale and remove the OREO from the balance sheet. The bank then records a loan receivable.

For example, an institution that meets all the criteria above wants to sell OREO that has a book value of $1,000,000. Three possible sales scenarios follow: (A) cash of $100,000 and a loan of $900,000; (B) cash of $100,000 and a loan of $850,000; (C) cash of $150,000 and a loan of $900,000. The entries below show how the bank would book each sale using the full accrual method.

(A) Dr.	Cash	$ 100,000	
Dr.	Loan Receivable	900,000	
Cr.	OREO		$ 1,000,000
(B) Dr.	Cash	$100,000	
Dr.	Loan Receivable	850,000	
Dr.	Loss on Sale of OREO	50,000	
Cr.	OREO		$ 1,000,000
(C) Dr.	Cash	$150,000	
Dr.	Loan Receivable	900,000	
Cr.	OREO		$ 1,000,000
Cr.	Gain on Sale of OREO		50,000

Cost Recovery Method

The *cost recovery method* of accounting (accounting for the OREO sale as a real sale only when the carrying value of OREO is received) should be used if the following circumstances exist.

1. The recovery of the cost of the property is *not* reasonably assured.
2. The buyer defaults.
3. The cost has already been recovered and collection of the additional amounts is uncertain.

Under such circumstances, there is no sale. OREO must remain on the books until payments equal or exceed the seller's cost of the property sold. If that does not happen, OREO remains on the books. Below is an example of accounting for OREO using the cost recovery method.

OREO is sold for $2,000,000 when its book value or cost is $1,000,000. The financial institution records accumulated payments in a deferred sales contract account until accumulated payments equal $1,000,000. At that time, the financial institution can record the sale. Any additional payments received are recorded as a gain on the sale of OREO.

Journal Entries

1. When payments are received:

Dr.	Cash	$50,000	
Cr.	Deferred Sales Contracts		$50,000

2. When the deferred sales contract account accumulates to $1,000,000:

Dr.	Deferred Sales Contracts	$1,000,000	
Cr.	OREO		$1,000,000

3. Any additional payments over the $1,000,000:

Dr.	Cash	XXXX	
Cr.	Gain on Sale of OREO		XXXX

Note that OREO stays on the books until the cost is recovered.

Deposit Method

The *deposit method* (accounting for the OREO sale as a real sale when a predetermined deposit amount is received) should be used when the buyer's initial investment does *not* meet SFAS 66's criteria for down payments (see Figure 10.7), but the recovery of the cost of the property is reasonably assured if the buyer defaults.

FIGURE 10.7 SFAS 66 CRITERIA FOR DOWN PAYMENTS

Minimum Initial Investment Expressed as a Percentage of Sales Value under the Provisions of SFAS 66

	%
LAND	
• Held for commercial, industrial or residential development to commence *within* two years after sale	20%
• Held for commercial, industrial or residential development to commence *after* two years	25%
COMMERCIAL & INDUSTRIAL PROPERTY	
Office and industrial buildings, shopping centers, etc.	
• Properties subject to lease on a long-term basis to parties with satisfactory credit rating; cash flow currently sufficient to service all indebtedness	10%
• Single-tenancy properties sold to a buyer with a satisfactory credit rating	15%
• All other	20%
• Cash flow currently sufficient to service all indebtedness	15%
• Start-up situations or current deficiencies in cash flow	25%
MULTIFAMILY RESIDENTIAL PROPERTY	
Primary residence:	
• Cash flow currently sufficient to service all indebtedness	10%
• Start-up situations or current deficiencies in cash flow	15%
Secondary or recreational residence:	
• Cash flow currently sufficient to service all indebtedness	15%
• Start-up situations or current deficiencies in cash flow	25%
SINGLE-FAMILY RESIDENTIAL PROPERTY (INCLUDING CONDOMINIUMS)	
• Primary residence of the buyer	5%
• Secondary or recreational residence	10%

Source: Financial Accounting Standards Board, *Accounting for Sales of Real Estate*, Appendix A (October 1982).

The deposit method does *not* reflect a receivable until the buyer has made the appropriate down payment. The institution continues to carry OREO on the books and discloses in the notes to its financial statements that the property is subject to a sales contract. Cash received from the buyer is reported as a deposit. Below are two examples of accounting for OREO using the deposit method. The first example focuses on the basic OREO accounting and when OREO is removed from the books and records; the second focuses on the proper recognition of interest income, especially in the first year of the sale.

ACCOUNTING FOR THE SALE OF OREO

Two methods of accounting for the sale of OREO are (1) basic OREO accounting with the deposit method and (2) OREO accounting with recognition of interest income. Each method is detailed below.

Basic OREO Accounting with the Deposit Method

OREO with a book value of $2,000,000 is sold for $2,000,000 with the financial institution financing 100% of the sales price. The OREO is a multifamily dwelling, which under SFAS 66 requires a 10% down payment.

Journal Entries

1. When cash is received:

Dr.	Cash	$100,000	
Cr.	Deposit on OREO Sales Contracts		$100,000

2. When the deposit on OREO sales contracts account equals $200,000 (10% of $2,000,000):

Dr.	Deposit on Sales Contracts	$200,000	
Dr.	Loan Receivable	$1,800,000	
Cr.	OREO		$2,000,000

SFAS 66 is about substance over form. For accounting purposes, OREO is not sold until the required minimum investment is received—regardless of the actual arrangement.

OREO Accounting with Recognition of Interest Income

Assume that a financial institution has a multifamily dwelling in its OREO account. Under SFAS 66, if the institution uses the full accrual method, a down payment equal to 10% of the sales value is required.

Assume that all other criteria are met except the down payment. The carrying value of the OREO is $100,000, and the institution sells the OREO and finances the sale with a mortgage loan for 10 years at a market rate of interest of 12%.

Selling price	$ 100,000
Actual down payment	0
Amount financed	100%
Interest rate	12%
FASB required minimum down payment	10%

OREO should remain in other assets on the balance sheet. No loan receivable should be recognized on the financial statements until the institution has received $10,000 (10% of $100,000).

Journal Entries

1. As cash payments are received:

Dr.	Cash	XXX
Cr.	Deposit on OREO Sales Contracts (Liability Account)	XXX

2. Once cash deposits equal $10,000:

Dr.	Deposit on OREO Sales Contracts	$ 10,000
Dr.	Loan Receivable	$ 90,000
Cr.	OREO	$100,000

Figure 10.8 shows how the depository institution should properly recognize interest income. The institution must maintain the financial integrity of the loan.

FIGURE 10.8 RECOGNITION OF INTEREST INCOME

	Per Customer Records (at 12%)				Per Bank (at 13.91%)			
Year	Payment	Interest	Principal	Net [1] Carrying Amount	Interest	Principal	Net [2] Carrying Amount	Net Interest
0				100000			100000	
Jan to July						10000	90000	
Aug to Dec	17700	12000	5700	94300	5446[3]	2254	87746	(6544)
2	17700	11316	6384	87916	12205	5495	82251	889
3	17700	10550	7150	80766	11441	6259	75992	891
4	17700	9692	8008	72758	10570	7130	68862	878
5	17700	8731	8969	63789	9579	8121	60741	848
6	17700	7655	10045	53744	8449	9251	51490	794
7	17700	6449	11251	42493	7162	10538	40952	713
8	17700	5099	12601	29892	5696	12004	28948	597
9	17700	3587	14113	15779	4027	13673	15275	440
10	17700	1921	15779	0	2425	15275	0	504
	177000	77000	100000		77000	100000		0

[1] Stated interest rate 12%
[2] Effective interest rate 13.91%
[3] Amount of interest income recognized in first year
  90,000 x [(1.00 - .565) x .1391]
  90,000 x .060508 = 5446

The effective rate of interest must be computed as follows:

1. Using present value of annuity tables or a calculator, the computed yearly payment on $100,000 at 12% for 10 periods is $17,700. The yearly payment of $17,700 divided by 12 equals a monthly payment of $1,475.

2. Compute the *period of non–interest bearing payments*:
   Minimum down payment ÷ monthly payment = months of non–interest bearing payments ÷ 12 = years of non–interest bearing payments

   $10,000/$1,475 = 6.78 mos./12 = .565 yrs. (period of non–interest bearing payments)

3. Compute the *number of interest bearing periods*:
   Original loan period - Non–interest bearing period = number of interest bearing periods
   10.000 yrs. - .565 yrs. = 9.435 yrs.

4. Compute the *effective yield*:
   $17,700   Payment amount
   $90,000   Principal amount ($100,000 - $10,000)
   9.435 yrs   Payment period

Prior to SFAS 66, some financial institutions recorded $12,000 interest income in the first year—not the correct amount of $5,446. This created material overstatements of interest income. SFAS 66 attempted to fix the overstatement problem.

In this chapter, you learned about accounting issues that are of immediate concern to community financial institutions. The next chapter will acquaint you with possibilities for the future of accounting.

CHAPTER 11

Current Trends

This chapter presents a summary of current trends in the accounting profession. It focuses on the need for more disclosure about related party transactions. It speculates about future accounting, auditing and consulting expectations and reviews the clearly evident fair value, risk disclosure and balance sheet emphasis trends.

After studying this chapter you should be able to
- summarize the related party disclosure and other disclosure concerns of SOX
- list and discuss the emphasis on the current fair value, risk disclosure and balance sheet trends
- identify potential future expectations
- identify the new fair value accounting requirements

Related Party Disclosures

Much of the Enron affair and other failures centered on the management's unwillingness to disclose certain relationships with carefully created Special Purpose Entities. A *Special Purpose Entity (SPE)* is a business (usually a corporation) set up to provide a particular service for another entity. Such services include providing research and development, servicing sold loans, handling employees' stock option plans, servicing debt, etc. In the Enron situation, the CPAs who performed the Enron audit were severely criticized for not disclosing Enron's activities with the SPEs from a related party disclosure point of view.

GAAP financial statements must provide the reader with pertinent information about related parties. SFAS 57, *Related Party Disclosures*, specifically defines a related party. Figure 11.1 details the definition.

FIGURE 11.1 EXAMPLES OF RELATED PARTIES

> Examples of related party transactions include transactions between
> (a) a parent company and its subsidiaries;
> (b) subsidiaries of a common parent;
> (c) an enterprise and trusts for the benefit of employees, such as pension and profit-sharing trusts that are managed by or under the trusteeship of the enterprises's management;
> (d) an enterprise and its principal owners, management, or members of their immediate families; and
> (e) affiliates.

Source: Financial Accounting Standards Board, SFAS 57, *Related Party Disclosures* (1982).

The following disclosures are required whenever material transactions between related parties have occurred.

1. **NATURE OF THE RELATIONSHIPS**—Identify the parties involved in the transactions: the party with which the company did business (for example, its officers, its stockholders, its parent company, its subsidiary).

2. **DESCRIPTION OF THE TRANSACTIONS**—For each income statement presented, describe the nature of all material related party transactions. For example, disclose whether the related party transaction is a loan, a guarantee, a leasing arrangement, a purchase or a sale of products or assets, etc. Regardless of whether there was any dollar amount involved, disclose all material transactions.

3. **DOLLAR AMOUNTS OF TRANSACTIONS**—For each income statement presented, quantify the total amount of various types of related party transactions, as well as year-end balances. If similar types of transactions took place between one type of related party, add these transactions together and disclose the total amount. For instance, a company may buy goods and services from a vendor in the normal course of business. If the vendor or several vendors are owned or controlled, for example, by the spouse of a principal owner, the company would have to disclose the total dollar amounts of transactions with the related party vendor(s).

4. **EFFECT OF ANY CHANGES IN THE TERMS OF THE TRANSACTIONS**—Disclose any factor that affects comparability. If the terms of any related party transactions have changed from the prior period, disclose the change.

5. **BALANCES, TERMS AND SETTLEMENT OF RELATED PARTY RECEIVABLES AND PAYABLES**—The nature of any control relationship that could significantly impact the business must be disclosed, regardless of whether

any transactions occurred between the parties. If common management or common ownership exists between companies, that fact can affect their financial positions, even if the two companies did not conduct business together.

The authoritative literature presumes that related parties have *better rights* than others. Because of that, to protect the others, related party activity must be disclosed.

Title IV (Enhanced Financial Disclosures) of the Sarbanes-Oxley Act of 2002 addresses some related party and other disclosure issues. A summary follows.

1. **ACCURACY OF FINANCIAL REPORTS**—Each financial report that contains financial statements and that is required to be prepared in accordance with (or reconciled to) generally accepted accounting principles must reflect all material correcting adjustments that have been identified by a registered public accounting firm in accordance with generally accepted principles and the rules and regulations of the SEC.

2. **OFF-BALANCE-SHEET TRANSACTIONS**—Each annual and quarterly financial report required to be filed with the SEC must disclose all material off-balance-sheet transactions, arrangements, obligations (including contingent obligations) and other relationships of the issuer with unconsolidated entities or other persons that may have a material current or future effect on financial condition, changes in financial condition, results of operations, liquidity, capital expenditures, capital resources or significant components of revenues or expenses.

3. **CODE OF ETHICS DISCLOSURE**—Each public company must disclose whether or not (and if not, the reason) it has adopted a code of ethics for senior financial officers that applies to its principal financial officer and comptroller, principal accounting officer or anyone who performs similar functions. Immediate disclosure is required for any change in or waiver of the code of ethics for senior financial officers.

The term *code of ethics* means standards that are reasonably necessary to promote

- honest and ethical conduct, including the ethical handling of actual or apparent personal and professional conflicts of interest
- full, fair, accurate, timely and understandable disclosure in periodic reports
- substantial compliance with applicable governmental rules and regulations

4. **DISCLOSURE OF AUDIT COMMITTEE FINANCIAL EXPERT**—Public companies must disclose whether or not (and if not, the reasons) their audit committees are comprised of at least one member who is a financial expert, as defined by the Commission (see Figure 11.2).

FIGURE 11.2 SOX DEFINITION OF FINANCIAL EXPERT

> Definition of Financial Expert
> on
> Audit Committee
>
> (a) **RULES DEFINING "FINANCIAL EXPERT"**—The Commission shall issue rules, as necessary or appropriate in the public interest and consistent with the protection of investors, to require each issuer, together with periodic reports required pursuant to sections 13(a) and 15(d) of the Securities Exchange Act of 1934, to disclose whether or not, and if not, the reasons therefor, the audit committee of that issuer is comprised of at least 1 member who is a financial expert, as such term is defined by the Commission.
>
> (b) **CONSIDERATIONS**—In defining the term "financial expert" for purposes of subsection (a), the Commission shall consider whether a person has, through education and experience as a public accountant or auditor or a principal financial officer, comptroller, or principal accounting officer of an issuer, or from a position involving the performance of similar functions—
> (1) an understanding of generally accepted accounting principles and financial statements;
> (2) experience in—
>   (A) the preparation or auditing of financial statements of generally comparable issuers; and
>   (B) the application of such principles in connection with the accounting for estimates, accruals, and reserves;
> (3) experience with internal accounting controls; and
> (4) an understanding of audit committee functions

Source: Sarbanes-Oxley Act of 2002, Section 407.

5. **ENHANCED REVIEW OF PERIODIC DISCLOSURES BY ISSUERS**—The Commission will review disclosures made by issuers, including their financial statements.

   For purposes of scheduling the reviews required by subsection (a), the Commission will consider, among other factors, the following:

   * Issuers that have issued material restatements of financial results
   * Issuers that experience significant volatility in their stock prices as compared to other issuers
   * Issuers that have the largest market capitalization
   * Emerging companies with disparities in price-to-earning ratios

- Issuers whose operations significantly affect any material sector of the economy
- Any other factors that the Commission may consider relevant

Issuers will be reviewed at least every three years.

Future Expectations

As a result of the events that occurred in the financial world in late 2008 and early 2009, the auditing, consulting and accounting professions are likely to experience many changes in the coming years.

FUTURE AUDITING EXPECTATIONS

Auditors and those who use their services can anticipate many changes.
- More will be expected of auditors.
- Auditors will have to audit!
- More evidence will be sought; more audit work will be performed.
- More professional skepticism will be required.
- A "show me" attitude will be pervasive.
- Fraudulent financial reporting concerns will be more carefully and more fully considered.
- Audit committee disclosure will be improved.
- Auditors will report to the audit committee.
- More partner supervision and review will be required.
- Audit proposed adjustments will be made by audit clients.
- Materiality will be reassessed.
- Revenue recognition will be scrutinized.
- Related party disclosures will be scrutinized.
- Independence will be constantly reviewed.
- Auditors will be less willing to back off from a position.
- Audit partners will be rotated every five years.
- Audit fees will rise sharply.

FUTURE CONSULTING EXPECTATIONS

The field of financial consulting may also experience changes.
- Consulting by CPA firms will continue and even increase for non-audit clients.
- Consulting services will need audit committee preapproval and SEC prohibited services exemption.
- SEC auditor prohibited services will be needed and nonaudit CPAs will be sought to perform the following prohibited services:
  – tax services
  – bookkeeping
  – systems design and implementation (for financial systems)
  – appraisal or valuation

- internal auditing
- actuarial services
- human resource services
- investment advisor services

FUTURE ACCOUNTING EXPECTATIONS

The field of accounting will probably undergo modifications.

- Accounting rules will not change much.
- Accounting rules will be followed to the letter and spirit.
- The SEC oversight board will more carefully review accounting pronouncements.
- Alternative GAAP will start to disappear.
- Stock compensation will be compensation. The intrinsic value approach will disappear. The *intrinsic value approach* resulted in no compensation expense being recorded for stock compensation paid by employers in the form of stock options unless on the grant date the employees' exercise price was less than the market price of shares granted.
- SPEs will be consolidated.
- Related party transactions will be revisited for proper accounting and disclosure.
- Revenue recognition rules will be revisited.
- Accountants will be accountants. Auditors will be auditors.
- Accounting fees will rise.

Recent Trends

Some of the more obvious trends in financial reporting are the (1) fair value trend; (2) risk disclosure trend; (3) balance sheet emphasis trend. Below is a summary of each.

FAIR VALUE TREND

Many believe that GAAP financial statements are misleading because they are not adjusted to show value or purchasing power changes.

Those who cling to the historical cost model dislike fair value financial statements because they believe fair values (however determined) are "soft" numbers. The fair value amounts, however, don't seem to be any softer than the historical amounts that are currently used in financial statements.

If the financial statements don't give readers what they want and need—information about value—then they will have no usefulness and will become obsolete.

Examples of current value trends include:

- Accounting for investments
- Marking-to-market the receivables and/or payables of taxing authorities

- Fair value reporting of derivatives
- Carrying impaired loans at fair value

The trend toward fair value financial reporting is rapid. In fact in the financial services industry, fair value financial statements are almost a reality.

Much more work is needed in the use of following:
- Appraisal values
- Selling prices
- Replacement costs
- Exit values
- Price-level adjusted amounts
- Pricing models

See the appendix to this chapter for fair value information.

RISK DISCLOSURE TREND

The FASB has become very sensitive to issues that are not covered in the body of financial statements, and it has required extended disclosures for items such as the following:
- Cash disclosures (operations, financing, investing activities)
- Financial guarantees
- Risks and uncertainties
- Off-balance-sheet credit and market risk
- Concentration of credit risk
- Environmental risk issues
- Going concern issues
- Financial instrument risk and disclosure issues

More and more readers of financial statements look to the footnotes for risk disclosure information. Until fair values are recognized in financial statements, footnote disclosures of business risks will continue to be important. (For a discussion of business risks, see Chapter 4.)

BALANCE SHEET EMPHASIS TREND

Financial standards have favored, and will continue to favor, the development of a reasonable balance sheet at the expense of the income statement. This is the opposite of trends in past years.

Examples of this trend include emphasis on the following issues:
- Pension liability (particularly unfunded liability) rather than pension expense
- Income taxes receivable and payable rather than income tax expense
- Asset impairment—especially loan impairment
- Asset valuation—removal of R & D from assets
- Lease asset and liability recognition

Figure 11.3 lists accounting Web sites that are valuable resources for keeping abreast of trends and changes in the accounting profession.

FIGURE 11.3 ACCOUNTING WEB SITES

Accounting Research Network
http://www.ssrn.com

AccountingWeb
http://www.accountingweb.com/

AICPA AcSEC Update Newsletter
http://www.aicpa.org/members/div/acctstd/acsec/index.htm

AICPA Daily News Alert
http://www.aicpa.org/index.htm

American Institute of Certified Public Accountants
http://www.aicpa.org

The Center for Audit Quality
http://www.thecaq.org

EDGAR Online
http://www.edgar-online.com/people

Electronic Accountant
http://www.webcpa.com

Financial Accounting Standards Board
http://www.fasb.org/

Financial Accounting Standards Board Exposure Drafts
http://www.fasb.org/draft/

Financial Accounting Standards Board Summaries and Status
http://www.fasb.org/st/

FASB Emerging Issues Task Force
http://www.fasb.org/eitf/

Public Company Accounting Oversight Board
http://www.pcaobus.org

SEC Proposed Rules
http://www.sec.gov/rules/proposed.shtml

SEC Staff Accounting Bulletins
http://www.sec.gov/interps/account.shtml

Accounting is an evolving, ever-changing field that will continue to record, classify and interpret economic transactions and events for businesses. Those interested in an exciting future in accounting might use this book to get on board and start the journey. Good luck!

APPENDIX

Fair Value Information

Some FASB pronouncements (for example, Statements 107, 115, 133, 156) have required or allowed financial statement preparers an option to use fair value. These pronouncements, however, did not contain specific guidance on how to determine the amount that is fair value.

Finally, in SFAS 157, *Fair Value Measurements*, the FASB provided guidance on how to measure fair value for financial and nonfinancial assets and liabilities that are required or are permitted to be measured at fair value under GAAP literature.

Any item on the face of the financial statements or in the footnotes that was shown at fair value prior to SFAS 157 must now be shown at fair value using the SFAS 157 measurement criteria.

This appendix is a brief summary of the GAAP fair value measurement approach set forth in SFAS 157.

DEFINITION OF FAIR VALUE

Fair value is the measure that assumes an asset is sold or a liability is transferred in an orderly transaction between market participants at the measurement date. Fair value is somewhat fuzzy. It's not a black or white issue. Fair values are "soft" numbers based on ever-changing inputs. Some fair value estimates are more reliable than others.

Orderly Transaction

An *orderly transaction* is a hypothetical transaction that assumes exposure to the market for a period prior to the measurement date to allow for marketing activities that are usual and customary for transactions involving such assets or liabilities. It is not a forced transaction (for example, a forced liquidation or distress sale).

Hypothetical Transactions

The transaction to sell the asset or transfer the liability is a *hypothetical transaction* at the measurement date, considered from the perspective of a market participant that holds the asset or owes the liability.

Exit Values

The objective of a fair value measurement is to determine the price that would be received to sell the asset or paid to transfer the liability at the measurement date *(an exit price)*.

Assumed Markets

The measurement assumes the hypothetical transaction occurs in the principal market for the asset or liability or, in the absence of a principal market, in the most advantageous market for the asset or liability.

The *principal market* is the market in which the reporting entity would sell the asset or transfer the liability with the greatest volume and level of activity for the asset or liability.

The *most advantageous market* is the market in which the reporting entity would sell the asset or transfer the liability with the price that maximizes the amount that would be received for the asset or minimizes the amount that would be paid to transfer the liability, considering transaction costs in the respective markets.

In either case, the market and the market participants should be considered from the perspective of the reporting entity.

If there is a principal market for the asset or liability, the fair value measurement shall represent the price in *that* market (whether that price is directly observable or otherwise determined using a valuation technique), even if the price in a different market is potentially more advantageous at the measurement date.

The price in either market that is used to measure the fair value of the asset or liability should *not* be adjusted for transaction costs, which represent the incremental direct costs to sell the asset or transfer the liability in the market used.

Valuation Techniques

To properly measure fair value, valuation techniques must be used consistently with the following three approaches:

1. Market approach
2. Income approach
3. Cost approach

Valuation techniques that are appropriate in the circumstances and for which sufficient data are available shall be used to measure fair value. In some cases, a single valuation technique will be appropriate (for example, when valuing an asset or liability using quoted prices in an active market for *identical* assets or liabilities).

In other cases, multiple valuation techniques will be appropriate (for example, as might be the case when valuing a reporting unit). If multiple valuation techniques are used to measure fair value, the results (respective indications of fair value) shall be evaluated and weighted, as appropriate, considering the reasonableness of the range indicated by those results. A fair value measurement is the point within that range that is most representative of fair value in the circumstances.

Valuation techniques used to measure fair value shall be consistently applied.

Inputs to Valuation Techniques

Inputs refer broadly to the assumptions that market participants would use in pricing the asset or liability, including assumptions about risk.

For example, the risk inherent in a particular valuation technique used to measure fair value (such as a pricing model) and/or the risk inherent in the inputs to the valuation technique.

Inputs may be observable or unobservable:
- **Observable inputs** reflect the assumptions market participants would use in pricing the asset or liability developed based on market data obtained from *sources independent* of the reporting entity.
- **Unobservable inputs** reflect the reporting *entity's own assumptions* about the assumptions market participants would use in pricing the asset or liability developed based on the best information available in the circumstances.

Valuation techniques used to measure fair value shall maximize the use of observable inputs and minimize the use of unobservable inputs.

FAIR VALUE HIERARCHY

The fair value hierarchy prioritizes the inputs to valuation techniques used to measure fair value into three broad levels.

Level 1

Sometimes called *marking to market*. The most precise level.

Valuations are based on *quoted prices in active markets for identical assets or liabilities*. Prices appear on computer screens.

Assets in this category: Publicly traded stocks, listed futures and options, government and agency bonds and mutual funds.

Level 2

Called *marking to matrix* by some. Less precise.

Valuations are based on *observable market data* for *similar or comparable assets*, such as dealer-pricing services based on surveys or other market bids and offers. Fewer screen prices.

Assets in this category: Emerging-market government bonds, some infrequently traded corporate and municipal bonds, structured notes, some mortgage and asset-backed securities and some derivatives that don't trade publicly.

Level 3

Called *marking to model*. Involves the most guesswork.

Valuations are based on management's best judgment and involve management's *own assumptions about the assumptions market participants would use in pricing the asset*. The process can employ pricing models based on estimates of future cash flows or other formulas.

Assets in this category: Some real-estate and private-equity investments, certain loan commitments, some long-term options and less easily tradable asset-backed bonds.

EFFECTIVE DATE

SFAS 157 became effective for financial statements issued for fiscal years beginning after November 15, 2007, and interim periods within those fiscal years. For calendar-year companies SFAS 157 was used for 2008.

The FASB went one step further in SFAS 159, which permits entities to *choose* to measure many financial instruments and certain other items at fair value.

SFAS 159 also became effective as of the beginning of an entity's first fiscal year that begins after November 15, 2007. It was effective for calendar year 2008, if the entity elected to measure selected financial instruments at fair value. In 2009 the election will extend to nonfinancial assets, such as property, plant and equipment.

In the financial and credit markets, determining fair value for asset-backed securities became extremely difficult if not impossible throughout 2008. The credit crunch turmoil put additional pressure on accountants who believed fair value should be used in place of historical cost.

The fair value accounting story is not over yet.

PART THREE

FINANCIAL STATEMENTS

Financial Statements

This part of *Accounting Basics for Community Financial Institutions* contains copies of the financial statements of Fictitious Depository Corporation that are discussed in detail in Chapters 6, 7 and 9. These copies are provided for your convenience. You can remove these perforated financial statements for easy reference as you go through the chapters.

Accounting Basics for Community Financial Institutions, 2nd edition, Copyright © 2009 by Financial Managers Society, Inc. All rights reserved. Limited permission is granted to the original purchaser to photocopy Part 3, Financial Statements.

BALANCE SHEET (ASSETS) (FIGURE 6.2)

Fictitious Depository Corporation
Consolidated Balance Sheet
(In thousands, except share data)

THE LEFT-HAND SIDE OF THE BALANCE SHEET

	Current Year	Prior Year
ASSETS		
Cash and cash equivalents	$ 21,100	$ 20,600
Money market investments:		
Interest bearing deposits with banks	18,300	12,200
Federal funds sold	21,750	9,600
Total money market investments	40,050	21,800
Securities available-for-sale:	115,750	113,350
Loans	366,650	298,200
Less:		
Unearned interest	17,400	14,600
Reserve for loan losses	3,600	3,050
Net loans	345,650	280,550
Premises and equipment	11,200	9,850
Accrued interest receivable	3,450	3,600
Other assets	6,600	3,600
Total assets	$ 543,800	$ 453,350

Accounting Basics for Community Financial Institutions, 2nd edition, Copyright © 2009 by Financial Managers Society, Inc. All rights reserved. Limited permission is granted to the original purchaser to photocopy Part 3, Financial Statements.

BALANCE SHEET (LIABILITIES) (FIGURE 6.3)

THE RIGHT-HAND SIDE OF THE BALANCE SHEET

LIABILITIES

Deposits:		
Non–interest bearing	$ 59,900	$ 50,450
Interest bearing	418,550	354,050
Total deposits	478,450	404,500
Federal funds purchased and securities sold under agreements to repurchase	6,200	4,450
Accrued interest payable	1,050	1,650
Other liabilities	2,900	550
Advances from Federal Home Loan Bank	9,250	4,450
Total liabilities	497,850	415,600

SHAREHOLDERS' EQUITY

Preferred stock:		
No par value; Authorized shares 2,000,000	–	–
Common stock:		
Par value, $5.00; Authorized shares 10,000,000; Shares issued: 3,390,000 for (current year) and 3,140,000 for (prior year)	9,100	7,850
Additional paid-in capital	14,550	8,200
Retained earnings	19,900	19,250
Net unrealized holding gains on securities available for sale	2,400	2,450
Total shareholders' equity	$ 45,950	$ 37,750
Total liabilities and shareholders' equity	$ 543,800	$ 453,350

Accounting Basics for Community Financial Institutions, 2nd edition, Copyright © 2009 by Financial Managers Society, Inc. All rights reserved. Limited permission is granted to the original purchaser to photocopy Part 3, Financial Statements.

INCOME STATEMENT (FIGURE 6.4)

Fictitious Depository Corporation
Consolidated Statement of Income
(In thousands, except shares and per share data)

	Years Ended December 31,	
	Current Year	**Prior Year**
INTEREST INCOME		
Loans, including fees	$ 25,150	$ 25,050
Securities:		
Taxable	7,100	7,900
Tax-exempt	100	150
Deposits with banks	950	1,250
Federal funds sold	200	800
Total interest income	33,500	35,150
INTEREST EXPENSE		
Deposits	11,250	14,000
Federal funds purchased and securities sold under agreements to repurchase	100	250
Advances from FHLB	200	300
Total interest expense	11,550	14,550
NET INTEREST INCOME	21,950	20,600
Provision for loan losses	1,000	1,450
Net interest income after provision for loan losses	20,950	19,150
OTHER INCOME		
Trust income	850	800
Fees for other services	1,750	1,450
Security gains	–	100
Other income	600	450
Total other income	3,200	2,800

Accounting Basics for Community Financial Institutions, 2nd edition, Copyright © 2009 by Financial Managers Society, Inc. All rights reserved. Limited permission is granted to the original purchaser to photocopy Part 3, Financial Statements.

OTHER EXPENSES

Salaries and wages	7,000	6,550
Pension and other employee benefits	1,600	1,500
Net occupancy expense	1,550	1,450
Equipment expense	1,300	1,200
F.D.I.C. insurance	900	850
Amortization of intangible assets	550	400
Other operating expense	4,150	3,900
Total other expense	17,050	15,850
Income before income taxes	7,100	6,100
Provision for income taxes	2,400	1,750
NET INCOME	$ 4,700	$ 4,350
Net income per share	$ 1.39	$ 1.39

The accompanying notes* are an integral part of the consolidated financial statements.

* Extensive footnote disclosures would accompany the actual financial statement. Selected footnote disclosures are included in this book.

Accounting Basics for Community Financial Institutions, 2nd edition, Copyright © 2009 by Financial Managers Society, Inc. All rights reserved. Limited permission is granted to the original purchaser to photocopy Part 3, Financial Statements.

STATEMENT OF CASH FLOWS (FIGURE 6.5)

Fictitious Depository Corporation
Consolidated Statement of Cash Flows
(In thousands)

	Years Ended December 31,	
	Current Year	Prior Year
CASH FLOWS FROM OPERATING ACTIVITIES:		
Net income	$ 4,700	$ 4,350
Adjustments to reconcile net income to net cash provided by operating activities:		
Provision for loan losses	1,000	1,450
Provision for depreciation and amortization	1,100	1,050
Amortization of intangible assets	550	400
Amortization of premium, net of accretion of discount on loans and investments	(50)	(100)
Deferred income taxes	(400)	(300)
Realized securities (gains) losses		(100)
Decrease (increase) in interest receivable	150	50
Decrease (increase) in interest payable	(600)	(600)
Decrease (increase) in other assets and liabilities, net	(800)	(850)
Net cash provided by operating activities	5,650	5,350
CASH FLOWS FROM INVESTING ACTIVITIES:		
Proceeds from sales of securities	18,250	8,800
Repayments and maturities of securities	27,150	18,600
Purchase of securities	(47,850)	(40,750)
Net decrease (increase) in money market investments	(18,250)	20,350
Net increase in loans	(66,050)	(3,950)
Purchases of premises and equipment	(2,450)	(2,050)
Net cash provided by (used in) investing activities	(89,200)	1,000

Accounting Basics for Community Financial Institutions, 2nd edition, Copyright © 2009 by Financial Managers Society, Inc. All rights reserved. Limited permission is granted to the original purchaser to photocopy Part 3, Financial Statements.

CASH FLOWS FROM FINANCING ACTIVITIES:

Cash from issuance of common stock	5,250	0
Net increase in deposits	73,950	5,200
Net increase (decrease) in federal funds purchased and securities sold under agreements to repurchase	1,750	(5,700)
Cash dividends paid	(1,700)	(1,500)
Net increase (decrease) in advances from FHLB	4,800	(1,250)
Net cash provided by (used in) financing activities	84,050	(3,250)
Increase (decrease) in cash and cash equivalents	500	3,100
Cash and cash equivalents at beginning of year	20,600	17,500
Cash and cash equivalents at end of year	$ 21,100	$ 20,600

Supplemental disclosures of cash flow information:

Cash paid during the year for:

Interest on deposits and other borrowings	$ 12,200	$ 15,200
Federal income taxes, net of refunds	2,500	2,000

The accompanying notes* are an integral part of the consolidated financial statements.

* Extensive footnote disclosures would accompany the actual financial statement. Selected footnote disclosures are included in this book.

SELECTED SUPPLEMENTAL DATA (FIGURE 9.1)

Fictitious Depository Corporation
Supplemental Financial Data
(in thousands, except per share data)
Years Ended December 31

	Current*	Prior*	2nd Prior	3rd Prior	4th Prior
SELECTED DATA					
Total assets	$ 543,800	$453,350	$450,000	$449,000	$446,500
Loans, net of unearned interest	349,250	283,600	279,000	275,000	270,000
Securities available-for-sale	115,750	113,350	110,000	109,500	108,000
Total deposits	478,450	404,500	401,600	400,900	398,900
FHLB advances	9,250	4,450	4,000	3,900	3,800
Total shareholders' equity	45,950	37,750	36,500	36,300	35,100
Net loans charged off [1]	450	950	770	700	730
Dividends	1,700	1,500	1,400	1,400	1,300
Net income (after tax)	4,700	4,350	4,100	4,000	3,900
Average shares outstanding	3,390	3,140	3,140	3,140	3,140

	Current	Prior	2nd Prior	3rd Prior	4th Prior
PER SHARE DATA					
Net income [2]	$1.39	$1.39	$1.30	$1.27	$1.25
Cash dividends declared [3]	0.50	0.48	0.45	0.45	0.41
Year-end book value [4]	13.55	12.02	11.62	11.56	11.18

* Readers should be able to locate these amounts in the financial statements in Chapter 6.
(1) See the Footnote Disclosure in the Reserve for Loan Losses section in Chapter 7.
(2) $4,700 ÷ 3,390 shares = $1.39 current; $4,350 ÷ 3,140 shares = $1.39
(3) $1,700 ÷ 3,390 shares = $0.50; $1,500 ÷ 3,140 shares = $0.48
(4) $45,950 ÷ 3,390 shares = $13.55; $37,750 ÷ 3,140 shares = $12.02

Accounting Basics for Community Financial Institutions, 2nd edition, Copyright © 2009 by Financial Managers Society, Inc. All rights reserved. Limited permission is granted to the original purchaser to photocopy Part 3, Financial Statements.

FINANCIAL RATIOS (FIGURE 9.2)

Fictitious Depository Corporation
Supplemental Financial Data
Financial Ratios
Years Ended December 31

	Current	Prior	2nd Prior	3rd Prior	4th Prior
Return on average assets	0.94%	0.96%	0.91%	0.89%	0.87%
Return on average shareholders' equity	11.23%	11.72%	11.26%	11.20%	11.11%
Net yield on earning assets (Interest Income Ratio)	7.31%	6.90%	6.60%	6.55%	6.50%
Common stock dividend payout %	36.17%	34.48%	34.15%	35.00%	33.33%
Average shareholders' equity to average assets	8.39%	8.22%	8.10%	8.01%	7.86%
Net charge-offs to average loans, net of unearned interest (Net Charge-off Ratio)	0.14%	0.33%	0.28%	0.26%	0.26%
Reserve for loan losses to period-end loans, net of unearned interest	1.03%	1.08%	0.92%	0.99%	1.02%

NOTE: The reader should try to calculate ratios based on the Supplemental Financial Data in this chapter and the financial statements in Chapter 6.

This figure also appears in Section 3. It is perforated so it may be torn from the book and used for reference while reading.

Accounting Basics for Community Financial Institutions, 2nd edition, Copyright © 2009 by Financial Managers Society, Inc. All rights reserved. Limited permission is granted to the original purchaser to photocopy Part 3, Financial Statements.

Glossary

AAA. Acronym for *American Accounting Association*.

A/C. Abbreviation for *account*.

account. A device for grouping additions and subtractions that apply to items included in the financial statements that keeps track of what the business owns, owes, spends, receives, incurs or earns.

accounting. A field of business that records, classifies and interprets the economic transactions of a business enterprise.

Accounting Principles Board (APB). Successor to the Committee on Accounting Procedure. Formed in 1959 by the AICPA to (1) advance the written expression of accounting principles; (2) determine appropriate accounting practices; (3) narrow the areas of difference and inconsistency in practice. Replaced by the FASB in 1973. *See also* **Committee on Accounting Procedure; Financial Accounting Standards Board.**

accounting system. A record-keeping method that encompasses the entire process of recording, classifying, reporting and interpreting transaction data.

accounts payable. A current business expense that will be paid for at a later time.

accounts receivable. Receivables other than loan receivables. They include utility, space rental and other required deposits. Also included are advances made to trusts for conducting trust business.

accrual. A recorded transaction that affects the income statement (recorded revenue or recorded expense) but has no effect on cash flows because no cash changes hands. *Contrast* **deferral.**

accrual basis. Method of accounting that recognizes income or expense independent of when the cash is actually received or disbursed. The company credits revenues in the accounting period in which they are earned and charges or debits expenses in the accounting period in which they are incurred. *Contrast* **cash basis.**

accrued interest payable. Interest earned by depositors and others to whom the institution owes money.

accrued interest receivable. Interest earned but not yet received on interest bearing deposits and investments.

AFS. Abbreviation for *available-for-sale (security)*.

AICPA. Acronym for *American Institute of Certified Public Accountants*.

allowance for loan losses. *See* **reserve for loan losses.**

American Institute of Certified Public Accountants (AICPA). The national professional organization of Certified Public Accountants. It has been a significant player in the development of GAAP.

American option. Call (put) option for which the buyer can exercise his or her right to buy (sell) the underlying security on any date up to the expiration date. *Contrast* **European option.**

amortization. Systematic allocation of an item from the balance sheet to the income statement over time. For example, a company may have a patent or copyright that has value and is an asset on the balance sheet. The value is used up over the legal life or over the economic life of the patent or copyright. The asset is taken off the balance sheet and transferred to the income statement on a systematic and logical basis (for example, straight-line or the same amount each year) over the shorter of the legal life or economic life of the asset.

ARB. Acronym for *Accounting Research Bulletin*.

asset. Resource a business owns.

asset account. An account that accumulates balances for the items the business owns: cash, inventory, receivables and fixed assets. *Contrast* **liability account.**

asset leverage ratio. Capital ratio that is a basic measure of leverage. It shows how far equity is stretched. It shows to what extent dollar amounts of assets are carried by limited equity levels. All depository institutions are leveraged. This ratio shows how much. Asset Leverage Ratio = Average Total Assets ÷ Average Shareholders' Equity.

asset quality ratio. (1) In general, a ratio that shows the relationship between "good" assets, "bad" assets, write-offs and resources. Ratio that provides a measure of how good the assets are. That is, it measures the quality of the assets. (2) Specific ratio that is a standard ratio used by federal regulators. A ratio of 1.0 or more requires immediate corrective action. A low ratio is good. High is bad. Asset Quality Ratio = Classified Assets ÷ Risk-Based Capital + Loan Loss Allowance Not Counted as Risk-Based Capital.

asset-sensitive institution. Financial institution whose interest-sensitive assets will mature faster than its interest-sensitive liabilities. Most financial institutions are liability sensitive (interest-sensitive liabilities mature faster than interest-sensitive assets). However, during certain periods (for example, the next three months, the next six months) a financial institution could be asset sensitive. Asset-sensitive institutions fear rate declines since the faster maturing assets will be reinvested at lower rates, causing income to go down. *Contrast* **liability-sensitive institution.**

asset valuation. Concept that requires that assets initially be recorded at cost and then be adjusted to reflect proper accounting values.

Auditing Standard 2 (AS2). Guidance to CPAs on how to audit management's internal controls for public companies; issued by the Public Company Accounting Oversight Board (PCAOB).

Auditing Standard 5 (AS5). A standard issued by the Public Company Accounting Oversight Board (PCAOB) that superceded Auditing Standard 2 (AS2); attempts to eliminate unnecessary requirements while preserving the key principles in AS2.

available-for-sale security. Security that cannot be classified as a held-to-maturity or trading security. *Contrast* **held-to-maturity security; trading security.**

balance sheet. A financial report that is the culmination of the accounting cycle activity. It displays the fundamental accounting equation (Assets = Liabilities + Stockholders' Equity) as of a single point in time (the period end date). Also called *statement of financial position*.

banker's acceptance. Outstanding draft or bill of exchange a bank has accepted.

call option. Agreement granting the right to buy a fixed quantity of a bond or a bond future, at a specified price, for a specified period. The seller (or writer) of a call option is exposed to unlimited loss potential because of the obligation to sell the underlying security at the strike price—regardless of its market price—if and when the option is exercised. *Contrast* **put option.** *See also* **option.**

Call Report. Detailed government form that must be filed by each depository institution with the institution's primary regulator (FDIC, Federal Reserve Bank, NCUA, etc.) each calendar quarter.

capital adequacy ratio. Capital ratio that is a basic measure of an institution's capital adequacy. A measure of financial condition. High is good. Low is bad. (Note that this is *not* the regulatory risk-weighted capital ratio.) Capital Adequacy = Total Equity ÷ Total Assets.

capital ratio. Relationship between assets and equity. Ratio that measures the adequacy of equity levels in light of the assets carried by the limited amounts of equity of depository institutions.

capital risk. Possibility that an organization cannot attract (or internally create) adequate capital on favorable terms.

carrying amount. The net amount of a loan.

cash. This includes cash on hand (coins, currency, undeposited checks, money orders and drafts) and deposits in financial institutions.

cash and cash equivalents. Balance sheet asset category that generally consists of (1) cash on hand; (2) cash items; (3) clearings and exchanges; (4) due from correspondent banks. Also called *cash and due from banks*.

cash and due from banks. *See* **cash and cash equivalents.**

cash basis. A method of accounting that credits income when cash is received and debits expenses when cash is disbursed. *Contrast* **accrual basis.**

cash equivalent. A short-term, highly liquid investment that is readily convertible to known amounts of cash and is so near its maturity period that it presents insignificant risk to changes in value because of changes in interest rates. Investments that have original maturities of three months or less when the investment is made: Treasury bills, commercial paper, money market funds, federal funds sold, etc.

cash flow hedge. Hedge of exposure to variable cash flows of a forecasted transaction. *See also* **hedging.**

cashier's check. Check a financial institution draws on itself. The financial institution is both the drawer and the drawee. Not a certified check. Financial institutions often use cashier's checks to pay out loan proceeds to customers, to pay suppliers, vendors, etc. Cashier's checks may also be sold to customers for a fee. Also called *official check* or *treasurer's check*.

cash items. Instruments other than coin or currency that are held for conversion to cash: food stamps, maturing coupons and bonds, petty cash vouchers, returned checks, due bills, unposted debits and other items pending disposition.

cash letter. Transmittal letter sent with each batch of checks to other institutions. *See also* **foreign check.**

cash on hand. Currency and coins in the possession of tellers plus reserve cash in the financial institution's vault.

certificate of deposit (CD). Time deposit that requires that the customer keep the deposit account for a minimum period (generally one month to five years). It may be redeemed before maturity, but the depositor usually pays a penalty for the early withdrawal. *See also* **time deposit.**

certified check. Draft for which the drawee financial institution assumes liability and sets aside the necessary funds.

check. Demand draft drawn on a bank. *See also* **draft.**

Check Clearing for the 21st Century Act (Check 21 Act). Federal legislation that authorizes community financial institutions and other depository institutions to substitute an electronic check for the original hard-copy check.

checking account. Deposit account that a depositor uses for disbursements. The customer can easily order the financial institution to make payments from these accounts simply by making a check. *See also* **check.**

clearing and exchange item. Check deposited at one institution that is drawn on another institution. *Contrast* **on us check.**

clearinghouse. An association of local financial institutions that is used for clearing checks drawn on member institutions.

closing entries. Year-end entries that put all the revenue balances (credits) into the income summary account as a credit and all the expense balances (debits) into the income summary account as a debit. *See also* **income summary account.**

Club account. Savings account for which the depositor makes regular weekly or monthly deposits. Christmas, Hanukkah and Holiday accounts are examples.

code of ethics. Standards that are reasonably necessary to promote (1) honest and ethical conduct, including the ethical handling of actual or apparent personal and professional conflicts of interest; (2) full, fair, accurate, timely and understandable disclosure in periodic reports; (3) substantial compliance with applicable governmental rules and regulations.

collateral risk. Exposure to losses if a security interest is not perfected; if collateral is not safeguarded; if collateral values decline; if collateral cannot be realized.

collection method. A revenue recognition method used only if the receipt of cash is uncertain. Under this method, the seller waits to record the sale until cash is received. *See also* **revenue recognition principle.**

Committee of Sponsoring Organizations (COSO). Committee formed by private sector organizations to support implementation of the Treadway recommendations. *See also* **COSO report; National Commission on Fraudulent Financial Reporting.**

Committee on Accounting Procedure (CAP). Committee of the AICPA from 1939 to 1959 that preceded the Accounting Principles Board. *See also* **Accounting Principles Board; American Institute of Certified Public Accountants.**

comparability. Accounting concept that deals with the period-to-period display of accounting information (financial statements) in the same manner.

compensating balance. Deposit balance maintained or fee paid as compensation to a financial institution for holding a credit line available. *See also* **line of credit.**

completed-contract method. Conservative revenue recognition approach used for construction projects. All revenue is recognized when the construction project is completed. *Contrast* **percentage-of-completion method.** *See also* **revenue recognition principle.**

compound journal entry. An entry that includes debits to more than one account or credits to more than one account.

concentration risk. Possibility that losses could be sustained because the portfolio (loans, investments) is not properly diversified. This risk is assumed when there is high concentration in particular industries or geographic regions. It also occurs when the financial institution has a large number of activities with relatively few customers.

consistency concept. Accounting concept that deals with the period-to-period application of the same accounting principles.

consolidated financial statement. Financial statement that includes all subsidiaries, units, branches, departments, etc., of an entity.

continuity concept. *See* **going concern concept.**

continuous departmental accountability. One department or branch can have accounts that are affected by activity in another department or branch.

core deposit. Stable, relatively inexpensive (low interest cost) deposit that remains with the typical community financial institution. Rates can go up or down but, in most cases, total core deposit amounts remain stable.

correspondent bank. A "banker's bank" that acts on behalf of its customers—other financial institutions. It provides services such as collecting out-of-state amounts due, buying and selling securities, providing asset/liability management services, providing investment advice, wire-transfer receipts and payments to smaller financial institutions.

COSO Report. Report of the Committee of Sponsoring Organizations. The report (1) defined internal control; (2) described internal control components; (3) provided criteria for management and others to assess control systems; (4) provided guidance on public reporting on internal control; (5) provided tools for conducting an evaluation of an internal control system. *See also* **Committee of Sponsoring Organizations; National Commission on Fraudulent Financial Reporting.**

cost recovery method of accounting. Accounting for an OREO sale as a real sale only when the carrying value of OREO is received. *Contrast* **deposit method of accounting; full accrual accounting.** *See also* **Other Real Estate Owned.**

counterparty. Party on the other side of a transaction.

country risk. Risk that exists when a particular country's conditions (political or legal) will adversely affect a U.S. organization's ability to repatriate U.S. dollars.

covered call. Call for which the seller (or writer) holds the underlying security on which the option is written. *Contrast* **naked call.** *See also* **call option; option.**

CPA. Acronym for *Certified Public Accountant*.

Cr. Abbreviation for *credit*.

credit. An accounting term that indicates that funds are transferred from an account; the amount is recorded on the right side of the account. *Contrast* **debit.** *See also* **double-entry bookkeeping.**

credit risk. (1) Probability that the borrower cannot, or will not, repay the original loan amount due (principal and interest). (2) Possibility that the issuer of debt securities will not be able to pay off the entire principal and interest as scheduled. (3) Factor in trading, investing and repo transactions where the potential exists that the party on the other side of the transaction (the counterparty) will be unable or unwilling to deliver securities and/or cash when due.

current asset. An item a business owns that it can reasonably expect to convert into cash, sell or consume within one year (or within the operating cycle, if it is longer): cash and cash equivalents, short-term investments, receivables, inventories and prepaid expenses. *Contrast* **current liability.**

current liability. Amount the business owes that it expects to liquidate using current assets or the creation of other current liabilities. They generally include (1) obligations arising from the acquisition of goods and services entering the operating cycle; (2) collections of money in advance for the future delivery of goods or performance of services; (3) other obligations maturing within the current year to be met through the use of current assets. *Contrast* **current asset.**

customer acceptance liability. Balance sheet category that indicates a receivable from the institution's customers for banker's acceptances. *Contrast* **banker's acceptance.**

DDA. Acronym for *demand deposit account.*

debit. An accounting term that indicates that funds are transferred to an account; the amount is recorded on the left side of the account. *Contrast* **credit.** *See also* **double-entry bookkeeping.**

defalcation. Misappropriation of assets. *See also* **irregularity.**

deferral. A recorded transaction for which cash is received or paid, but the cash transaction has no impact on the income statement. *Contrast* **accrual.**

deferred provision for income tax. GAAP income tax expense that takes into account those temporary differences between GAAP income (book net income) and taxable income that will theoretically turn around in the future.

delivery price. Specified price in a forward contract. *See also* **forward contract.**

demand CD. Certificate of deposit that the bank must honor whenever it is presented for payment—whether it is negotiable or nonnegotiable.

demand deposit. Liability of a community financial institution that represents customers' cash that is on deposit. The major types of demand deposits include checking accounts, official checks, demand CDs and escrow deposits.

demand instrument. An instrument payable upon presentation, for example, a check. *Contrast* **time instrument.**

demand loan. Loan that generally contains a provision for maturity or renewal or provides for periodic review of the loan status. It is often continued or renewed, assuming no deterioration in the borrower's credit risk. *Contrast* **time loan.**

deposit account. Liability account that is the due to customer account. Its credit balance represents the customer's funds currently held by the depository institution. *See also* **due to account.**

deposit method of accounting. Accounting for an OREO sale as a real sale when a predetermined deposit amount is received. *Contrast* **cost recovery method of accounting; full accrual accounting.** *See also* **Other Real Estate Owned.**

depreciation. Systematic allocation of fixed asset costs from the balance sheet to the income statement over the estimated useful life of the fixed assets.

derecognize. To take an amount off the books.

derivative. Financial instrument that has no value in and of itself. It derives its value from elsewhere—from outside itself—for example, from the performance of underlying assets, interest rates, currency rates, various indices, etc.

disclosure principle. GAAP principle that holds that a company's financial statements should report enough information for readers to make knowledgeable decisions about the company.

discount. Upward adjustment of the stated rate of interest to the market yield at purchase when obligations (bonds) are bought at a market price less than face value. *Contrast* **premium.**

discounted basis. Describes a loan on which interest (discount) is added to the amount loaned to the consumer to determine the loan receivable.

dividend. A return a corporation pays to a stockholder.

doctrine of conservatism. Concept that states that accounting should never anticipate gains or profits but should always recognize losses when they are probable. Loss contingencies should immediately be recognized. Gain contingencies should not be recognized until they are realized. *See also* **gain contingency; loss contingency.**

double-entry bookkeeping. A method for recording transactions by tracking where cash comes from and where it goes. Every transaction has at least one debit and one credit. And, for every transaction, the total debits (left-side amounts) equal the total credits (right-side amounts). *See also* **credit, debit.**

doubtful loan. Loan that has the same weaknesses as a substandard loan. However, the weaknesses of doubtful loans are so severe that collection in full is highly questionable or unlikely, given current facts, conditions and values. *See also* **loan classification; substandard loan.**

Dr. Abbreviation for *debit*.

draft. Standard, simplified form of a letter of instruction in which one party orders the holder of a credit balance (the financial institution) to make payment to a third party. *See also* **drawee; drawer, payee.**

drawee. The party who is told to make the payment specified in a draft; the party on whom the draft is drawn. Also called the *payor bank*. *See also* **draft.**

drawer. The party who executes and issues a draft.

due from banks. Balance sheet asset category that reports correspondent bank accounts used for check collection and other banking services between financial institutions. *See also* **correspondent bank.**

due from correspondents account. Represents the receivable from or the payable to a correspondent bank. *Contrast* **due to account.** *See also* **correspondent bank.**

due to account. A deposit account. The institution's balance sheet should present due from accounts net of due to accounts.

duration. The effective period until an instrument can be repriced.

earning asset. Asset that generates a monetary return, generally in the form of interest income: loans, investments, federal funds sold, etc.

effective-interest method. *See* **interest method of amortization.**

efficiency ratio. Profitability ratio that shows overhead expenses as a percentage of assets. Increases can be influenced by unusual transactions. Decreases can be the result of unrecorded expenses. Low is good. High is bad. Efficiency Ratio = Non-interest Expense ÷ Avg. Total Assets.

Emerging Issues Task Force (EITF). Task force composed of 13 members who represent CPA firms and preparers of financial statements. Observers from the SEC and AICPA also attend EITF meetings. The EITF's goal is to reach a consensus on how to account for new and unusual transactions that may create inconsistent financial reporting practices.

entity concept. The most basic accounting concept. It draws a boundary around the organization. The transactions of each entity are accounted for separately from the transactions of the owners or of other entities. The concept applies equally to all types and sizes of organizations. It requires that the financial statements of the entity include all departments, divisions, branches, subsidiaries, etc.

equity. The amount of net assets (Assets = Liabilities + Equity) of the business.

equity account. An account that represents the value of the initial infusion of cash into the business plus the profits or minus the losses of the business.

equity method of accounting. Accounting method in which an investment is recorded on the books of an investor at the cost of acquisition; an increase or decrease in carrying value of the investment and income thereon is recognized based on accrual of the investor's share of the investee's post-acquisition net income or loss. Dividends received reduce the carrying value of the investment.

error. Unintentional misstatement or omission of amounts or disclosures in financial statements. *Contrast* **irregularity.**

escrow deposit. Represents real estate taxes and insurance payments remitted to the financial institution with customer mortgage payments. Such amounts are received in advance of the date they are payable to the taxing authority or insurance company, and they are liabilities until they are paid.

European option. Call (put) option for which the buyer can only exercise his or her right to buy (sell) the underlying security on its expiration date. *Contrast* **American option.** *See also* **option.**

exercise price. *See* **strike price.**

exit price. The price that would be received to sell an asset or paid to transfer a liability at the measurement date. *See also* **fair value.**

expense account. An account that accumulates the amounts the organization spends, or incurs, to run the business (cost of goods sold, salaries, heat, power); a temporary account.

expense recognition principle. A principle of GAAP that requires that expenses be recorded when incurred.

fair presentation. GAAP principle that requires that a full set of GAAP financial statements with all appropriate disclosures be presented to the organization, the regulators and the public.

fair value. The measure that assumes an asset is sold or a liability is transferred in an orderly transaction between market participants at a measurement date; the determination of the fair value measure is currently governed by SFAS 157.

fair value hedge. Hedge of exposure to changes in the fair value of a recognized asset or liability or firm commitment. *See also* **hedging.**

Federal Deposit Insurance Corporation Improvement Act of 1991 (FDICIA). Federal act that addresses the problems that occurred during the 1980s and 1990s. It specifically regulates the banking industry. It sets forth requirements for all depository institutions (public or private) that have $500 million or more in assets.

federal funds purchased. Buyer's term for bank-to-bank loans of excess Federal Reserve balances. *Contrast* **federal funds sold.**

federal funds sold. Seller's term for bank-to-bank loans of excess Federal Reserve balances. *Contrast* **federal funds purchased.**

fee-based service. An activity that generates income based on service performed rather than based on funds invested or loaned.

FEI. Acronym for *Financial Executives Institute*.

FHLB. Acronym for *Federal Home Loan Bank*.

FIFO. Acronym for *first in first out*.

Financial Accounting Standards Advisory Council (FASAC). A council responsible for consulting with the FASB on major policy and technical issues and for helping select task force members. *See also* **Financial Accounting Standards Board.**

Financial Accounting Standards Board (FASB). AICPA created the FASB in 1973 to replace the Accounting Principles Board as the accounting rule-making body in the private sector. Its purpose is to establish and improve standards of financial accounting and reporting. It develops standards designed to guide and educate issuers, auditors and users of financial statements. *See also* **Accounting Principles Board; American Institute of Certified Public Accountants.**

financial statement. The synthesis of massive amounts of data representing financial transactions (principally the balance sheet and income statement); usually the final product of accounting.

floor-ceiling agreement. *See* **interest rate collar.**

FMV. Acronym for *fair market value*.

footnote. *See* **note to the financial statements.**

foreign check. Check written on checking accounts of other institutions that must be sent to those institutions for clearing. *Contrast* **on us checks.** *See also* **cash letter.**

foreign exchange risk. Loss exposure a depository institution faces when adverse changes occur in the value of the dollar vis-à-vis other currencies.

forward contract. Agreement to buy or sell an asset at a specified future time for a specific price. The contract is usually written by a financial institution and is not normally traded on an exchange. (It is an over-the-counter financial instrument.) *Contrast* **futures contract.**

forward rate agreement (FRA). Forward contract on interest rates. The buyers and sellers are referred to as counterparties. FRAs are like a one-period interest rate swap in which the fixed rate is set at the signing date and the floating rate is set at a specified forward date, called the *reset date*. *See also* **forward contract.**

FRA. Acronym for *forward rate agreement*.

fraud risk. Possibility that business deals, such as loans, investments and other types of transactions, are not genuine or bona fide.

FRB. Acronym for *Federal Reserve Bank*.

full accrual accounting. Method of accounting for an OREO sale as a genuine, bona fide sale. *Contrast* **cost recovery method of accounting; deposit method of accounting.** *See also* **Other Real Estate Owned.**

fundamental accounting equation. An important accounting concept: Assets = Liabilities + Equity.

funding. Obtaining cash to carry the assets of a financial institution.

funding risk. Possibility that the depository institution will not be able to renew or roll over its liabilities when they mature.

futures contract. Binding agreement to deliver or accept delivery of a standard quantity of securities, currencies, commodities, etc., on a certain date and place at a price established at the time the agreement is made. An institution can use financial futures to match the maturities of assets and liabilities by locking in the cost of funds or by locking in a current yield for future investments. Futures are exchange-traded contracts. *Contrast* **forward contract.**

GAAP. Acronym for *generally accepted accounting principles*.

GAAS. Acronym for *Generally Accepted Auditing Standards*.

gain contingency. Probable gain.

general obligation muni. Municipal issue backed by the full taxing power ("full faith and credit") of the issuer. *See also* **municipal issue.**

generally accepted accounting principles (GAAP). A technical term that encompasses the conventions, rules and procedures needed to define acceptable accounting practice at a particular time.

going concern concept. In the absence of contrary evidence, accountants assume the entity will continue operating for the foreseeable future (at least one year subsequent to the balance sheet date). Also called *continuity concept*.

HC. Abbreviation for *Holiday Club deposit account*.

hedging. Act of taking a temporary position in the futures market that is equal to and opposite to the cash market position. The purpose of hedging is to protect the cash position against loss due to price fluctuations. It is a very useful tool for the management of interest rate risk.

held-to-maturity security. Security the company has the positive *intent* and *ability* to hold until it matures. *Contrast* **available-for-sale-security; trading security.**

historical cost concept. *See* **stable monetary unit concept.**

holding. Ownership interest of a holding company. *See also* **holding company.**

holding company. Nonoperating corporate entity whose assets are investments in financial institutions and investments in any other operating entities (leasing companies, mortgage service companies, etc.).

holdover. *See* **rejected item.**

home equity line of credit. Loan that gives borrowers the ability to draw funds as needed up to a specified amount. The repayment terms are usually flexible, and interest rates are lower than those for installment loans. It is secured by liens on the equity a borrower has in the home. *Contrast* **home improvement loan; installment loan.**

home improvement loan. Loan made to individuals who want to expand, remodel, improve or otherwise work on their homes. It is secured by a second mortgage on the home. *Contrast* **home equity line of credit.**

HTM. Acronym for *held-to-maturity (security)*.

IASB. Acronym for *International Accounting Standards Board*.

IFRS. Acronym for *International Financial Reporting Standards*.

IIA. Acronym for *Institute of Internal Auditors*.

IMA. Acronym for *Institute of Management Accountants*—Formerly the National Association of Accountants (NAA).

impaired loan. Loan for which, based on current information, it is probable that the financial institution will be unable to collect all amounts due based on the original loan agreement. Most impairments are for loans presumed to be good loans.

income statement. Financial statement that measures performance for a given period. It is used to determine profitability, value and creditworthiness. It shows the results of the financial institution's operations. Also called *statement of earnings* or *statement of income*.

income statement account. A temporary account that explains the change in owner's equity resulting from the operations of the business. It provides the link between the prior and current balance sheets. At the end of each year, it is reset to a zero balance by using closing entries. *See also* **closing entries; income summary account.**

income summary account. A fictitious account into which the balances of all the income statement accounts are transferred at year-end. Each revenue and expense account is "zeroed out" by means of closing entries, and each balance is transferred to the income summary account. *See also* **closing entries; income statement account.**

individual retirement account (IRA). Tax-deferred investment account for retirement savings. It may be maintained as a CD or as a separate form of time deposit. *See also* **time deposit.**

insider risk. Potential that executives, directors, principal owners and related parties may obtain privileges beyond those offered to others in the normal course of business. Also called *Regulation O risk*.

installment loan. Loan for which the note is repayable in installments, usually in equal monthly amounts. The period depends on the nature of the loan and type of collateral, if any.

installment method. A revenue recognition collection method used for installment sales. *See also* **revenue recognition principle.**

intangible asset. Asset such as a trademark, patent, copyright or organizational cost.

interest bearing deposit. Certificate of deposit or other interest bearing account a financial institution maintains in other financial institutions.

interest bearing liability. Funds the financial institution uses for its operations for which interest costs are incurred. A liability that must be paid for. Generally, all liabilities other than demand deposits that are interest free.

interest expense. Amount an institution incurs for use of other people's money (OPM).

interest expense ratio. Profitability ratio that shows the average rate paid for the use of interest bearing liabilities. The ratio shows the cost of funding. The trend in this ratio generally follows prevailing interest ratios. High is bad. Low is good. Interest Expense Ratio = Interest Expense ÷ Avg. Interest Bearing Liabilities.

interest income. Principal source of revenue for a financial institution. It has several sources: loans (including fees); securities (taxable and tax-exempt); deposits with others; fed funds sold; securities bought under agreement to resell (reverse repos).

interest income ratio. Profitability ratio that shows the yield on earning assets for the year. Unless the institution has many fixed-rate assets, the trend in this ratio should follow prevailing interest rates. High is good. Low is bad. Interest Income Ratio = Interest Income ÷ Avg. Earning Assets.

interest method of amortization. Amortization method that computes periodic interest expense based on the same effective interest rate determined at inception of the related transaction. The fixed rate multiplied by the ever-changing carrying amount determines the periodic interest expense. Also called the *effective-interest method.* Contrast **straight-line method of amortization.** *See also* **amortization.**

interest-only strip receivable. Future inflow of cash from the interest—not the principal—paid on a transferred loan for which the initiating financial institution retained servicing.

interest rate cap. Off-balance-sheet financial instrument that pays the holder of the cap the difference between the cap (or strike) rate and an index (that is, rate to be capped) rate. An interest rate cap is designed to provide borrowers with protection against the cap rate rising above the index rate. *Contrast* **interest rate floor.**

interest rate collar. Off-balance-sheet financial instrument that specifies both the upper and lower limits for the rate that would be charged. The collar agreement is activated only if rates move up or down by a predetermined level. *Also called* a *floor-ceiling agreement* or a *range swap.*

interest rate floor. Off-balance-sheet financial instrument that is designed to provide lenders (investors) with protection against the interest rate on a floating-rate loan going below a specified rate level. *Contrast* **interest rate cap.**

interest rate risk. Possibility that a financial institution will sustain losses because of improper matching of asset and liability maturities.

interest rate swap. Private agreement between two counterparties to exchange cash flows in the future according to a prearranged formula.

interest ROA. Profitability ratio that shows the portion of ROA produced from net interest margin. The trend in this ratio should generally follow prevailing interest rates. High is good. Low is bad. Interest ROA = Net Interest Income after Loan Loss Provision ÷ Avg. Total Assets.

internal capital generation rate. Capital ratio that shows to what extent earnings on invested equity are retained in the business. For expansion-minded entities, high is good. For entities that pay a large portion of earnings to owners, low is good. (Note that net income after dividend declaration divided by net income is the retention rate.) Internal Capital Generation Rate = ROE x Earnings Retention Rate.

internal control. Procedure management puts in place to safeguard assets, to generate financial statements that are free of material misstatements and to help management achieve its objectives.

International Accounting Standards Board (IASB). An independent accounting body based in London that issued the International Financial Reporting Standards. *See also* **International Financial Reporting Standards (IFRS).**

International Financial Reporting Standards (IFRS). Principle-based accounting standards issued after 2001 by the International Accounting Standards Board.

interpretation. Modification or extension of existing standards by the FASB. Interpretations have the same authority as standards. *See also* **Financial Accounting Standards Board.**

intrinsic value approach. Accounting approach that results in no compensation expense being recorded for stock compensation paid by employers in the form of stock options unless on the grant date the employees' exercise price is less than the market price of shares granted.

inventory. An asset that includes goods on hand that are held for sale. The basis of evaluation and the methods of pricing must be disclosed.

investing. Conversion of non-lendable funds into financial instruments that generate investment income.

IRA. Acronym for *individual retirement account.*

IRD. Acronym for *image replacement document.*

irregularity. Intentional misstatement or omission of amounts or disclosures in financial statements. Irregularities include fraudulent financial reporting undertaken to render financial statements misleading *(management fraud)* and misappropriation of assets (defalcations). *Contrast* **error.**

I/S. Abbreviation for *income statement.*

issuer. Company that issues shares to the public.

journal. The original, chronological record of all transactions that occurred in the life of a business.

jumbo CD (jumbo). Certificate of deposit for $100,000 or more. *See also* **certificate of deposit.**

jumbo deposit ratio. Liquidity ratio that measures volatility of the deposit base. Jumbos and brokered deposits are not desirable. They are the least stable funding sources. They are subject to flight and often do not renew. High is bad. High ratio indicates high liquidity risk. Jumbo Deposit Ratio = Jumbo Deposits and Brokered Deposits ÷ Total Deposits.

Keogh account. Tax-deferred retirement account for a self-employed person. It may be maintained as a CD or as a separate form of time deposit. *See also* **time deposit.**

lending. Disbursement of funds to borrowers who agree to pay back the funds plus interest over time; it is the primary business of the community financial institution.

liability. Claim against the resources of a business.

liability account. An account that accumulates the balances the company owes: accounts payable, short-term debt and long-term debt. *Contrast* **asset account.**

liability-sensitive institution. Institution that has liabilities maturing at a faster rate than the maturing assets, which creates sensitivity to higher interest rates. Liability-sensitive institutions fear rising interest rates since the faster maturing liabilities will be renewed at higher costs, causing income to go down. *Contrast* **asset-sensitive institution.**

LIBOR. Acronym for *London Interbank Offered Rate*.

LIFO. Acronym for *last in first out*.

line of credit. Commercial lending arrangement under which the financial institution gives the borrower a maximum borrowing limit for a specified period, at a stated interest rate.

liquidation accounting. Type of accounting that shows all assets and liabilities on the balance sheet at values that the business expects to realize when the assets are sold and the values it expects to pay for established liabilities. The amounts would be substantially different from GAAP amounts.

liquidity ratio. Relationship between the assets and liabilities and among the types of assets. Ratio that measures the degree to which the assets can readily be converted to cash—the most liquid asset.

loan classification. Classification that describes the amount of risk a particular loan represents to an institution and indicates the likelihood that the institution can recover loaned funds. Loan classifications generally fall into four categories. *See also* **doubtful loan; loss; substandard loan; unclassified loan.**

loans to earning assets ratio. Liquidity ratio that shows the portion of earning assets invested in loans. Since loans are most profitable if properly controlled for credit quality, high is good. Low is bad. Loans to Earning Assets Ratio = Average Loans ÷ Average Earning Assets.

loan to deposit ratio. Liquidity ratio that shows the extent to which funds from deposits are invested in loans. A high ratio indicates liquidity risk. A low ratio indicates ample (perhaps, excess) availability of funds for loans. Loan to Deposit Ratio = Total Loans ÷ Total Deposits.

LOCOM. Acronym for *lower of cost or market*; sometimes referred to as *LOCM*.

long-term investments. Investments in debt and equity securities intended to be held to maturity, tangible assets, investments held in sinking funds, pension funds, amounts held for financial institution expansion, cash surrender values of life insurance policies, etc.

loss. Loan classification in which the loan is considered uncollectible with little or no recovery or salvage value. Loss classifications typically cover only portions of loans rather than entire loan balances. *See also* **loan classification.**

loss contingency. Probable loss for which amounts are reasonably estimable.

L/P. Abbreviation for *ledger page*.

macro hedge. Hedge used for the entire balance sheet. Compare micro hedge. *See also* **hedging.**

management fraud. Fraudulent financial reporting undertaken to render financial statements misleading. *See also* **irregularity.**

management risk. Possibility that the competency, judgment and integrity of management and its actions will jeopardize the value of net assets.

margin. Gross profit from deposit, lending and investing activities.

marked-to-market. Indicates that a security is carried at fair value.

market risk. Possibility that the value of loans, investments, etc., will decline because of fluctuating markets. It is the risk that a financial institution may not be properly hedged.

matching. Principle that governs the recording and reporting of expenses. It requires that expenses related to revenue be recorded in the same period as the revenues. Income is revenue minus expense. The company first measures its revenues then identifies and measures all the expenses it incurred during the period to earn the revenues. To *match the expenses against the revenue* means to subtract the expenses from the revenues.

materiality. Concept that requires that financial statements not include a dollar misstatement or omission that would adversely influence the financial statement reader.

MD & A. Acronym for *management's discussion and analysis*.

memorandum account. An account maintained separately from the general ledger. It is a summary of nonrecorded potential liabilities.

micro hedge. Hedge used for specific assets or liabilities. *Contrast* **macro hedge.** *See also* **hedging.**

MIS. Acronym for *management information system*.

most advantageous market. The market in which a reporting entity would sell an asset or transfer a liability at a price that maximizes the amount that would be received for the asset or minimizes the amount that would be paid to transfer the liability, considering transaction costs in the respective markets. *See also* **fair value.**

municipal issue (muni). Bonds issued by any government or agency of government other than the federal government (for example, issues of state, city, county, town, school district, turnpike authority).

naked call. Call for which the seller (or writer) does not hold the underlying security on which the option is written. *Contrast* **covered call.** *See also* **call option; option.**

National Commission on Fraudulent Financial Reporting. Federal commission formed in 1985 to identify factors that cause fraudulent financial reporting and to make recommendations to reduce the incidences of such reporting. Also known as the *Treadway Commission*.

negative amortization. An instance in which an outstanding loan balance goes up, rather than going down as it should.

net charge-off ratio. Asset quality ratio that shows the portion of a financial institution's loans that have gone sour during the period. It measures the collectibility of loans. It is an indication of credit standards and/or economic conditions. High is bad. Low is good. Net Charge-off Ratio = Net Loan Charge-offs ÷ Average Loans before Reserve for Loan Losses.

net income (NI or N/I). If the revenue account balances are greater than the expense account balances, the business has *net income*. Revenue - Expense = Net Income.

net interest income (NII). Difference between interest income and interest expense. The institution's margin (gross profit) from deposit, lending and investing activities.

net interest margin. Interest income less interest expense less provision for loan losses. The company's spread.

net interest margin ratio. Profitability ratio that shows the institution's gross profit for the period. High is good. Low is bad. Net Interest Margin = Interest Income Ratio - Interest Expense Ratio.

net realizable value. Amount that is expected to be collected. The present value of the future cash flows.

net working capital (NWC). Current assets minus current liabilities equal NWC. NWC represents the margin of safety available to meet the financial demands of the operating cycle.

NI (N/I). Abbreviation for *net income*.

NII. Abbreviation for *net interest income*.

noncurrent assets. Items the business owns that it *cannot* reasonably expect to convert into cash, sell or consume within one year (or within the operating cycle): long-term investments; property, plant and equipment; intangible assets.

noncurrent liabilities. Amounts the business owes that it *does not* expect to liquidate using current assets or the creation of other current liabilities. They generally include (1) obligations arising through the acquisition of assets; (2) obligations arising out of the normal course of operations; (3) contingent liabilities involving uncertainty as to possible losses; (4) noncurrent capital lease obligations.

nondilutive. Indicates that new capital can be raised without reducing or watering down the value of existing capital before raising the new capital.

non-interest expense ratio. Productivity ratio that is a basic measure of expenses from sources other than the basic business of the financial institution—lending. Low is good. High is bad. Non-interest Expense Ratio = Non-interest Expense ÷ Average Total Assets.

non-interest ROA. Profitability ratio that shows the portion of ROA from sources of income other than interest income. Unusual transactions can result in significant fluctuations in this ratio from period to period. It measures fee-based income as a percentage of assets. High is good. Low is bad. Non-interest ROA = Non-interest Income ÷ Avg. Total Assets.

nonmarketable securities. Balance sheet category that includes securities that cannot immediately be converted to cash by sale in the open market. Generally, this includes the stock that represents the financial institution's investment to become a member of the Federal Reserve Bank or the Federal Home Loan Bank.

nonperforming assets reserved ratio. Asset quality ratio that shows the portion of the overall loan loss cushion reserved for nonperformers. High is generally good, but an excess amount could be reserved for nonperformers. Low is bad. Nonperforming Assets Reserved Ratio = Loan Loss Reserve ÷ Nonperforming Loans.

nonperforming ratio. Asset quality ratio that shows how much of the assets are tied up in bad loans (nonperformers). An indicator of overall loan portfolio quality. High is bad. Low is good. Nonperforming Ratio = Nonperforming Assets (Nonaccrual Loans + Renegotiated Loans + OREO) ÷ Total Assets.

note to the financial statements. Footnote that is an integral part of the financial statements. The financial statements and footnotes together represent management's presentation of the corporation's financial position as of, and results of operations for, the year ended. The financial statements and footnotes are inseparable. Also called *footnote*.

notional amount. Predetermined amount.

NSF check. Abbreviation for *insufficient funds check*.

NWC. Acronym for *net working capital*.

OCBOA. Acronym for *Other Comprehensive Basis of Accounting*.

OCI. Acronym for *other comprehensive income*.

official check. *See* **cashier's check.**

OLEM. Acronym for *Other Loans Especially Mentioned*.

on us check. Check drawn against a customer account at the financial institution where the deposit was made. *Contrast* **clearing and exchange item.**

operations risk. Possibility that inadequate, ineffective or incompetent back office activities will interfere with normal business functions.

OPM. Acronym for *other people's money*.

option. Agreement granting the right to buy (call) or sell (put) a fixed quantity of a bond or a bond future, at a specified price, for a specified period.

orderly transaction. A hypothetical transaction for determining fair value measurement that assumes exposure to the market for a period prior to the measurement date to allow for marketing activities that are usual and customary for transactions involving such assets or liabilities. *See also* **fair value.**

OREO. Acronym for *Other Real Estate Owned*.

other assets. Accounts that do not fit into the current or noncurrent categories: long-term prepaid expenses, deferred taxes, noncurrent receivables, restricted cash. *See also* **current assets; noncurrent assets.**

other liabilities. Accounts that do not fit into the current or noncurrent categories: deferred credits, deferred income taxes payable, etc. *See also* **current liabilities; noncurrent liabilities.**

Other Loans Especially Mentioned (OLEM). Category of assets regulators recognize that applies to assets with special weaknesses that deserve management's attention. Also called *special mention.*

Other Real Estate Owned (OREO). Real property (other than premises the financial institution uses) that was acquired through a foreclosure.

overall efficiency ratio. Productivity ratio that shows portion of total expenses covered by average assets. Total expenses include interest expense, provision for loan losses, other expenses and provision for income taxes. Efficient financial institutions have low total expenses as a percentage of assets. Low is good. High is bad. Overall Efficiency Ratio = Total Expenses ÷ Average Total Assets.

overdraft loan. Type of revolving credit loan that financial institutions offer individuals in the form of overdraft privileges. When an overdraft loan agreement is in place, if a customer issues a check in excess of his or her demand deposit balance, the financial institution sets up a loan and credits the checking account for the overdraft.

owners' equity. *See* **stockholders' equity.**

payee. The beneficiary who is to receive the payment from a draft. *See also* **draft.**

payor bank. *See* **drawee.**

PCAOB. Acronym for *Public Company Accounting Oversight Board.*

percentage-of-completion method. Preferred method of revenue recognition for construction contracts. Revenues are recognized as the work is performed. *Contrast* **completed-contract method.** *See also* **revenue recognition principle.**

plain vanilla interest rate swap. Locks in fixed rate funding (for example, pay fixed/receive variable). *See also* **interest rate swap.**

premises and equipment. Fixed assets, including office buildings, equipment, leasehold improvements, furniture and fixtures, that are required for use in operating a financial institution.

premium. Downward adjustment of the stated rate of interest to reflect the market yield at purchase when obligations (bonds) are bought at a market price in excess of face value. *Contrast* **discount.**

prepaid expenses. Assets created by the prepayment of cash or the incurrence of a liability. They expire and become expenses with the passage of time, usage or events. Examples are prepaid rent and prepaid insurance.

prepaid item. Item paid for in advance: insurance, taxes, FDIC assessments, etc.

present value table. Table that provides factors for the partial payment needed to pay off (amortize) one dollar over time at certain interest rates.

principal market. The market in which a reporting entity would sell an asset or transfer a liability where there is the greatest volume and level of activity for the asset or liability. *See also* **fair value.**

productivity ratio. Relationship between expenses and assets and expenses and revenue. Ratio that shows how well or how poorly funds are spent.

profitability ratio. Relationship that helps explain to what extent the company is generating income, given the assets and equity that are available.

Proof Department. The central unit in a financial institution that sorts, distributes and arrives at control figures for all transactions.

property, plant and equipment. Assets that include machinery, equipment, buildings, vehicles, furniture, fixtures, natural resources, land, etc.

public company. Company whose shares trade in public markets such as the New York Stock Exchange, American Stock Exchange, National Association of Securities Dealers Automated Quotation Market.

Public Company Accounting Oversight Board (PCAOB). Board created by the Sarbanes-Oxley Act to oversee the audit of public companies. Its goal is to protect the interests of investors and further the public interest in the preparation of informative, accurate and independent audit reports.

put option. Agreement granting the right to sell a fixed quantity of a bond or a bond future, at a specified price, for a specified period. The seller (or writer) of a put option is exposed to limited loss potential because if the price of the bond falls to zero, the seller of the put option is obligated to buy the bond at the strike price. Thus, the potential loss to the seller of a put option cannot exceed an amount equal to the strike price. *Contrast* **call option.** *See also* **strike price.**

PV factor. Statistic that (given an established interest rate) allows one to easily compute (1) the future value of $1.00; (2) the future value of $1.00 per period; (3) the present value of $1.00; (4) the present value of $1.00 per period and other values. PV factors come from carefully designed, mathematically accurate tables based on mathematical formulae.

PV of annuity factor. Statistic that when multiplied by the periodic payment will result in the future amount. Conversely, the future amount divided by that factor will result in the amount of periodic payment.

quoted market value. Number of trading units times the market price per trading unit in the financial instrument's most active market.

range swap. *See* **interest rate collar.**

RAP. Acronym for *Regulatory Accounting Principles*.

ratio analysis. Analytical review technique that uses financial statement information to study plausible relationships among data.

real estate mortgage loan. A loan secured by a first mortgage lien on real property—commercial or residential.

realizable/realized. Revenues are realizable or realized when goods or services or other assets are exchanged for cash or claims to cash.

receivable. Unpaid bill or other money not yet received for goods or services sold.

receivables. Assets that include accounts receivable, notes receivable, receivables from affiliates, receivables from officers and employees, etc.

receive fixed counterparty. Seller of a FRA. *See also* **forward rate agreement.**

receive floating counterparty. Buyer of a FRA. *See also* **forward rate agreement.**

recognize. In accounting, to record (book) a transaction.

recourse obligation. Contingent liability of the transferor (seller) of loans. The transferor agrees to take back the sold loans if certain conditions are not met—for example, the borrower does not pay as required. This obligation gives the transferee (buyer) the right under certain conditions to "put" the loans back to the transferor. *See also* **put option.**

Ref. Abbreviation for *reference* that is used in the column of a journal that gives the journal page number on which the entry originally appears.

Regulation O risk. *See* **insider risk.**

regulatory capital ratio. Capital ratio that shows the amount by which the institution exceeds minimum requirements. If this is less than 1.0, the institution is not properly capitalized. More than 1.0 is good, but a very high number might indicate overcapitalization and possible underutilization of capital. Regulatory Capital Ratio = Regulatory Capital ÷ Minimum Regulatory Capital.

regulatory risk. Possibility the financial institution may engage in transactions that violate laws, statutes, regulations, etc.

rejected item. Check that is not posted because it is missorted, lacking endorsement, subject to stop-payment orders, etc. Also called a *holdover*.

related party transaction. According to the FASB, transactions between (1) a parent company and its subsidiaries; (2) subsidiaries of a common parent; (3) an enterprise and trusts for the benefit of employees, such as pension and profit-sharing trusts that are managed by or under the trusteeship of the enterprises's management; (4) an enterprise and its principal owners, management or members of their immediate families and (5) affiliates.

repurchase agreement (repo). Funding transaction that requires a financial institution to put up government securities as collateral for the cash the financial institution receives. Sale of government securities to a counterparty with a simultaneous agreement to buy back the same security on a specific date (usually overnight) at a specific price. *Contrast* **reverse repurchase agreement.**

resell agreement. *See* **reverse repurchase agreement.**

reserve for loan losses. Account that is similar to the allowance for bad debts account for an industrial company. The balance in the account at a particular balance sheet date is management's best estimate of the amount of probable losses in the loan portfolio. Also called *allowance for loan losses*.

reset date. *See* **forward rate agreement.**

retained earnings account. A balance sheet account that appears in the owner's equity section of the balance sheet. It has a credit balance and presents the accumulated earnings available for dividends.

return on average assets (ROA). Profitability ratio that shows the relationship of net income after taxes—the bottom line—to average total assets. Shows how profitably the assets have been employed. High is good. Low is bad. ROA = Net Income (NI) ÷ Avg. Total Assets.

return on average equity (ROE). Profitability ratio that shows how profitably the net assets (equity) have been employed. High is good. Low is bad. ROE = NI ÷ Avg. Total Stockholders' Equity (SE).

revenue account. An account that accumulates the values of the goods or services the business sells; considered a temporary account.

revenue bond. Municipal issue that is not backed by the taxing power of the issuer. It is backed by the income expected from a specific project, for example, port authority, power authority, turnpike authority. *See also* **municipal issue.**

revenue per employee ratio. Productivity ratio that shows how much the institution grosses per employee. The more revenue each employee generates, the more funds will be available to cover operating costs. That is, the more productive the entity will be. High is good. Low is bad. Revenue Per Employee Ratio = Total Revenue ÷ No. of Employees.

revenue recognition principle. A GAAP principle that requires that revenues and gains be recognized (recorded, incorporated into the financial records as assets, liabilities, equity, revenue or expense) when measurable and when realized or realizable or earned. Revenue should be recorded in the period earned. *See also* **realizable/realized.**

reverse repurchase agreement (reverse repo). Lending transaction that involves the purchase of government securities from a counterparty with a simultaneous agreement to sell back the same security on a specific date at a specific price. Also called *resell agreement. Contrast* **repurchase agreement.**

revolving credit agreement. Credit arrangement that increases the amount available for subsequent borrowing when repayment of prior borrowings is made.

right of setoff. Debtor's legal right, by contract or otherwise, to discharge all or a portion of the debt owed to another party by applying against the debt an amount that the other party owes to the debtor.

ROA. Acronym for *return on average assets*.

ROE. Acronym for *return on average equity*.

Sarbanes-Oxley Act of 2002 (SOX). Federal act that addresses the serious financial irregularity problems of the 1990s. It was designed to thwart the future efforts of corporate management, external auditors and others who might consider using deceitful accounting practices to mislead investors, creditors and others and to benefit themselves. The act sets forth requirements for all publicly owned companies; it has no asset-size test.

savings account. Time deposit that allows depositors to withdraw cash on demand. Checks cannot be drawn against these accounts. They generally offer higher interest rates than interest bearing checking accounts. *See also* **time deposit.**

SE (S/E). Abbreviation for *stockholders' equity.*

SEC. Acronym for *Securities and Exchange Commission.*

Securities and Exchange Commission (SEC). The federal government established the SEC to help develop and standardize financial information presented to stockholders. It is a federal agency that administers the Securities Exchange Act of 1934 and several other acts.

servicing agent. Agent that collects the mortgage payments for purchased loans for the purchasing financial institution. The agent is usually the originator of the mortgage.

servicing asset. Exclusive right (that has current value) of the transferor (seller) to service the loans transferred. The transferor has the right to collect principal and interest, pay real estate taxes, pay insurance premiums, maintain customer accounting and tax records, etc.

SFAS. Acronym for *Statement of Financial Accounting Standards.*

SFAS 5. *Accounting for Contingencies.*

SFAS 57. *Related Party Disclosures.*

SFAS 66. *Accounting for Sales of Real Estate.*

SFAS 91. *Accounting for Nonrefundable Fees and Costs Associated with Originating or Acquiring Loans and Initial Direct Costs of Leases.*

SFAS 95. *Accounting for Cash Flows.*

SFAS 109. *Accounting for Income Taxes.*

SFAS 114. *Accounting by Creditors for Impairment of a Loan—an Amendment of FASB Statements 5 and 15.*

SFAS 115. *Accounting for Certain Investments in Debt and Equity Securities.*

SFAS 118. *Accounting by Creditors for Impairment of a Loan—Income Recognition and Disclosures.*

SFAS 133. *Accounting for Derivative Instruments and Hedging Activities.*

SFAS 140. *Accounting for Transfers and Servicing of Financial Assets, and Extinguishments of Liabilities.*

SFAS 157. *Fair Value Measurements.*

shareholders' equity. *See* **stockholders' equity.**

short-term investment. A readily marketable security.

short-term investment ratio. Liquidity ratio that measures the liquidity of the investment portfolio. Short-term investments generally are more liquid. Thus, a high ratio is good. A low ratio is bad. Short-Term Investment Ratio = Short-Term Investments ÷ Total Investment Portfolio.

single-entry ticket. Ticket that is used to post only one side of the entry in double-entry bookkeeping to record a transaction.

SOX. Acronym for *Sarbanes-Oxley Act of 2002.*

SPE. Acronym for *Special Purpose Entity.*

special mention. *See* **Other Loans Especially Mentioned (OLEM).**

Special Purpose Entity (SPE). A business (usually a corporation) set up to provide a particular service for another entity. Such services include providing research and development, servicing sold loans, handling employees' stock option plans, servicing debt, etc.

stable monetary unit concept. Accounting concept that ignores the effect of inflation. "A dollar is a dollar, regardless of time." A year 2000 dollar is equal to a year 1900 dollar for accounting purposes. Also called *historical cost concept.*

statement of cash flows. Financial report that shows what the organization did with its cash and cash equivalents during the year. Summary of the institution's cash flows from all sources: operating activities, investing activities and financing activities.

statement of changes in stockholders' equity. Report that shows the activity in each of the categories in the shareholders' equity section of the balance sheet for several years (each ending on a balance sheet date). It shows number of shares issued, redeemed, etc., as well as the related dollar amounts for capital stock, paid-in capital, retained earnings, treasury stock, etc.

statement of earnings. *See* **income statement.**

Statement of Financial Accounting Concepts. Statement that sets forth fundamental objectives the FASB will use in developing standards of financial accounting and reporting. They are intended to form a conceptual framework that will consistently serve as a tool for solving existing and emerging problems. *A Statement of Financial Accounting Concepts does not establish GAAP.*

Statement of Financial Accounting Standards (SFAS). Financial accounting standard issued by the FASB. An SFAS is considered generally accepted accounting principles. *See also* **Financial Accounting Standards Board.**

statement of financial position. *See* **balance sheet.**

statement of income. *See* **income statement.**

stockholder. An investor who infuses cash (equity) into the business by purchasing shares of capital stock.

stockholders' equity. Equity that arises from investments by owners. Generally, stockholders' equity is increased by additional owners' investments or net income and is reduced by distributions to the owners or net losses. A company's residual—what it owns minus what it owes. It is the carrying amount of the assets less the carrying amount of the liabilities. It represents the book value of the company. Also called *owners' equity; shareholders' equity. See also* **equity.**

straight-line method of amortization. Amortization method that computes interest expense evenly over the life of the obligation and results in a fixed dollar amount each period—not a fixed interest rate each period. *Contrast* **interest method of amortization.** *See also* **amortization.**

strategy risk. Potential that the organization may not carefully establish viable plans for operations, finance and asset/liability management.

strike price. Predetermined sale or purchase price of the security underlying an option. Also called an *exercise price*. *See also* **option.**

subprime loan. A type of loan made at higher than normal rates or with adjustable rates to borrowers who might not qualify for a traditional loan. Many such loans were "no income verification" loans or "stated income" loans for which the borrower never had to verify that he or she had enough income to pay back the loan.

subsidiary ledger. Group of accounts with individual balances that in total equal the balance in a general ledger account.

substandard loan. Loan (1) that is inadequately protected by the current financial condition and paying capacity of the borrower or (2) for which the value of the collateral is classified as substandard. Substandard assets have a well-defined weakness or weaknesses that jeopardize the collectibility of the loan. *See also* **loan classification.**

support activity. An activity that is not directly related to the primary businesses of banking (funding, lending, investing, trading, fee-based services) but aids, assists or supports the line activities.

swap. *See* **interest rate swap.**

TD. Abbreviation for *time deposit account*.

3/27 loan. A 30-year loan that had a relatively low fixed interest rate for the first three years and then was adjusted to a much higher adjustable rate for the subsequent twenty-seven years. *Compare* **2/28 loan.**

time deposit. Liability of a financial institution that represents customer deposits that will not be drawn upon for disbursement purposes; these deposits are expected to be in the financial institution for long periods.

time instrument. An instrument that requires payment in a given time, for example, 90 days. *Contrast* **demand instrument.**

time loan. Generally made for relatively long periods and contains provisions for payment in installments or at maturity. *Contrast* **demand loan.**

trading security. Security a financial institution holds principally to sell in the near term. *Contrast* **available-for-sale security; held-to-maturity security.**

transferee. Buyer of financial assets.

transferor. Seller of financial assets.

Treadway Commission. *See* **National Commission on Fraudulent Financial Reporting.**

treasurer's check. *See* **cashier's check.**

trial balance. A listing of all account balances; total debit balance accounts must equal total credit balance accounts.

2/28 loan. A 30-year loan that had a relatively low fixed interest rate for the first two years and then was adjusted to a much higher adjustable rate for the subsequent twenty-eight years. *Compare* **3/27 loan.**

UBPR. Acronym for *Uniform Bank Performance Report.*

unclassified loan. Loan that is not considered a greater-than-normal risk. This rating may also be referred to as "pass" or "good." *See also* **loan classification.**

unearned interest. Interest the financial institution has not yet earned that is charged to a customer for a loan.

Uniform Bank Performance Report (UBPR). Report the government issues each quarter that shows a host of ratios for banks within various peer groups. This free service for banks uses the actual numbers filed by depository institutions on their quarterly Call Reports. *See also* **Call Report.**

Uniform Thrift Performance Report (UTPR). Report the government issues each quarter that shows a host of ratios for thrifts within various peer groups. This free service for thrifts uses the actual numbers filed on their quarterly Thrift Financial Reports.

upstreamed. Describes cash that is sent to the parent by an affiliate.

U.S. government agency security. Short-, intermediate- or long-term obligation of the Federal National Mortgage Association, the Federal Home Loan Bank, the Federal Farm Credit Bank, the Student Loan Marketing Association, the Government National Mortgage Association, the Tennessee Value Authority and others. It is readily marketable and generates investment income.

U.S. Treasury obligation. Debt security issued by the government to help finance government activities. A fully guaranteed obligation of the U.S. government, including U.S. Treasury bills, notes and bonds.

UTPR. Acronym for *Uniform Thrift Performance Report.*

value in use. The present value of cash flows expected to be derived from a receivable.

Y/E. Abbreviation for *year-end.*

Index

AAA (American Accounting Association), 94
Accountability. *See also* Internal control
   for cash items, 66
   for checks, 63–65
   for clearing and exchange items, 66–68
   for drafts, 63
   for due from correspondents, 68
   for interest bearing deposits, 68–69
Accounting
   defined, 3
   future of, 228
   information sources on, 230
   role of, 3–4
Accounting cycle
   balance sheet preparation, 13–17, 30 (*See also* Balance sheet)
   closing the books, 21–25, 30
   correcting entries, 21, 30 (*See also* Errors)
   end-of-period adjustments, 12–13, 30
   frequency of, 58
   income statement preparation, 17–21, 27–29 (*See also* Income statement)
   journalizing transactions, 9–10, 11, 30
   posting to ledger, 10, 11, 30, 69–70
   summary of, 8, 30
   trial balance preparation, 10, 12, 26, 30 (*See also* Trial balance)
Accounting equation, 6
Accounting Principles Board (APB), 41–42
Accounting Research Bulletins (ARBs), 41, 43, 45, 49
Accounting Research Network, 230
Accounting systems, defined, 4. *See also* Accounting cycle
AccountingWeb, 230

Accounts. *See also specific*
   balancing, 61
   defined, 4
   types of, 4–6, 7–8
Accounts receivable, 15, 153
Accrual basis, 13, 50. *See also* Full accrual accounting
Accruals, defined, 34
Accrued interest payable, 164–165
Accrued interest receivable, 151
Adequacy, of internal controls, 98–99. *See also* Internal control
Adjusting entries, 12–13, 30
Advances, from FHLB, 71, 91–92, 165–166
AFS securities. *See* Available-for-sale (AFS) securities
AICPA. *See* American Institute of Certified Public Accountants (AICPA)
AICPA AcSEC Update Newsletter, 230
AICPA Daily News Alert, 230
Allocation, 12, 33
Allowance for loan losses. *See* Reserve for loan losses
American Accounting Association (AAA), 94
American Institute of Certified Public Accountants (AICPA)
   on audit reports, 113
   EITF and, 43
   in GAAP hierarchy, 44
   on IFRS implementation, 54
   role of, 40–41
   on Treadway Commission, 94
   Web addresses, 230
American options, 205
Amortization. *See also* Depreciation
   of bond discounts, 197–198
   of fees, 187–190
   interest method of, 132
   and loan payments, 133–135, 137–140
   negative, 157–159
Annual reports, 102–106, 109, 111–112, 175. *See also* Financial statements; *specific statements*
APB (Accounting Principles Board), 41–42
AS2 (*Auditing Standards 2*) (PCAOB), 107
AS5 (*Auditing Standards 5*) (PCAOB), 107–108
Asset accounts, 5, 7, 8
Asset leverage ratio, 177, 185
Asset quality ratio, 178, 185–186
Assets. *See also specific*
   in accounting equation, 6
   control over, 212
   current, 14–15

defined, 51, 110
   noncurrent, 15
   noncurrent liability from purchase of, 16–17
   other, 16, 152–154
Asset transfers, 212–213
Asset valuation concept, 39
Assumed markets, 231–232
Assurances, from trial balance, 12
Attestation Report on Management's Assertion about the Effectiveness of Internal Control over Financial Reporting, 112
Audit committees, 46, 47, 101, 102, 225–226
Auditing. *See also* Certified Public Accountants (CPAs)
   auditor independence in, 46–47, 101, 102, 227
   federal standards for, 107–108
   future of, 227
   legislation on, 107–108
   related party disclosure in, 223–227
   reporting results of, 105–106, 111, 112, 113
Auditing Standards 2 (AS2) (PCAOB), 107
Auditing Standards 5 (AS5) (PCAOB), 107–108
Auditor's reports, 105–106, 111, 112, 113
Available-for-sale (AFS) securities
   accounting for, 191–197
   balance sheet reporting of, 125–126
   defined, 191
   footnote disclosure on, 126–130
   valuation of, 38, 39

Balance sheet. *See also* Loans; Reserve for loan losses; Securities
   accrued interest receivable on, 151
   cash and cash equivalents on, 122–124
   in closing process, 21–22, 30
   current emphasis on, 229–230
   disclosure on, 225
   examples, 114–115, 238–239
   IFRS versus GAAP on, 51
   liabilities on, 162–166
   money market investments on, 125
   other assets on, 152–154
   premises and equipment on, 150–151
   preparing, 13–17, 21
   role of, 110
   shareholders' equity on, 166–167
   unearned interest on, 135–140

Banker's acceptance, 152
Banker's banks, 67–68
Bearish strategy, 205
Bills, U.S. Treasury issuing, 80–81
Bond coupons, 66
Bonds, 81, 197–198
Borrowings
    FHLB, 90–92, 165–166
    IFRS versus GAAP on, 52
Branch banks, 62–63, 74
Bullish strategy, 205
Business functions. *See also* Funding; Investing
    fee-based services, 83–84
    internal accounting, reporting, and compliance, 85 (*See also* Internal control)
    lending, 76–78 (*See also* Loans)
    support activities, 84
    types of, 71

Call options, 205, 207
Call Report, 109, 180
Capital adequacy ratio, 177, 185
Capital ratios, 177, 185–186
Capital risk, 85–86
Captions, 206
Carrying amount, 188
Cash and cash equivalents, 15, 66, 122–124
Cash and due from banks. *See* Cash and cash equivalents
Cash basis, 13
Cash flow hedges, 207, 208, 210–211
Cash flows. *See* Statement of cash flows
Cashier's checks, 65, 72
Cash items, 66, 122–123
Cash letters, 67
Cash on hand, 122
Cause-and-effect relationships, 33
CDs (certificates of deposit), 73–74
The Center for Audit Quality, 230
Certificates of deposit (CDs), 73–74
Certified checks, 64–65
Certified Public Accountants (CPAs), 41, 48, 112. *See also* American Institute of Certified Public Accountants (AICPA); Auditing; Consulting
Check Clearing for the 21st Century Act (Check 21 Act), 70
Checking accounts, 72
Checks
    cashier's, 72

    certified, 64–65
    defined, 63–64
    foreign, 67
    official, 72
    paper versus electronic, 70
    sent to clearing house, 67
    on us, 67
Chicago Board of Trade, 204
Classified loans, 144–147
Clearing and exchange items, 66–68, 123
Clearinghouses, 66, 67
Closing entries, 22–23
Closing process, 21–25, 30. *See also* Accounting cycle
Club accounts, 62, 74
Code of ethics, 225
Collars, interest rate, 206
Collateral, 81–83, 91–92, 131
Collateral risk, 86, 100
Collection method, 37
Committee of Sponsoring Organizations (COSO), 94–96. *See also* Internal control
Committee on Accounting Procedure (CAP), 41
Communication systems, 96, 97
Community financial institutions
    continuous departmental accountability at, 63–69
    daily balancing and posting by, 58–61
    paper versus electronic documents in, 70
    proof function in, 69
    separate ledger and memo accounts in, 69–70
    single-entry tickets in, 61–63
Comparability concept, 36
Compensating balances, 131
Compensation, stock as, 228
Completed-contract method, 37
Compliance, 85, 96, 97. *See also* Accountability; Internal control
Concentration risk, 86, 99
Conceptual framework, 32, 35–40. *See also* Generally accepted accounting principles (GAAP)
Condensed income statement, 18, 29
Conservatism, doctrine of, 38
Consistency concept, 36
Consolidated financial statements, 109. *See also* Financial statements; *specific statements*
Construction projects, revenue recognition on, 37–38
Consulting, 46, 227–228. *See also* Auditing; Certified Public Accountants (CPAs)
Consumer loans, 131–133
Contingencies, IFRS versus GAAP on, 54

Contingent gains and losses, 38
Contingent liabilities, 17
Continuity concept. *See* Going concern concept
Continuous departmental accountability, 63. *See also* Accountability
Control, 63, 96, 97, 212. *See also* Internal control
Cooling-off period, 47
Core deposits, 71–72, 92
Corporations, defined, 5
Correcting entries, 21, 30. *See also* Errors
Correspondent banks, 67–68
COSO (Committee of Sponsoring Organizations), 94–96. *See also* Internal control
Cost approach, 232
Cost recovery method, 216
Country risk, 86
Covered calls, 205, 207
CPA. *See* American Institute of Certified Public Accountants (AICPA); Certified Public Accountants (CPAs)
Credit card financing, 132–133
Credit risk
   defined, 87
   internal control measures and, 99, 100
   investing activities and, 80, 81
   on time and demand loans, 131
Credits, versus debits, 6–8
Current assets, 14–15
Current liabilities, 16
Customer acceptance liability, 152

DDAs (demand deposit accounts), 62, 72–73
Debits, versus credits, 6–8
Debt covenant violations, 54
Defalcations, 98
Deferrals, defined, 34–35
Deferred provisions, 168
Deficiency letters, 41
Delivery price, in forward contracts, 204
Demand CDs, 72–73
Demand deposit accounts (DDAs), 62, 72–73
Demand deposits, types of, 72–73
Demand drafts. *See* Checks
Demand instruments, 64. *See also* Checks
Demand loans, 130–131
Departmental accountability, continuous, 63. *See also* Accountability
Department of Justice, 41

Department of Veterans Affairs (DVA), 131
Deposit accounts, 58, 132
Deposit method, 216–218
Deposits
   balance sheet reporting of, 162–163
   demand, 62, 72–73
   in ratio analysis, 178–179
   recording, 58–61, 74
   time, 73–74
Depreciation, 150. *See also* Amortization
Derivatives, 203–211. *See also* Hedging
Direct method, for cash flow reporting, 110
Disclosure. *See also* Supplemental data to the financial statements
   accounting method change, 37
   business risk, 229
   cash and cash equivalents, 124
   deposit liability, 162–163
   FHLB advance, 165–166
   income tax reporting, 170–172
   investment accounting, 126–130
   loans, 134–135, 140, 148–149
   money market investments, 125
   premises and equipment, 150–151
   related party transactions, 223–227
   risk-related information, 229
   in supplemental data to the financial statements, 244
Disclosure principle, 40
Discounted basis on installment loans, 132
Discounts, 197–198
Diversification, 80–81, 86
Dividends, 5, 16, 17
Doctrine of conservatism, 38
Documentation, 70, 99–100. *See also* Internal control
Double-entry bookkeeping, 6–8
Doubtful loans, 146
Drafts, 63. *See also* Checks
Drawee, 63
Drawer, 63
Due from accounts, 123
Due from banks, 123
Due from correspondents, 68
Due to accounts, 123
Due to customer account, 58
DVA (Department of Veterans Affairs), 131

Earned revenue, 33
EDGAR Online, 230
Effective controls, 97–98. *See also* Internal control
Effective-interest method, 132, 138, 139, 188–190. *See also* Amortization
Efficiency ratio, 179, 186
EITF (Emerging Issues Task Force), 43, 230
Electronic Accountant, 230
Emerging Issues Task Force (EITF), 43, 230
Employees
    affecting internal control, 95
    IFRS versus GAAP on cost of, 53
End-of-period adjustments. *See* Adjusting entries
Enron, 46, 223
Entity concept, 35
Equipment. *See* Premises and equipment
Equity. *See also* Balance sheet
    in accounting equation, 6
    defined, 17, 51
    return on, 176, 181
    shareholders', 17, 110, 111, 166–167
Equity accounts, 5, 8
Equity method, 152–153
Errors
    correcting entries for, 21, 30
    defined, 98
    in trial balance, 12
Escrow deposits, 73
European options, 205
Excess funds, placement of, 79
Exchange items. *See* Clearing and exchange items
Exercise price, 205
Exit price, 231
Expense accounts, 5–6, 8, 23–24
Expense recognition principle, 33
Expenses, unrecorded, 13
External users, 4

Fair presentation concept, 39
Fair value
    defined, 231
    estimation methods, 231–233
    guideline effective dates, 233–234
    reporting trends, 228–229
    valuation techniques, 232–233

Fair value accounting, 36
Fair value assets, 39
Fair value hedges, 207, 208, 209–210
FASAC (Financial Accounting Standards Advisory Council), 42
FASB. *See* Financial Accounting Standards Board (FASB)
Federal Deposit Insurance Corporation Improvement Act of 1991 (FDICIA), 94, 100–101, 102. *See also* Internal control
Federal Farm Credit Bank, 81
Federal funds purchased, 75, 163–164
Federal funds sold, 75, 78, 125
Federal Home Loan Banks (FHLBs)
  advances from, 71, 91, 165–166
  check clearing by, 67
  government securities from, 81
  overview, 90–92
Federal Housing Administration (FHA), 131
Federal National Mortgage Association, 81
Federal Reserve Banks (FRBs), 67, 81–82, 92, 123
Federal Savings and Loan Insurance Corporation (FSLIC), 92
Fee-based services, 83–84. *See also* Nonrefundable fees
FEI (Financial Executives Institute), 94
FFIEC Interagency Policy Statement on the Allowance for Loan and Lease Losses, 141, 148
FHLB. *See* Federal Home Loan Banks (FHLBs)
Financial Accounting Standards Advisory Council (FASAC), 42
Financial Accounting Standards Board (FASB). *See also* Statements of Financial Accounting Standards (SFASs)
  on cash flow reporting, 110
  codification of, 44–45
  on comparability, 36
  Emerging Issues Task Force, 230
  Exposure Drafts, 230
  on investment accounting, 190–191
  overview, 42–43
  on risk disclosure, 229
  SEC partnership with, 41
  steps in releasing new standards, 49
  Summaries and Status, 230
  Web address, 230
Financial components approach, 212
Financial Executives Institute (FEI), 94
Financial experts, 225–226
Financial Institutions Reform, Recovery and Enforcement Act (FIRREA), 92
Financial ratios. *See* Ratio analysis
Financial statements. *See also specific*
  analyzing (*see* Ratio analysis)

beyond GAAP requirements, 111–112
defined, 4
depreciation method and, 150
examples, 112–119, 238–245
fair value trend in, 228–229
GAAP requirements, 109–111
IFRS versus GAAP on, 50–51
legislation on accuracy of, 225
management discussion and analysis in, 112
supplemental data in, 111, 244

Financing activities, 110. *See also* Statement of cash flows
FIRREA (Financial Institutions Reform, Recovery and Enforcement Act), 92
Floor-ceiling agreements, 206
Food stamps, 66
Footnotes. *See* Disclosure; Notes to the financial statements
Foreign checks, 67
Foreign Corrupt Practices Act of 1977, 107
Foreign currency exposure, 87, 207
Foreign exchange risk, 87
Forward contracts, 204
Forward rate agreements (FRAs), 204
Fraud, 46, 98. *See also* Internal control
Fraud Commission. *See* Treadway Commission
Fraud risk, 87
FRBs (Federal Reserve Banks), 67, 81–82, 92, 123
FSLIC (Federal Savings and Loan Insurance Corporation), 92
Full accrual accounting, 215. *See also* Accrual basis
Functions. *See* Business functions
Funding
   demand deposits, 72–73
   federal funds purchased, 75
   introduction to, 71–72
   recording deposits, 74
   repurchase agreements, 75–76
   time deposits, 73–74
Funding risk, 87
Futures contracts, 203–204

GAAP. *See* Generally accepted accounting principles (GAAP)
Gain contingencies, 38
Gains. *See also specific financial instruments*
   contingencies for, 38
   in hedging, 207
   real versus holding, 80
   specific identification method for, 127

Generally accepted accounting principles (GAAP)
   on accruals and deferrals, 13, 34–35
   alternative, 36, 228
   conceptual framework of, 32, 35–40
   defined, 3
   on deposit liability, 162
   on depreciation, 150
   developers of, 40–43 (*See also specific organizations*)
   on expense recognition, 33
   FASB Concept Statements and, 43
   financial reporting requirements, 109–111
   hierarchy of, 43–44
   IFRS versus, 50–54
   investing excess funds and, 79
   on related party disclosure, 223
   on reserve accounts, 148
   on revenue recognition, 32–33
General obligation munis, 81
Going concern concept, 35–36, 50
Government National Mortgage Association, 81
Gross profit from deposit, lending, and investing, 167

HC (Holiday Club) deposit accounts, 62
Hedging. *See also* Derivatives
   accounting for, 209–211
   defined, 206
   market risk and, 88
   strategies for, 206–211
Held-to-maturity (HTM) securities
   accounting for, 191–197
   balance sheet reporting of, 126
   defined, 191
   premiums and discounts on, 197–198
   valuation of, 38, 39
Historical cost concept, 36, 228
Holding companies, 109–110
Holding gains, 80
Holding losses, 80
Holdovers, 72
Holiday Club (HC) deposit accounts, 62
Home equity lines of credit, 132
Home improvement loans, 132
HTM securities. *See* Held-to-maturity (HTM) securities
Hypothetical transactions, 231

IASB (International Accounting Standards Board), 50
IFRS (International Financial Reporting Standards), 50–54
IIA (Institute of Internal Auditors), 94
IMA (Institute of Management Accountants), 94
Image replacement document (IRD), 70
Immediate recognition, 33
Impairments. *See also* Loans
    FASB on, 140–141, 142, 143–144, 199
    probability of, 199
    recording, 78, 198–202
Income
    from interest, 83, 110, 167, 219–221 (*See also* Interest income ratio)
    net, 5–6
    other, 168
    as portfolio goal, 80
    unearned, 132
Income approach, 232
Income statement
    in closing process, 22, 30
    condensed, 18, 29
    examples, 116–117, 240–241
    IFRS versus GAAP on, 51
    income taxes on, 168–172
    interest income and expense on, 167
    multiple-step, 18, 28
    other income and expense on, 168
    preparing, 17–21, 27–29
    role of, 110
    segment information on, 172–173
    single-step, 18, 27
Income summary, 5
Income summary account, 17, 22–23, 24–25
Income taxes, IFRS versus GAAP on, 53. *See also* Taxes
Independence of auditors, 46–47, 101, 227
Indirect method, for cash flow reporting, 110
Individual retirement accounts (IRAs), 74
Information systems, and internal control, 96, 97
Inputs, into valuation techniques, 232–233
Insider risk, 88
Installment loans, 131–132
Installment method, 37
Institute of Internal Auditors (IIA), 94
Institute of Management Accountants (IMA), 94
Insufficient funds (NSF) checks, 66
Intangible assets, 15

Interest
    accrued and payable, 164–165
    accrued and receivable, 151
    income from, 83, 110, 167, 219–221 (*See also* Interest income ratio)
    unearned, 135–140
Interest bearing deposits, 68–69
Interest bearing liabilities, 176
Interest expense, 167
Interest expense ratio, 176, 184
Interest income, 167, 219–221
Interest income ratio, 176, 184
Interest method of amortization, 132. *See also* Amortization
Interest rate caps, 205–206
Interest rate collars, 206
Interest rate floors, 206
Interest rate risk, 88. *See also* Hedging
Interest rate swaps, 203–204, 210
Interest ROA ratio, 176, 181
Internal capital generation rate, 177, 185
Internal control
    adequacy of, 98–99
    as business function, 85
    in certified check handling, 64
    daily account balancing as, 61
    defined, 93, 95
    documentation for, 70, 99–100
    effectiveness of, 97–98
    FDICIA versus SOX, 100–101
    legislation on, 93–94, 98, 100–101 (*See also* Sarbanes-Oxley Act of 2002 (SOX))
    objectives and components of, 96–97
    operations risk and, 89
    recent initiatives, 93–94
Internal Control-Integrated Framework (Committee of Sponsoring Organizations), 94, 95
Internal users, 3
International Accounting Standards Board (IASB), 50
International Financial Reporting Standards (IFRS), 50–54
Interpretations, 42
Intrinsic value approach, 228
Inventories, 15, 52, 54, 58
Investing. *See also* Securities
    as business function, 79–83
    introduction to, 78–79
Investing activities, 110. *See also* Statement of cash flows
IRAs (individual retirement accounts), 74
IRD (image replacement document), 70
Irregularities, 98–99

Journals, recording transactions in, 9–10, 11, 30, 59. *See also* Accounting cycle
Jumbo CDs, 73
Jumbo deposit ratio, 179

Keogh accounts, 74

Leases, noncurrent capital, 17. *See also* Loans
Ledger accounts, 10, 11, 18–19. *See also* Accounting cycle
Ledgers, subsidiary, 59, 60–61
Lending, 76–78. *See also* Loans
Liabilities. *See also specific*
   in accounting equation, 6
   balance sheet reporting of, 162–166
   current, 16
   customer acceptance, 152
   defined, 51, 110, 162
   Interest bearing, 176
   noncurrent, 16–17
   other, 17, 165
Liability accounts, 5, 7, 8
Liability-sensitive financial institution, 203
LIBOR (London Interbank Offered Rate), 203, 204
Lines of credit, 131, 132
Liquidation accounting, 35–36
Liquidity, 63, 80
Liquidity ratios, 178–179, 186
Loan classifications, 144–147
Loan review system, 155
Loans
   classification of, 144–147
   disclosure on, 134–135
   fees on, 187–190
   installment, 131–132
   internal control documentation for, 99–100
   losses on (*See* Reserve for loan losses)
   overview, 76–78
   payment and amortization of, 133–135
   recording impairments to, 78, 198–202 (*See also* Impairments)
   subprime and negative amortizing, 157–159
   types of, 77, 130–133
Loans secured by deposit accounts, 132
Loans to earning assets ratio, 179, 186

Loan to deposit ratio, 178, 186
LOCOM (lower of cost or market), 213–214
London Interbank Offered Rate (LIBOR), 203, 204
Long-term investments, 15
Losses. *See also* Reserve for loan losses; *specific financial instruments*
   contingencies for, 38
   in hedging, 207
   real versus holding, 80
   specific identification method for, 127
Loss loans, 146–147
Lower of cost or market (LOCOM), 213–214

Macro hedges, 206
Management discussion and analysis (MD & A), 112
Management fraud, 98
Management information systems (MISs), 172–173
Management responsibilities, 102–104
Management risk, 88, 100
Management's Report on the Effectiveness of Internal Control over Financial Reporting, 112
Margin from deposit, lending, and investing, 167
Marked-to-market, 190. *See also* Fair value; Marking to market
Market approach, 232
Market risk, 80, 81, 88
Marking to market, 233. *See also* Fair value; Marked-to-market
Marking to matrix, 233
Marking to model, 233
Matching principle, 38–39
Materiality concept, 38–39
MD & A (Management discussion and analysis), 112
Memorandum accounts, 69–70
Micro hedges, 206
MISs (management information systems), 172–173
Mistakes. *See* Errors
Money market investments, 125
Money orders, 72
Monitoring systems, 96, 97
Moody's, 79
Mortgage loans, 131. *See also* Loans; Other Real Estate Owned (OREO)
Most advantageous market, 232
Multiple-step income statement, 18, 28
Municipal issues (munis), 81

NAA (National Association of Accountants). *See* Institute of Management Accountants (IMA)
Naked calls, 205
National Association of Accountants (NAA). *See* Institute of Management Accountants (IMA)
National Commission on Fraudulent Financial Reporting, 94
Negative amortizing loans, 157–159
Net charge-off ratio, 178, 186
Net income, 5–6
Net interest income, 83, 110, 167
Net interest margin ratio, 176, 184
Net realizable value (NRV), 39, 78, 140
Net working capital (NWC), 16
New York Futures Exchange, 204
Noncurrent assets, 15
Noncurrent liabilities, 16–17
Nondilutive capital funding, 85
Non-interest expense ratio, 179, 186
Non-interest ROA ratio, 177, 184
Nonmarketable securities, 153
Nonperforming assets reserved ratio, 178
Nonperforming ratio, 178
Nonrefundable fees, 187–190. *See also* Fee-based services
Notes, U.S. Treasury issuing, 81
Notes to the financial statements, 111. *See also* Disclosure; Supplemental data to the financial statements
Notional amounts, 203
NRV (net realizable value), 39, 78, 140
NSF (insufficient funds) checks, 66
NWC (net working capital), 16

Official checks. *See* Cashier's checks
OLEM (Other Loans Especially Mentioned), 147
On-line banking, 62
On us checks, 67
Open repo agreements, 75
Operating activities
  cash flows from, 110 (*See also* Statement of cash flows)
  internal control in, 96
  noncurrent liabilities arising from, 16
Operations risk, 89, 99, 100
OPM (other people's money), 58, 86, 167
Options, 205, 206, 207
Orderly transactions, 231
OREO. *See* Other Real Estate Owned (OREO)

Other assets, 16, 152–154
Other expenses, 168
Other income, 168
Other issues, 81
Other liabilities, 165
Other Loans Especially Mentioned (OLEM), 147
Other people's money (OPM), 58, 86, 167
Other Real Estate Owned (OREO)
    accounting for sales of, 218–221
    booking, 213–214
    defined, 213
    methods of selling, 215–218
    reporting value of, 153
    revenue recognition on sale of, 37
Outsourcing, 101
Overall efficiency ratio, 179, 186
Overdraft loans, 133
Overhead burden ratio, 177, 184
Overnight repo agreements, 75
Owners' equity, 110. *See also* Equity

Payables, IFRS versus GAAP on, 52
Payees, 63
Payor financial institution, 63
PCAOB (Public Company Accounting Oversight Board), 47–48, 107–108, 230
People, internal control affected by, 95
Percentage-of-completion method, 37–38
Plain vanilla interest rate swaps, 203
Poor credits, 99–100
Portfolio, balance in, 80–81
Post-closing trial balance, 26, 30
PPE (property, plant and equipment), 15, 51–52
Premises and equipment, 150–151
Premiums, 197–198
Prepaid expenses, 15
Prepaid items, 154
Present value, 78, 133, 136, 195, 199–200, 202
Present value factor, 136
Present value tables, 133
Principal market, 231–232
Probability, of impairment, 199
Process, internal control as, 95
Productivity ratios, 179, 186
Profitability ratios, 176–177, 181, 184–185
Profitability reporting, 172–173

Proof departments, 67, 69. *See also* Accountability; Compliance; Internal control
Property, plant and equipment (PPE), 15, 51–52
Provision for loan losses. *See* Reserve for loan losses
Provisions, IFRS versus GAAP on, 52
Public Company Accounting Oversight Board (PCAOB), 47–48, 107–108, 230
Put options, 205, 206
PV factor, 136

Quarterly reports, 141. *See also* Financial statements; *specific statements*
Quoted market value, 195. *See also* Fair value

Range swaps, 206
RAP (regulatory accounting principles), 148
Ratio analysis
   asset quality, 178, 185–186
   defined, 175
   equity adequacy, 177, 185
   examples, 181–186, 245
   limitations of, 180
   liquidity, 178–179, 186
   in peer group analysis, 180–181
   productivity, 179, 186
   profitability, 176–177, 181, 184–185
   in supplemental data, 111
Rational allocation, 33
Real estate mortgage loans, 131. *See also* Other Real Estate Owned (OREO)
Real gains, 80
Realizable revenue, 32–33, 37–38
Realized revenue, 32–33, 37–38
Real losses, 80
Reasonable assurance, 95
Receivables
   accounts receivable, 153
   credit card, 132–133
   defined, 15
   related party, 224–225
   valuation of, 39, 52, 140
Receive fixed counterparties, 204
Receive floating counterparties, 204
Recognition
   of expenses, 33
   of loan impairment, 201–202
   of revenue, 32–33, 37–38, 54

Regulation O risk, 88
Regulatory accounting principles (RAP), 148
Regulatory capital ratio, 177, 185
Regulatory risk, 89, 100
Related party disclosures, 223–227
Reporting. *See also* Annual reports; Disclosure; Financial statements
   as business function, 85
   internal control over, 96, 102, 105–106
Report of independent public accountants, 113. *See also* Auditor's reports
Repurchase agreements (repos). *See also* Reverse repurchase agreements (repos)
   as collateral, 82
   as funding source, 75–76
   reporting of, 163–164
Resell agreements, 78, 163. *See also* Reverse repurchase agreements (repos)
Reserve for loan losses. *See also* Loans
   account activity, 140–141
   controversy about, 148
   determining allowance for, 142–144, 155–156
   disclosure on, 148–149
   on income statement, 110
   NRV in reporting, 140
Reset date, 204
Retail loans, 131–132
Retained earnings, 5
Retirement accounts, 74
Return on average assets (ROA), 176, 181. *See also* Non-interest ROA ratio
Return on average equity (ROE), 176, 181
Revenue
   collected in advance, 12
   earned, 33
   IFRS versus GAAP on, 52–53, 54
   realized/realizable, 32–33, 37–38
   unrecorded, 13
Revenue accounts, 5, 8, 22–23
Revenue bonds, 81
Revenue per employee ratio, 179
Revenue realization/recognition concept, 37–38
Revenue recognition principle, 32–33
Reverse repurchase agreements (repos). *See also* Repurchase agreements (repos)
   accounting for, 82
   defined, 78, 83
   interest income from, 167
   reporting of, 163–164
Revolving credit agreements, 131
Right of setoff, 123–124

Risk
    disclosure trends, 229
    hedging against (*see* Derivatives; Hedging)
    and internal control, 96, 97
    in investing function, 79–80
    management assessment of, 99–100
    in municipal issues, 81
    types of, 85–89
    in U.S. Treasury obligations, 80–81
Risk assessment, 96, 97
RMA, 180
ROA (return on average assets), 176, 181. *See also* Non-interest ROA ratio
Robert Morris Associates, 180
ROE (return on average equity), 176, 181

Safety, as portfolio goal, 80
Sarbanes-Oxley Act of 2002 (SOX). *See also* Internal control
    on audit procedures, 102, 105–106
    FDICIA versus, 100–101
    on internal control adequacy, 98–99
    on management responsibilities, 102–104
    origin of, 94
    on outsourcing, 101
    on related party disclosure, 225–227
    role of, 46–47, 48
SDLC (System Development Life Cycle), 84
SEC. *See* Securities and Exchange Commission (SEC)
Securities. *See also specific*
    classification of (*See* Available-for-sale (AFS) securities; Held-to-maturity (HTM) securities; Trading securities)
    nonmarketable, 153
    U.S. government agency, 81
    valuation of, 38, 190–191
Securities and Exchange Commission (SEC)
    on auditor independence, 101, 227
    in FASB codification, 45
    on financial report accuracy, 225
    Proposed Rules, 230
    role of, 40–41, 228
    Staff Accounting Bulletins, 230
Securities available-for-sale. *See* Available-for-sale (AFS) securities
Securities Exchange Act of 1934, 40
Securities purchased under reverse repurchase agreements. *See* Reverse repurchase agreements (repos)
Securities sold under agreements to repurchase. *See* Repurchase agreements (repos)
Securitizations, 213

Security, departmental accountability for, 63. *See also* Internal control
Segments, reporting on, 172–173
Servicing agents, 131
SFASs. *See* Statements of Financial Accounting Standards (SFASs)
Shareholders' equity, 17, 110, 166–167. *See also* Equity
Sheshunoff, 180
Short-term investment ratio, 179, 186
Short-term investments, 15
Significant accounting policies, disclosure of, 124
Single-entry ticket approach, 61–63
Single-step income statement, 18, 27
SOX. *See* Sarbanes-Oxley Act of 2002 (SOX)
Special mention assets, 147
Special Purpose Entities (SPEs), 223, 228. *See also* Related party disclosures
Specific identification method, 127
SPEs (Special Purpose Entities), 223, 228. *See also* Related party disclosures
Stable monetary unit concept, 36
Standard & Poor's, 80
Statement of cash flows
    examples, 118–119, 242–243
    IFRS versus GAAP on, 53
    role of, 110, 173–174
Statement of changes in stockholders' equity, 111
Statement of earnings. *See* Income statement
Statement of financial position. *See* Balance sheet
Statement of income. *See* Income statement
Statements of Financial Accounting Concepts, 43
Statements of Financial Accounting Standards (SFASs). *See also* Financial Accounting Standards Board (FASB)
    SFAS 5, *Accounting for Contingencies*, 141, 142
    SFAS 57, *Related Party Disclosures*, 223–224
    SFAS 66, *Accounting for Sales of Real Estate*, 215–218, 219, 221
    SFAS 91, *Accounting for Nonrefundable Fees and Costs Associated with Originating or Acquiring Loans and Initial Direct Costs of Leases*, 187–188
    SFAS 95, *Statement of Cash Flows*, 110
    SFAS 107, *Disclosure about Fair Value of Financial Instruments*, 231
    SFAS 109, *Accounting for Income Taxes,* 168–169
    SFAS 114, *Accounting by Creditors for Impairment of a Loan—An Amendment of FASB Statements 5 and 15*, 140–141, 142, 143–144, 199
    SFAS 115, *Accounting for Certain Investments in Debt and Equity Securities*, 38, 125–126, 128–130, 190–191, 231
    SFAS 133, *Accounting for Derivative Instruments and Hedging Activities*, 207, 231
    SFAS 140, *Accounting for Transfers and Servicing of Financial Assets, and Extinguishments of Liabilities*, 212
    SFAS 151, *Inventory Costs*, 45
    SFAS 156, *Accounting for Servicing of Financial Assets*, 231

SFAS 157, *Fair Value Measurement*, 231–233
SFAS 159, *The Fair Value Option for Financial Assets and Financial Liabilities*, 234
source of, 42, 49
Stock compensation, 228
Stockholders, 5
Stockholders' equity. *See* Owners' equity; Shareholders' equity; Statement of changes in stockholders' equity
Stop orders, 41
Stop payments, 64–65
Straight-line method of amortization, 132
Strategy risk, 89
Strike price, 205
Student Loan Marketing Association, 81
Student loans, 132
Subprime loans, 157–159
Subsidiary ledgers, 59, 60–61
Substandard loans, 145
Supplemental data to the financial statements, 111, 244. *See also* Disclosure
Support activities, as business function, 84
Swaps, 203, 206, 208
Systematic allocation, 33
Systems Development Life Cycle (SDLC), 84

T accounts, 6–7
Taxes
   depreciation method for reporting, 150
   escrow deposits and, 73
   FHLB borrowings and, 90, 92
   IFRS versus GAAP on, 53
   loan impairments benefiting, 199
   reporting provision for, 168–172
TDs (time deposits), 73–74. *See also specific*
Technical Bulletins, 43
Temporary accounts, 22
Tennessee Valley Authority, 81
Term repo agreements, 75
Thrift Financial Report, 109, 180
Time deposits (TDs), 73–74. *See also specific*
Time instruments, 64
Time loans, 130–131
Trading securities
   accounting for, 191–197
   balance sheet reporting of, 126–130
   defined, 191
   valuation of, 38, 39

Transfers, of financial assets, 212–213
Treadway Commission, 94
Treasurer's checks. *See* Cashier's checks
Trial balance
　adjusted, 30
　daily balancing and posting to, 58–61
　post-closing, 26, 30
　preliminary, 10, 12, 30
　revised, 20

U*BPR (Uniform Bank Performance Report)*, 180
Unclassified loans, 145
Unearned discounts, 132
Unearned income accounts, 132
Unearned interest, 135–140
Uniform Bank Performance Report (UBPR), 180
U.S. government agency securities, 81
U.S. Treasury obligations, 80–81, 82

V*alue in use*, 52

W*ithdrawals, recording*, 61
Write-downs, 54